222 Easy Italian Recipes Pasta

WHITE STAR PUBLISHERS

GRAPHIC DESIGN BY **MARIA CUCCHI**

WS White Star Publishers® is a registered trademark
property of Edizioni White Star s.r.l.

© 2011 Edizioni White Star s.r.l.
Via M. Germano, 10
13100 Vercelli, Italy
www.whitestar.it

Translation: Mary Doyle
Editing: Elizabeth Heath

ISBN 978-88-544-0618-6
1 2 3 4 5 6   15 14 13 12 11

Printed in China

EDITED BY

ACADEMIA BARILLA

PREFACE BY **CARLO CRACCO**

CONTENTS

PREFACE

Pasta, my first love

by Carlo Cracco

INNATE. PROFOUND. INTENSE. SUCH IS MY RELATIONSHIP WITH PASTA.

I REMEMBER MY MOTHER WOULD ALWAYS MAKE SPAGHETTI FOR LUNCH WHEN I WAS A CHILD. SHE WOULD MAKE IT WITH BOLOGNESE SAUCE, OR MORE OFTEN WITH TOMATO SAUCE, WHICH WERE MY FAVORITES. MY PARENTS HAD A SMALL VEGETABLE GARDEN NEAR THE HOUSE AND THE TOMATO PURÉE CAME FROM THOSE TOMATOES. MY MOTHER WOULD DRIZZLE SOME OLIVE OIL IN A PAN, ADD A CLOVE OF GARLIC FOR FLAVOR, AND THEN ADD THE HOMEMADE TOMATO PURÉE. SHE WOULD TOSS IT WITH THE SPAGHETTI AND SERVE IT.

PASTA PUTS ONE AT PEACE WITH THE WORLD. AS A CHILD I HAD A BIG APPETITE, ESPECIALLY WHEN I GOT HOME FROM SCHOOL, AND THAT SPAGHETTI CALMED MY HUNGER IN A VISCERAL WAY – IMMEDIATELY AND PERFECTLY.

SPAGHETTI IS THE PASTA *PAR EXCELLENCE*. IT'S A SYMBOL OF ITALY THAT I CONSIDER TO BE SACRED. AT MY RESTAURANT I ALWAYS HAVE SPAGHETTI WITH VARIOUS SAUCES ON THE MENU. IT'S ALSO IMPORTANT TO PRESERVE THE TRUE ORIGINS AND CULTURE OF SPAGHETTI. IT MAY NOT HAVE BEEN BORN IN ITALY, BUT THAT'S WHERE IT TRULY BECAME SPAGHETTI – A TERM THAT CAN'T BE TRANSLATED INTO ANY OTHER LANGUAGE IN THE WORLD. THAT'S WHERE THE PRACTICE OF TWIRLING IT ON A FORK BECAME AN EXPRESSION OF *JOIE DE VIVRE*. EVERYONE TRIES TO IMITATE SPAGHETTI, BUT IT WILL NEVER BE INTERNATIONAL. AND THAT'S BECAUSE ITALIAN CULTURE IS INIMITABLE.

ACADEMIA BARILLA

The Art of Italian Gastronomy

Since 2004, Academia Barilla has been a prestigious meeting place for international professionals and passionate devotees of Italian gastronomy and food culture. It was founded with the goal of spreading Italian gastronomic heritage and strengthening its value by promoting both the culinary culture and its high quality products around the world, encouraging interest in the country and its cuisine.

Academia Barilla is the international center for Italian gastronomy, and is part of the Barilla center in Parma. This splendid example of modern urban renewal, designed by architect Renzo Piano, is located on the grounds of the old Barilla factory.

Geographically, Academia Barilla is at the heart of the Italian food valley. Recognized as a culinary capital, Parma is in the center of a region with the highest quality agro-alimentary production in the world.

Academia Barilla was conceived to respond to a need for professional culinary training, and is equipped with a spectacular audi-

TORIUM, A MULTI-SENSORY LABORATORY, CLASSROOMS FOR DIDACTIC IN-STRUCTION AND PRACTICAL APPLICATION, AND ITS OWN INTERNAL RESTAU-RANT. IT ALSO HOUSES A VAST GASTRONOMIC LIBRARY WITH A COLLECTION OF MORE THAN 10,000 VOLUMES, COMBINING HISTORIC MENUS AND AN-TIQUE PRINTS – INDISPENSABLE TOOLS WHEN IT COMES TO SAFEGUARDING TRADITIONS – WITH THE MOST MODERN AND INNOVATIVE TECHNOLOGY. IN ORDER TO MAKE THIS RICH CULTURAL HERITAGE AVAILABLE TO THE PUBLIC, THE INSTITUTE HAS CREATED A WEBSITE WHERE ITS POSSIBLE TO SEARCH THE LIBRARY CATALOGUE AND ACCESS THE INDEX OF PRINTS AND MENUS ALONG WITH HUNDREDS OF DIGITIZED HISTORICAL TEXTS.

THE CENTER OFFERS AN EXTENSIVE ARRAY OF TRAINING COURSES, WHICH ARE ORGANIZED BY DURATION, CATEGORY, AND SKILL LEVEL, AND INTENDED FOR BOTH PROFESSIONALS AND CULINARY ENTHUSIASTS. THE TEACHING STAFF IS MADE UP OF PROFESSIONAL AND INTERNATIONALLY RENOWNED CHEFS, FULLY QUALIFIED TO PROVIDE COLLEAGUES, ENTHUSIASTS, OR COM-PANIES WITH AN EXCLUSIVE OPPORTUNITY FOR PERSONALIZED LEARNING, SEMINARS, THEMED COURSES, CONVENTIONS, ETC.

THE CENTER IS ALSO AN EXCELLENT STARTING POINT FOR INTERESTING GOURMET TOURS THAT WILL LEAD YOU TO DISCOVER A WORLD THAT OFFERS NOT ONLY BREATHTAKING LANDSCAPES, BUT UNIQUE ENOGASTRONOMIC TRADITIONS AND LOCAL PRODUCTS OF THE HIGHEST QUALITY.

TO GUARANTEE THE HIGHEST STANDARDS FOR FOOD PRODUCTS WITH A "MADE IN ITALY" LABEL, ACADEMIA BARILLA CHOOSES, APPROVES, AND DISTRIBUTES A WIDE RANGE OF ITALIAN SPECIALTIES THROUGH THEIR HIGHLY QUALIFIED CHEFS AND RESTAURATEURS, WHO SELECT SMALL-SCALE PRODUCERS AND ARTISANAL COMPANIES.

THE INSTITUTE IS ALSO PARTICULARLY ACTIVE ON THE CULTURAL FRONT – THE ACADEMIA BARILLA FILM AWARD CONTEST WAS INSTITUTED TO SPREAD KNOWLEDGE ABOUT ITALIAN GASTRONOMIC CULTURE, BOTH IN GENERAL AND RELATING TO SPECIFIC GEOGRAPHIC REGIONS, THROUGH SHORT FILMS (NARRATIVE OR DOCUMENTARY).

AS PART OF THE 2007 "PREMIO IMPRESA E CULTURA", ACADEMIA BARILLA WAS AWARDED FOR ITS WORK IN PROMOTING ITALIAN GASTRONOMIC CULTURE AND CREATIVITY THROUGHOUT THE WORLD.

INTRODUCTION

… BERGAMO AND NAPLES ARE ENEMIES,

AS MACCHERON'S TRUE HOME EACH YEARNS TO BE;

GREAT FIGHTING AND A GREATER FRACAS MADE

OVER MACCHERON THAN EVER TASSO CAUSED.

AND THUS THE QUARREL LEAVES TO US UNCERTAIN

THE PLACE THAT MACARON CALLS HOUSE AND HOMELAND,

AS TO THE GREEKS THE TRUTH IS STILL UNKNOWN

'BOUT WHICH PLACE THE FAMOUS HOMER CALLS HIS HOME.

LOST IN THE ANNALS OF TIME, THE ORIGINS OF PASTA HAVE ALWAYS BEEN AN INTRIGUING QUESTION THAT DOZENS OF AUTHORS HAVE ATTEMPTED TO ANSWER, AS THOUGH TRACING THE ANCESTRY OF THIS FOODSTUFF WAS VITAL TO ESTABLISHING THE NOBILITY OF A DISH THAT'S BECOME SYNONYMOUS WITH ITALY. COUNT FRANCESCO DI LEMENE (1634-1704) WAS A MAGISTRATE FROM LODI WHO SPENT HIS FREE TIME WRITING POETRY. HIS *DELLA DISCENDENZA E NOBILTÀ DE' MACCHERONI* ("ON THE ANCESTRY AND NOBILITY OF MACCHERONI") WAS PUBLISHED IN MODENA IN 1654. IT RECOUNTS THE FOLLOWING TALE: "FLOUR GAVE BIRTH

On the Ancestry and Nobility of Maccheroni

TO PASTA, A PROLIFIC MOTHER WHO GAVE BIRTH AS A WIDOW TO A SON CALLED GNOCCO (WHOSE TERRIBLE HABITS BROUGHT HIM TO A BAD END); BUT SHE ALREADY HAD OTHER SONS BY HER THREE HUSBANDS: CANNELLA (ROLLING PIN), GRAMOLA (KNEADING MACHINE), AND TORCHIO (HAND-CRANKED PRESS). WITH CANNELLA SHE HAD POLENTA AND LASAGNA, THE LATTER BEING MOTHER TO TORTA AND RAVIOLO. BUT IT WAS BY TORCHIO THAT PASTA BORE THE GREATEST CHILD OF THEM ALL, MACCARONE, FROM WHOM FIDELINO IS DESCENDED."

IN THIS WORDPLAY, WHICH IS NOT WITHOUT SOME IRONY, WE CAN CATCH AN EARLY ATTEMPT TO SORT OUT THIS COMPLICATED SUBJECT.

HISTORIANS AGREE THAT LIKE MANY HUMAN INVENTIONS, PASTA CAME ABOUT BY ACCIDENT. IT STARTED WITH A MIXTURE OF CRUSHED GRAINS AND WATER, WHICH WAS SOAKED IN COLD WATER AT FIRST, AND THEN SOAKED IN HOT WATER. THIS LED TO WHAT THE ANCIENT ROMANS CALLED *PULS*, BOTH A FOREFATHER OF *POLENTA* AND THE DOUGH FROM WHICH FRESH PASTA ORIGINATES. THE ROMANS' DIET WAS ACTUALLY DEPENDENT ON BARLEY (*TRITICUM TURGIDUM L. DICOCCUM*), AND THE SOUP THEY MADE FROM IT WAS A STAPLE IN THAT ERA. THIS EXPLAINS THE DELAY IN THE DEVELOPMENT OF PASTA, WHICH WAS MADE FROM WHEAT (COMMON WHEAT:

TRITICUM AESTIVUM L. DURUM; DURUM WHEAT: *TRITICUM TURGIDUM L. DURUM*). *LAGANA*, A DISH THAT CICERO ADORED, WAS REALLY STRIPS OF DOUGH, THOUGH THEY WERE LIKELY FRIED RATHER THAN BOILED.

AT VARIOUS PLACES AND TIMES, SEVERAL PRODUCTS WERE DEVELOPED FROM THAT VERY SAME CORE INGREDIENT: BREAD, LEAVENED OR UN-LEAVENED, WHICH WAS COOKED IN A DRY ENVIRONMENT; *POLENTA*, WHICH WAS COOKED IN WATER; FRITTERS, COOKED IN BOILING OIL; AND PASTA, FRESH OR DRIED, WHICH WAS COOKED IN WATER.

THE FIRST PRODUCTS WERE CHARACTERIZED BY THEIR SHORT SHELF LIFE AND THE NEED TO PREPARE THEM SHORTLY BEFORE THEY WERE TO BE CONSUMED. BUT DRIED PASTA DISTINGUISHED ITSELF AS A FORM OF "WHEAT PRESERVATION" AND IN-TRODUCED THE POSSIBILITY OF TRULY LONG TERM FOOD STORAGE. THIS IS THE QUALITY THAT WOULD LEAD IT TO BECOME SO WIDESPREAD AND SUCCESSFUL OVER TIME. RESEARCH ON THE ORIGINS OF PASTA GETS EVEN MORE COMPLICATED AS WE BEGIN TO FOLLOW THE PARALLEL PATHS OF DRIED AND FRESH PASTA.

MANY ANCIENT TEXTS REGARDING FOOD AND DIET USE THE TERMS *LASAGNA* AND *TRIA*. AS WE NOTED, THE FORMER WAS ALREADY KNOWN IN ROMAN TIMES (THE NAME PROBABLY DERIVES FROM THE GREEK *LÀGANON*) AND WAS A FORM OF FRESH PASTA DOUGH DESCENDED FROM THE *LAGANUM* OF THE CLASSICAL WORLD. IT WAS ROLLED OUT WITH THE HELP OF A ROLLING PIN, THEN CUT AND COOKED IN VARIOUS WAYS (*TAGLIATELLE, TAGLIERINI, TAGLIOLINI*, AND *MALTAGLIATI* ARE ALL TAKEN FROM

THE ITALIAN WORD *TAGLIARE*, "TO CUT"). THE SECOND, WHOSE NAME PROBABLY COMES FROM THE ARABIC *ITRIYAH*, PERHAPS IN TURN FROM THE GREEK *ÌTRION*, CAME IN LONGER SHAPES LIKE THREADS OR ROPES (*SPAGHETTI*, FROM *SPAGO*, MEANING "ROPE" OR "TWINE"; *TRENETTE*, FROM THE LIGURIAN *TRENNA*, A THIN STRIP OF COTTON OR SILK USED FOR TRIMMING). THESE DRIED PASTAS WERE MADE BY HAND AT FIRST, BUT THAT METHOD WAS LATER REPLACED BY MACHINES WITH AN EX-TRUDER AND A PERFORATED DISC, WHICH ORIGINATED "IN THE EASTERN PART OF THE ROMAN EMPIRE, IN THE FIRST CENTURIES OF OUR ERA," ACCORDING TO THE *TALMUD*. SOME BELIEVE THAT LONG FORM DRIED PASTA SPREAD THROUGHOUT THE MIDDLE EAST WITH THE FALL OF JERUSALEM (70 AD) AND THE DIASPORA. FROM THERE IT REACHED THE ISLAND OF SICILY DURING THE PERIOD OF ARAB RULE (9TH -11TH CEN-TURY). HISTORICAL EVIDENCE SHOWS THAT DRIED PASTA WAS BEING PRODUCED IN TRABÌA (PROVINCE OF PALERMO) IN 1154, AND THAT IT WAS DESTINED FOR EXPORT BY SEA. IT THEN SPREAD TO TWO PLACES: GENOA, AND THEREFORE ALL OF LIGURIA, WHERE THERE ARE HISTORICAL ACCOUNTS OF PASTA PRODUCTION BY THE *FIDELARI* (GENOAN PASTA-MAKERS GUILD) AS EARLY AS 1279; AND NAPLES, WHERE DRY PASTA WAS INTRODUCED IN THE 13TH CENTURY UNDER FEDERICO II.

BETWEEN THE 14TH AND 15TH CENTURY, THE PRODUCTS THAT WERE EVOLVING ALONG THE TWO MAIN PATHS (*LAGANA*: FRESH SHEETS OF PASTA DOUGH ORIGINATING IN ANCIENT ROME; *TRIA*: LONG FORM DRIED PASTA ORIGINATING IN THE MIDDLE EAST) STARTED TO GET MIXED UP, AND FINALLY MERGED INTO A SINGLE CATEGORY – PASTA.

BUT NO HISTORIAN COULD EVER KNOW THE NAMES OF ALL THE PEOPLE WHO INVENTED THE INFINITE VARIETIES – MORE THAN 300 – OF PASTA THAT HAVE DEVELOPED OVER SEVERAL CENTURIES. SURELY THE *TRAFILAI*, WHO SPECIALIZED IN THE CREATION AND IMPLEMENTATION OF PERFORATED DISCS FOR EXTRUSION, WERE THE ONES TO MODIFY THE SIMPLE ROUND HOLES OF THE *SPAGHETTI* DISC AND CREATE ALTERNATE VERSIONS, LEADING TO THE DEVELOPMENT OF MANY DIFFERENT TYPES OF PASTA. PRECISE CONTROL OVER THE SPEED AT WHICH THE EXITING DOUGH IS CUT CAN DETERMINE WHETHER THE PASTA WILL BE LONG, SHORT, OR EXTRA-SHORT. CHANGING THE ANGLE OR SHAPE OF THE HOLES CAN RESULT IN TWISTED OR HOLLOW PASTAS. AND COMBINING THESE TWO FACTORS GIVES WAY TO INFINITE SHAPES AND STYLES.

THE CREATIVITY OF THE *TRAFILAI* STIMULATED THE IMAGINATIONS OF MANY CHEFS. THROUGHOUT THE THOUSAND YEARS THAT PASTA HAS SPENT ON ITALIAN SOIL, THOSE CHEFS HAVE LEARNED TO ORCHESTRATE BEAUTIFUL SYMPHONIES WITH WONDERFUL BLENDS OF SHAPES, SAUCES, AND SPICES; GENUINE, IMMORTAL WORKS OF ART. *TRENETTE* WITH PESTO, *ORECCHIETTE* WITH TURNIP GREENS, AND *SPAGHETTI CARBONARA* EXEMPLIFY THE ART OF "BLENDING" THAT HAS SUCCESS-FULLY UNITED THE BEST LOCAL PRODUCTS IN PASTA-BASED DISHES.

THERE WERE ALSO THOSE IN THE MIDDLE AGES WHO WERE INSPIRED AT FIRST BY THE NEED TO USE UP LEFTOVERS, AND LATER BY THE GREAT RESULTS, WHO "DREAMED UP" STUFFED PASTAS (THE ENORMOUS *TORTELLI* FAMILY) BY WRAPPING

DOUGH AROUND FILLINGS MADE FROM VEGETABLES, CHEESE, MEAT, OR FISH, BASED ON REGION AND THE AVAILABILITY OF FOOD PRODUCTS.

THE FIRST STUFFED PASTA ON RECORD IS *RAVIOLI*, WHICH APPEARS IN A DOCUMENT FROM SAVONA DATING TO THE TURN OF THE 13TH CENTURY.

FRA' SALIMBENE DE ADAM (1221-1288), A 13TH CENTURY CHRONICLER FROM PARMA, RECOUNTS THAT SOME PEOPLE IN HIS TIME (WHOSE GLUTTONY HE CRITICIZES) HAD ACTUALLY CREATED A FORM OF TORTELLI "WITHOUT PASTA". *GNOCCHI, GNOCCHETTI, GNUDI, PISAREI, CHICCHE,* AND *CANEDERLI* SHARE THIS ORIGIN.

HOWEVER, THE OFFICIAL AND VERY WELL KNOWN CONSECRATION OF PASTA AND STUFFED PASTA CAME FROM THE *DECAMERON* BY GIOVANNI BOCCACCIO (1313-1375). IN THE 3RD NOVEL OF THE 8TH DAY, HE DESCRIBES THE DISTRICT OF BENGODI, "ON A MOUNTAIN, ALL OF GRATED PARMESAN CHEESE, DWELL FOLK THAT DO NOUGHT ELSE BUT MAKE MACARONI AND RAVIOLI, AND BOIL THEM IN CAPON'S BROTH, AND THEN THROW THEM DOWN…"

PASTA, IN ANY AGE, CAN BE A MOMENT OF JOY. THE PLEASURES OF GOOD COMPANY AND A GOOD FEAST ARE UNITED IN A CELEBRATION OF THE FLAVORS THAT THOUSANDS AND THOUSANDS OF RECIPES CAN IMPART – RECIPES THAT TELL COUNTLESS STORIES ABOUT PASTA WITHIN THESE PAGES. THEY ARE THE STORIES OF OUR OWN HISTORY, FROM THE PEOPLE WHO'VE MADE IT WITH LOVE AND CARE FOR OVER 1000 YEARS, TO THOSE WHO COOK IT AND EAT IT, ENJOYING THE MARRIAGE OF GOOD HEALTH AND GREAT FLAVOR IN A CULINARY MASTERPIECE.

DRIED PASTA

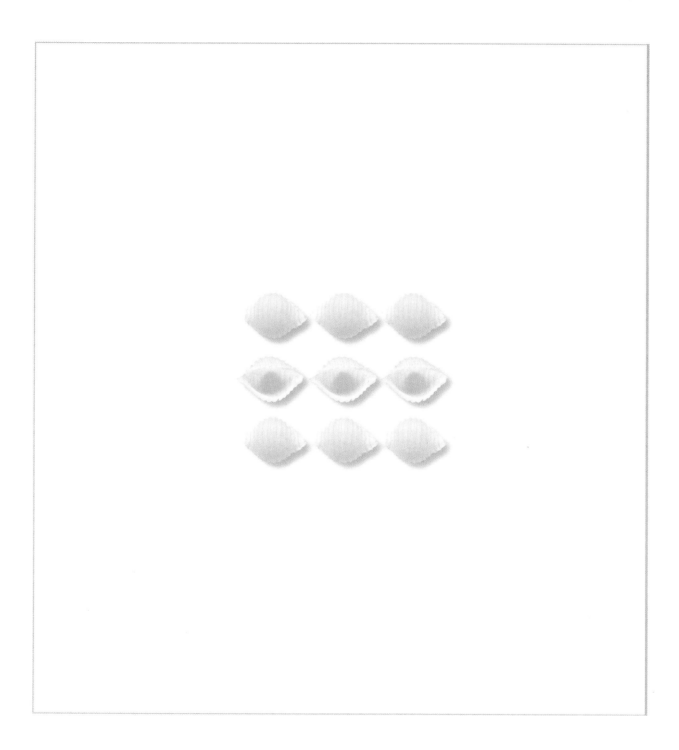

WHETHER IT'S MADE WITH WHITE FLOUR OR SEMOLINA, PASTA DOUGH ESSENTIALLY FALLS INTO ONE OF TWO LARGE CATEGORIES: DRIED AND FRESH. THE MAIN DIFFERENCE LIES IN THE DEHYDRATION PROCESS, WHICH FRESH PASTA DOES NOT UNDERGO, AND WHICH RESULTS IN ONE TYPE HAVING A MUCH LONGER SHELF LIFE THAN THE OTHER.

DESICCATED (OR DRIED, ACCORDING TO MODERN USAGE) SEMOLINA PASTA WAS FIRST USED IN SICILY IN THE 12TH CENTURY, AND SOON BECAME POPULAR ALL OVER ITALY. THE CULTURE OF *ITRYA* (PASTA) EXPANDED THROUGHOUT THE COUNTRY DURING THE TWO CENTURIES OF ARAB RULE, AND WENT ON TO TRAVEL FURTHER BY SEA, FIRST TO THE PORT OF GENOA AND THEN TO NAPLES.

BUT IT TOOK UNTIL THE 19TH CENTURY FOR PASTA TO BECOME A NATIONAL DISH. THE INTRODUCTION OF MODERN DEHYDRATION TECHNOLOGY FREED THE PRODUCTION PROCESS FROM THE CONFINES OF THE SPECIFIC MICROCLIMATES THAT WERE ONCE NECESSARY TO COMPLETE IT.

SEMOLINA PASTAS ARE STILL MADE FROM A MIXTURE OF WATER AND SEMOLINA, JUST AS THEY WERE BACK THEN. THE DOUGH PASSES THROUGH AN EXTRUDER, EITHER THE OLD-FASHIONED HAND-CRANKED VERSION OR A NEWER AUTOMATIC

MACHINE, WHICH PUSHES IT THROUGH A *TRAFILA*, A PERFORATED BRONZE DISC WITH DIFFERENTLY SHAPED HOLES FOR DIFFERENT KINDS OF PASTA. THE PASTA IS CUT BY A SERIES OF KNIVES AS IT COMES THROUGH THE DISC, AND THEIR SPEED DETERMINES THE LENGTH OF THE PASTA. DURING THE SUBSEQUENT DEHYDRATION PROCESS, THE PASTA SHRINKS IN VOLUME AND TAKES ON ITS DEFINITIVE SHAPE, TRANSFORMING INTO A PRODUCT WITH AN EXTENDED SHELF LIFE.

IN ITALY, MANY MODERN VARIETIES OF PASTA ARE LINKED TO REGIONAL GASTRONOMIC TRADITIONS THAT ARE BOTH ANCIENT AND DIVERSE. THERE ARE *PASTE LUNGHE* (LONG PASTAS) LIKE *SPAGHETTI, VERMICELLI, CAPELLINI, BUCATINI, ZITI, FUSILLI BUCATI, BAVETTE* AND *LINGUINE*; AND *PASTE CORTE* (SHORT PASTAS), WHICH CAN BE SMOOTH OR RIDGED, AND ARE AVAILABLE IN A SEEMINGLY INFINITE VARIETY OF SHAPES. THE SHORTER PASTAS TEND TO BE MORE WIDELY KNOWN: *PENNE, RIGATONI, MACCHERONI, MEZZE MANICHE, FUSILLI, ELICHE, CONCHIGLIE,* AND SO ON. THE EXTRA-SMALL PASTAS OR *PASTE DI MINESTRA* (SOUP PASTAS) MAY BE EVEN MORE NUMEROUS: *ANELLINI, DITALINI, STELLINE, SEMI, QUADRETTI, RISI...* AND THE TRULY ENDLESS LIST GOES ON.

Bavette al pesto di pomodoro
Bavette with Tomato Pesto

Servings 4
Difficulty Low
Prep Time 5'
Cook Time 8'

12.3 oz (350 g) bavette pasta – 1.76 lbs (800 g) ripe tomatoes (about 4 1/2 large tomatoes) – 1 oz (30 g) pine nuts (just under 1/4 cup) – 1 oz (30 g) shelled almonds (just under 1/4 cup whole or 1/3 cup sliced) – 1 oz (30 g) walnuts (1/4 cup whole or large pieces) – 1 garlic clove – 2/3 cup (60 g) Parmigiano Reggiano cheese, grated – 5 mint leaves – 3 tbsp (45 ml) extra-virgin olive oil – salt and pepper to taste.

Make an x-shaped incision on the bottom of each tomato and drop them into boiling water for 30-40 seconds. Use a slotted spoon to remove them from the pot (set the boiling water aside so the pasta can be cooked in it later) and put them right into a bowl of ice water. Once they've cooled thoroughly, peel off the skin. Then cut them into quarters and remove the seeds.

In a food processor combine the tomato quarters, pine nuts, almonds, walnuts, garlic (peeled and chopped), mint leaves, Parmigiano, and 2 tablespoons of extra-virgin olive oil. Blend until the mixture is smooth and consistent, then add a pinch of salt and pepper to taste.

Add a handful of coarse salt to the pot of water you set aside earlier. Bring it back to a boil and add the bavette. While the pasta cooks, transfer the pesto to a large bowl. When the pasta is done (it should be *al dente*), strain it and add it to the pesto. Add another tablespoon of olive oil and mix well.

Distribute the pasta among individual serving bowls, topping each portion with a dash of olive oil and sprinkling with more black pepper to taste.

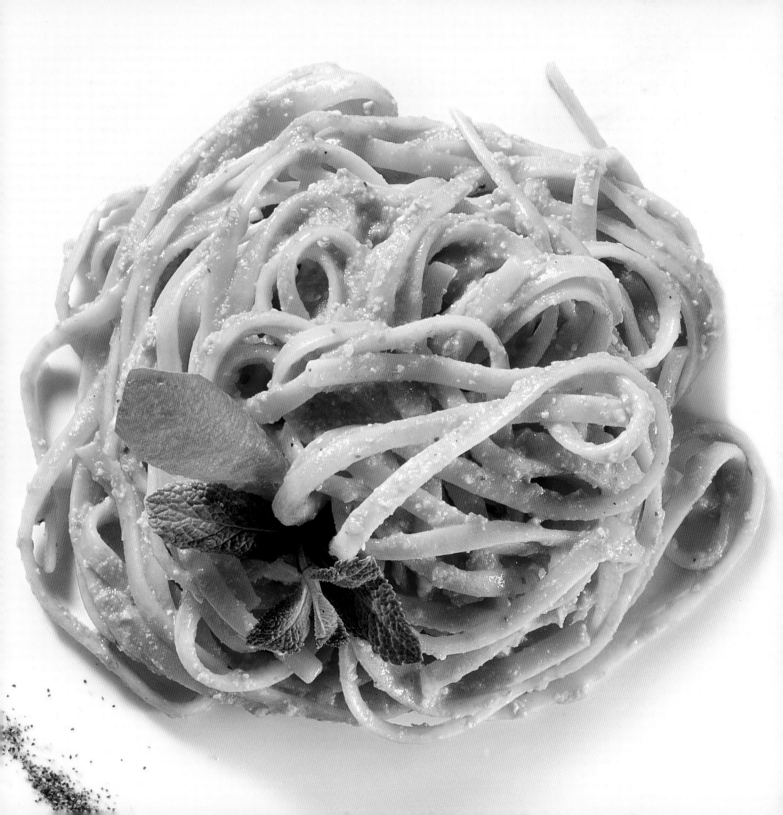

Bavette con gamberoni, Marsala e cipollotti freschi
Bavette with Jumbo Shrimp, Marsala, and Fresh Spring Onions

Servings 4
Difficulty Low
Prep Time 1h
Cook Time 8'

12.3 oz (350 g) bavette pasta – 0.88 lbs (400 g) jumbo shrimp – 2.5 oz (70 g) celery (about 2/3 cup chopped) – 2.8 oz (80 g) carrots (about 2/3 cup chopped) – 3.5 oz (100 g) onion (about 2/3 cup chopped) – 3.5 oz (100 g) spring onion (about 1 cup chopped) – 1 oz (25 g) tomato paste (about 1 1/2 tbsp) – 2 garlic cloves – 3/4 cup + 1 1/2 tbsp (200 ml) dry Marsala wine – 1/4 cup (60 ml) extra-virgin olive oil – salt and pepper to taste.

Clean the shrimp, removing the heads and shells, and cut them into small pieces.
Chop up the celery, carrots, and onion. Sauté them in a saucepan with half the oil and the 2 whole garlic cloves. After 5 minutes, add the shrimp shells and let them brown thoroughly. Then add the tomato paste and Marsala. Let all the liquid evaporate, then pour in 4 1/4 cups (1 L) of water. Let the sauce simmer for 30 minutes and season with salt and pepper. Filter the sauce when it's done. Finely chop the spring onion and sauté it in the rest of the oil. Add the shrimp and season with salt and pepper. Slowly add the filtered sauce and let it cook for a few minutes.
Boil the pasta in salted water and strain it when it's *al dente*. Add it to the shrimp sauce and cook it all together for a minute, stirring well to combine.

Chef's tips
For a more intense flavor, you can use the shrimp heads in the sauce. Just crush them with a meat pounder and add them along with the shells. The same technique can be used for other crustaceans, like lobster or scampi.

Bucatini all'amatriciana
Bucatini all'Amatriciana

Servings 4
Difficulty Low
Prep Time 15'
Cook Time 12'

12.3 oz (350 g) bucatini pasta – 5.3 oz (150 g) guanciale (cured pig's cheek) or pancetta – 4 ripe tomatoes – 1 hot red pepper – 1.4 oz (40 g) Pecorino Romano cheese, grated (about 1/3 cup + 1 tbsp) – salt and pepper to taste.

Slice the guanciale, then cut it into strips. Cook it in a pan on high heat with just a little bit of water to let the fat melt.

Blanch the tomatoes, peel them, cut them into quarters, and remove the seeds. Take the guanciale out of the pan and set it aside. Add the tomatoes, red pepper (crushed), and a pinch of salt and pepper to the melted fat. Cook it all together for 10 minutes and add the guanciale toward the end, just long enough for it to heat back up.

Meanwhile boil the bucatini in salted water. When they're *al dente*, strain them. Add them to the sauce along with the grated Pecorino. Mix well and serve hot.

Bucatini con seppie e piselli
Bucatini with Cuttlefish and Peas

Servings 4
Difficulty Low
Prep Time 30'
Cook Time 12'

12.3 oz (350 g) bucatini pasta – 12.3 oz (350 g) cuttlefish – 7 oz (200 g) peas, fresh or frozen (about 1 1/3 cup) – 3.5 oz (150 g) crushed tomatoes – 1 small onion – 1 garlic clove – 5-6 basil leaves – 1/3 cup + 1 1/2 tbsp (1 dl) dry white wine – 3 1/2 tbsp (50 ml) extra-virgin olive oil – salt and pepper to taste.

Peel and chop the onion and garlic. Clean and rinse the cuttlefish, then cut it into thin strips or very fine fillets, about 1/16-1/8 inch (2-3 mm) thick.

Drizzle a bit of olive oil in a pan and start browning the onion and garlic. Add the cuttlefish and cook for a few minutes, stirring continuously. Add the white wine, and when it's all been absorbed add the crushed tomatoes, peas, and basil leaves. Cook for another 15 minutes.

Meanwhile boil the pasta in salted water. When it's *al dente*, strain it well and transfer it to a large bowl. Toss the pasta with the cuttlefish sauce and serve it hot.

Chef's tips
The faster the cuttlefish cooks, the more tender it will be.
If you want the peas to have a vivid green color, you can blanch them separately. Boil them in lightly salted water for 3-4 minutes, then strain them and immediately put them in ice water to cool. Only add them to the cuttlefish for the last few minutes of cooking.

Caserecce con ricotta e cavolfiore fritto
Caserecce with Ricotta and Fried Cauliflower

Servings 4
Difficulty *Low*
Prep Time 30'
Cook Time 9'

12.3 oz (350 g) caserecce pasta – 0.88 lbs (400 g) cauliflower – 7 oz (200 g) ricotta – 1 tsp minced parsley – 3 1/2 tbsp (50 ml) extra-virgin olive oil – salt to taste – curry to taste (optional).

Wash the cauliflower and cut it into florets, removing the stems. Boil it in lightly salted water, making sure it doesn't get soft, and strain it. Let it cool, then fry it in very hot oil until it's browned on all sides.

Boil the pasta in a large pot of water with a handful of coarse salt.

Combine the ricotta, parsley, and 1/4 cup + 1 tablespoon (70 ml) of pasta water. If you prefer, you can also add curry to taste. Mix it all together until it's very creamy.

Strain the pasta as soon as it's *al dente* and transfer it to a large bowl. Stir in the fried cauliflower and seasoned ricotta, and serve immediately.

Chef's tips
Before boiling the cauliflower, dissolve a few tablespoons of flour in the water.

Castellane con palombo, olive e frutti di cappero
Castellane with Dogfish, Olives, and Caperberries

Servings 4
Difficulty Low
Prep Time 15'
Cook Time 12'

12.3 oz (350 g) castellane pasta – 1 lb (450 g) dogfish – 7 oz (200 g) cherry tomatoes (about 11 tomatoes) – 1.76 oz (50 g) black olives, pitted (about 11 large olives) – 8 pickled caperberries – 1 tbsp minced parsley – 1 garlic clove – 3 1/2 tbsp (50 ml) extra-virgin olive oil – salt and pepper to taste.

Sauté the entire garlic clove in half the olive oil. Dice the dogfish and add it to the pan, letting it cook for a few minutes. Cut the tomatoes into quarters and add them to the dogfish. Season with salt and pepper and cook it all for another 5 minutes.

Rinse the caperberries and cut them in half, thinly slice the olives, and add them both to the pan. Remove the garlic and keep the sauce warm.

In a small bowl or cup, mix the remaining olive oil with the minced parsley.

Meanwhile boil the castellane in salted water. Strain the pasta when it's *al dente* and combine it with the dogfish sauce.

Distribute it among serving plates and drizzle the olive oil and parsley mix over each portion.

Cellentani integrali con pere e Gorgonzola
Whole Wheat Cellentani with Pear and Gorgonzola

Servings 4
*Difficulty **Low***
Prep Time 30'
Cook Time 10'

12.3 oz (350 g) whole wheat cellentani pasta – 4.2 oz (120 g) Gorgonzola cheese – 1 1/2 tbsp (20 ml) extra-virgin olive oil – 2 heads of endive – 2 pears – 1 orange – 1 lemon – salt and pepper to taste.

Slice the endive and brown it in the oil for 3-4 minutes. Squeeze the orange and add the juice to the pan. Cook the endive for about 3 more minutes, then turn off the heat and add salt to taste.
Peel and dice the pears. Sprinkle them with lemon juice so they don't turn brown.
Boil the cellentani in a large pot of salted water. When the pasta is *al dente*, strain it and mix it with the endive. Let them cook together in the pan for a few minutes, adding the Gorgonzola (cut into pieces) and diced pear toward the end. Serve immediately.

Chef's tips
It's best to use a variety of pear that's "cooking-resistant" like or Decana or Kaiser.

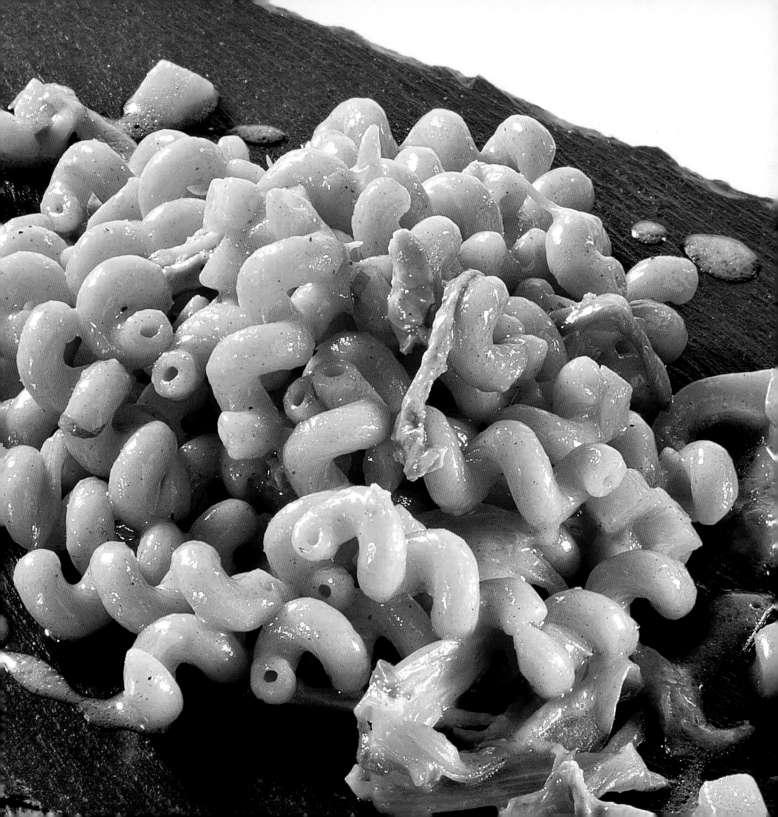

Chitarrine all'uovo con tonno fresco, porcini e zenzero
Egg Chitarrine with Fresh Tuna, Porcini, and Ginger

Servings 4
Difficulty Low
Prep Time 15'
Cook Time 9'

12.3 oz (350 g) egg chitarrine ("guitar string" pasta) – 8.8 oz (250 g) fresh tuna – 7 oz (200 g) fresh porcini mushrooms – fresh ginger to taste – 1 tsp minced parsley – 3 1/2 tbsp (50 ml) extra-virgin olive oil – salt and pepper to taste – 3 1/2 tbsp (50 ml) dry white wine.

Clean and rinse the mushrooms, and remove the stems. Drizzle a bit of olive oil in a pan and sauté the mushrooms with grated ginger to taste. When they're nice and browned, add the white wine and continue cooking on high heat until the liquid evaporates.

Cut the tuna into 1/3-1/2 inch (1 cm) cubes and cook it in a bit of oil. After a few minutes, once it's thoroughly cooked, add the mushrooms and season with salt to taste.

Boil the pasta in salted water and strain it as soon as it's *al dente*. Then combine it with the sauce, adding some fresh parsley and ground pepper.

Chef's tips
It's easier to grate the ginger if you freeze it first.

Ditaloni con cozze, patate e zafferano
Ditaloni with Mussels, Potatoes, and Saffron

Servings 4
Difficulty *Low*
Prep Time 20'
Cook Time 10'

12.7 oz (360 g) ditaloni rigati pasta – 1.1 lbs (500 g) mussels – 0.35 lbs (160 g) potatoes (about 1 cup diced) – 1/3 cup + 1 1/2 tbsp (100 ml) white wine – 1/4 cup (60 ml) extra-virgin olive oil – 1 garlic clove – 1 bay leaf – 1 tbsp minced parsley – 0.02 oz (0.5 g) saffron (about 3/4 tsp) – salt and pepper to taste.

Scrape the mussels clean and rinse them thoroughly. Combine them with the oil, bay leaf, whole garlic clove, and wine in a wide, shallow pan. Cover the pan and cook the mussels on high heat until they open. Remove some of the shells, then strain the liquid they cooked in and dissolve the saffron in it. Peel and cube the potatoes.

Boil the pasta and potatoes in a large pot of salted water. Strain it when they're very *al dente* and then finish cooking them in the pan with the mussels and saffron sauce.

Sprinkle with minced parsley, and serve with a dash of pepper and a drizzle of cold-pressed olive oil.

Ditalini rigati con acciughe e pomodori secchi
Ditalini Rigati with Anchovies and Sun-Dried Tomatoes

Servings 4
Difficulty *Low*
Prep Time 25'
Cook Time 9'

12.3 oz (350 g) ditalini rigati pasta – 2.8 oz (80 g) anchovies, packed in oil – 8 sun-dried tomatoes, packed in oil – 3 1/2 tbsp (50 ml) extra-virgin olive oil – half a garlic clove – 1 tsp minced parsley – 1/3 cup + 1 1/2 tbsp (100 ml) white wine – ground hot red pepper to taste – 1/3 cup (40 g) toasted breadcrumbs – salt to taste.

Boil the ditalini in salted water and strain them as soon as they're *al dente*.
Chop up the sun-dried tomatoes and anchovies. Drizzle some olive oil in a pan and cook the anchovies on very low heat until they dissolve, using a wooden spatula to help break them up. Be careful not to burn them; they should only need to cook for 1 minute at the most.
Add the chopped sun-dried tomatoes and mix well. Pour in the white wine and add the garlic (in one piece, not chopped up). Stir until the wine is almost completely evaporated.
Remove the garlic and add a pinch of hot pepper and minced parsley. Add the ditalini to the pan and mix well to blend the flavors, but don't let them cook past *al dente* stage.
Top with breadcrumbs (toasted in a very hot nonstick pan) to taste, and serve.

Chef's tips
Instead of sun-dried tomatoes marinated in oil, you can use those that aren't packed in liquid. Reconstitute the tomatoes by boiling them in a mixture of water, vinegar, and white wine for 5 minutes. Season the liquid with a bay leaf and other spices to taste, plus a pinch of salt and sugar.

Farfalle con ricotta e basilico
Farfalle with Ricotta and Basil

Servings 4
Difficulty Low
Prep Time 10'
Cook Time 10'

12.3 oz (350 g) farfalle pasta – 7 oz (200 g) ricotta – 3 1/2 tbsp (50 ml) heavy cream – 1 1/2 tbsp (20 ml) extra-virgin olive oil – 1/2 cup (50 g) Parmigiano Reggiano cheese, grated – 10 almonds, shelled and peeled – 15 basil leaves – half a garlic clove – salt – pepper.

Sift the ricotta into a large bowl and whisk it, slowly pouring in a bit of olive oil, until it's soft, creamy, and consistent.

Wash the basil and let it dry. Put it in a food processor with the almonds, Parmigiano, garlic, cream, and a pinch of salt and pepper. Blend until the sauce is smooth and carefully fold it into the ricotta. Boil the pasta in salted water and strain it when it's *al dente*. Add it to the bowl of ricotta sauce, mix well, and serve immediately.

Chef's tips
Add an ice cube to the mixture in the food processor. This will prevent overheating and keep the basil from turning a dark color.

Farfalle con salmone, finocchietto e zafferano
Farfalle with Salmon, Fennel, and Saffron

Servings 4
Difficulty *Low*
Prep Time *10'*
Cook Time *10'*

12.3 oz (350 g) farfalle pasta – 7 oz (200 g) smoked salmon – 3/4 cup + 1 1/2 tbsp (200 ml) heavy cream – 2 tbsp (30 g) butter – 4 bunches of fennel leaves – 0.02 oz (0.5 g) saffron (about 3/4 tsp) – salt and pepper to taste.

Cut the salmon into small pieces, about 1/8-1/4 inch square (5 x 5 mm). Sauté it in the butter for a few minutes, then add the cream, saffron, and fennel leaves. Remove it from the heat and season with salt to taste.

Boil the pasta in salted water. When it's *al dente*, strain it and combine it with the sauce. Mix well and serve with a sprinkling of white pepper.

Fiocchi rigati con trota salmonata in agrodolce
Fiocchi Rigati with Sweet and Sour Salmon Trout

Servings 4
Difficulty *Low*
Prep Time 35'
Cook Time 12'

12.3 oz (350 g) fiocchi rigati pasta – 0.66 lbs (300 g) salmon trout – 2.5 oz (70 g) celery (about 2 medium stalks) – 2.8 oz (80 g) carrots (about 1 1/2 small carrots) – 2.6 oz (75 g) onion (about 1 small onion) – 1.4 oz (40 g) raisins (about 1/4 cup packed) – 2 tbsp (30 ml) red wine vinegar – 2 tbsp (30 ml) extra-virgin olive oil – 2 sprigs of fresh oregano – 2 1/2 tbsp (20 g) toasted pine nuts (optional) – salt and pepper to taste.

Soak the raisins in water for 10 minutes. In the meantime, julienne the onion, celery, and carrot. Sauté the vegetables in the oil for about 5 minutes, then add the vinegar to deglaze the pan and let all the liquid evaporate. Add the raisins and cook everything together for a few minutes.
Clean, rinse, fillet, and debone the trout, then dice it and add it to the vegetables. Cook everything together for about 3-4 minutes, season with salt and pepper, and let it cool.
Boil the pasta in salted water and strain it when it's still very *al dente*. Quickly run cold water over the pasta and strain it again. Combine it with the trout sauce and garnish with oregano, stripped from the stem and finely chopped. You can also add the toasted pine nuts (just toss them in a very hot nonstick pan for about 30 seconds to toast them) at this point.

Chef's tips
Instead of cooling the pasta off by running cold water over it, you can strain it a few minutes before it should be ready according to package instructions. Spread it out in a large pan and drizzle it with some olive oil so it doesn't stick together, stirring frequently to encourage cooling.

Fusilli bucati corti con animelle
Fusilli Bucati Corti with Sweetbreads, Artichokes, and Smoked Ricotta

Servings 4
Difficulty **High**
Prep Time 10'
Cook Time 13'
For marinating 7h

12.3 oz (350 g) fusilli bucati corti – 0.88 lbs (400 g) sweetbreads – 3.5 oz (100 g) smoked ricotta – 5.3 oz (150 g) red onion (about 2 small onions) – 4 artichokes, 5.3–7 oz (150-200 g) each – 1 lemon – 5.3 oz (150 g) white onion (about 2 small onions) – 2.8 oz (80 g) carrots (about 1 1/2 small carrots) – 2.5 oz (70 g) celery (about 2 medium stalks) – 8 fresh mint leaves – 1/4 cup (60 ml) extra-virgin olive oil – salt and pepper to taste.
For the reduction sauce: 3/4 cup + 1 1/2 tbsp (200 ml) red wine – 2 1/2 tsp (10 g) sugar.

Soak the sweetbreads in cold water for a couple of hours to flush out any impurities. Put them in a pot with 8 1/2 cups (2 L) of cold water, a whole onion, a carrot, and a celery stalk. Bring the water to a boil, and let them cook for exactly 5 minutes from that point.

When they're done, strain them and let them cool. Put them in a strainer and place a weight on top of them (a meat tenderizer over a small plate for example). Let them sit there for 4-5 hours.

Peel the membrane from the sweetbreads, dice them, and sauté them in 1/3 of the oil. If you want, you can add a bit of salt.

In the meantime, reduce the wine and sugar over medium heat until the liquid reaches a syrupy consistency. Grate the lemon rind (only the yellow part) and juice the lemon. Clean the artichokes, removing the outer leaves and the stringy part in the middle. Slice them thinly, about 3/4-1 inch (2-3 cm) wide. Mix the lemon juice with water and soak the artichokes in it.

Peel the red onion and slice it, about 1/32 inch (1 mm) thick. Sauté it in 1/3 of the oil for 5-6 minutes, season with salt and pepper, and add the chopped mint leaves.

Stew the onion in the remaining oil. Add a ladleful of water and let it cook for another 10 minutes. Then add the artichokes, sweetbreads, and lemon zest. Season with salt and pepper to taste, and cook everything together for a few minutes to let the flavors blend.

Boil the pasta in salted water. Strain it when it's *al dente* and combine it with the sauce.

Transfer it to serving plates and top it with grated ricotta.

Gnocchetti sardi con capesante
Sardinian Gnocchetti with Scallops, Endive, and Chives

Servings 4
Difficulty Low
Prep Time 30'
Cook Time 14'

12.3 oz (350 g) Sardinian gnocchetti – 8 scallops – 2 heads of Belgian endive – 7 oz (200 g) whole plain yogurt – 3 1/2 tbsp (50 ml) extra-virgin olive oil – 1 shallot, minced – zest of 1 lemon – 1 tbsp minced chives – salt and pepper to taste.

Mix the shallot, lemon zest, and a pinch of salt and pepper with the yogurt. Set aside.
Rinse the scallops and quarter them. Wash the endive and cut the leaves into strips, then sauté them in a nonstick pan with half the oil and a pinch of salt. Remove the endive from the pan and transfer it to a plate. Sauté the scallops in the same pan, adding the remaining oil. Season with salt and return the endive to the pan.
Boil the pasta in salted water and strain it when it's *al dente*. Add it to the scallops and endive, and let everything cook together. Finish by mixing the gnocchetti with the seasoned yogurt, chives, and a drizzle of cold-pressed olive oil. Serve immediately.

Chef's tips
Cook the scallops for only 1-2 minutes on each side, over relatively high heat. Not only will they be more tender and flavorful, they won't shrink excessively.

Gnocchetti sardi con triglie e zafferano
Sardinian Gnocchetti with Mullet and Saffron

Servings 4
Difficulty **Medium**
Prep Time 40'
Cook Time 14'

12.3 oz (350 g) Sardinian gnocchetti – 8 small mullet – 7 oz (200 g) potatoes (about 1 medium) – 1.4 oz (40 g) celery (about 1/3 cup chopped) – 1.4 oz (40 g) carrot (about 1/3 cup chopped) – 1.4 oz (40 g) onion (about 1/4 cup chopped) – 0.02 oz (0.5 g) saffron (about 3/4 tsp) – 1 sprig of rosemary – 7 oz (200 g) tomatoes (about 1 1/2 medium) – 2 tbsp (30 g) butter – 1 1/2 tbsp (20 ml) extra-virgin olive oil – 2/3 cup (150 ml) heavy cream – salt and freshly ground pepper to taste.

Carefully scrape the scales from the fish. Use a very sharp knife to make the appropriate incisions and remove the head and bones.

Peel the potato and cut it into 1/3-1/2 inch (1 cm) cubes. Finely dice the celery, carrots, and onions. Sauté the vegetables in the butter for a few minutes.

Then add the cream and saffron and let it all boil for a few minutes. Season with salt and pepper to taste and keep the sauce warm.

Cut an X into the bottom of the tomato and blanch it in boiling water. Strain it, let it cool, and peel it. Remove any tougher parts from the inside and cut it into cubes.

Finely chop the rosemary and sauté it in the oil on low heat. Add the mullet and quickly cook them on both sides, starting on the side that has exposed flesh. When they're well browned, remove them from the pan and keep them warm. Transfer the saffron sauce to the pan.

Boil the gnocchetti in salted water and strain them when they're *al dente*. Combine them with the sauce, cubed tomatoes, and mullet fillets.

Gramigna con ragù di salsiccia
Gramigna with Sausage Ragù and Creamy Pea Sauce

Servings 4
Difficulty *Low*
Prep Time 20'
Cook Time 5'

12.3 oz (350 g) gramigna pasta.
For the ragù: 1 1/2 tbsp (20 ml) extra-virgin olive oil – 3.4 oz (100 g) Tropea red onion (about 1/3 of an onion) – 0.88 lbs (400 g) sausage – 3 1/2 tbsp (50 ml) red wine – 2 sprigs of fresh thyme – salt and pepper to taste.
For the pea sauce: 1 1/2 tbsp (20 ml) extra-virgin olive oil – 7 oz (200 g) peas (about 1 1/3 cups) – 1 oz (30 g) shallot (about 1 medium shallot) – 2 cups (500 ml) vegetable broth – salt and pepper to taste.

Slice the shallot and heat the oil in a pan. Sauté the shallot on low heat for a few minutes, then add the peas and the broth. Let it simmer for 15-20 minutes, adding salt and pepper to taste. Blend everything together until it's dense and creamy, and keep the sauce warm.

Mince the onion and sauté it in another pan with the olive oil and the whole sprig of thyme. Break up the sausage with your hands and add it to the onion. Brown the sausage for 3-4 minutes, then pour in the wine and let all the liquid evaporate. Cook it for another 10 minutes, adding a few tablespoons of hot water if necessary. Season with salt and pepper and remove the thyme sprig.

Boil the pasta in salted water. Strain it when it's *al dente* and mix it with the ragù. Spread a layer of pea sauce on each plate, top it with a portion of pasta, and serve.

Chef's tips
Try making this recipe with fennel sausage instead of regular sausage, or adding 1/2 teaspoon of roughly chopped fennel bulbs.

Lagane e fagioli
Lagane and Beans

Servings 4
Difficulty Low
Prep Time 1h
Cook Time 5'

For the pasta: 1 1/2 cups (250 g) re-milled durum wheat semolina – 1/2 cup (125 ml) water.
For the topping: 1.1 lbs (500 g) fresh beans (or dried) – 1 garlic clove – 3 1/2 tbsp (50 ml) extra-virgin olive oil – 1 tbsp minced rosemary – hot red pepper (fresh or dried) to taste – salt to taste.

Mix the semolina with the warm water until the dough is smooth and consistent. Wrap it in plastic and let it sit for about 30 minutes.
Boil the beans in a large amount of water, adding a handful of coarse salt at the end. If you prefer to use dried beans, soak them in cold water for at least 12 hours before using them.
To make the lagane, which are large tagliatelle, roll the dough out to about 1/32 inch (1 mm) thick. Cut it into strips about 1/3-1/2 inch (1 cm) wide. Lay the lagane out on a lightly floured surface.
Heat the oil in a pan. Sauté the whole garlic clove over medium heat with hot red pepper (fresh or dried) to taste. When it's golden brown, add the thoroughly strained beans and let them absorb the flavors.
Meanwhile boil the pasta in salted water. Strain it when it's *al dente* and combine it with the beans and rosemary.

Linguine all'astice
Linguine and Lobster

Servings 4
Difficulty Low
Prep Time 30'
Cook Time 10'

12.3 oz (350 g) linguine – 2 small lobsters, about 1.75 lbs (750/800 g) each – 17.6 oz (500 g) whole peeled tomatoes or crushed tomatoes – 3 1/2 tbsp (50 ml) extra-virgin olive oil – 1 tbsp minced parsley – 1 garlic clove – hot red pepper to taste – salt to taste.

Sauté the whole garlic clove with a bit of oil and hot pepper (fresh or dried) to taste. Divide the lobsters in half, lengthwise. Place them in the pan with the shell side up and let them cook.

After a few minutes, add the whole peeled tomatoes (chopped) or crushed tomatoes. Season with salt and pepper and cover the pan. Let it cook for 10 minutes.

Remove the garlic from the pan. Take the lobsters out and remove the shells, then chop the meat and return it to the pan.

Boil the pasta in salted water and strain it when it's very *al dente*. Add it to the lobster sauce along with the parsley, and let everything cook together for a minute.

Top each serving with a drizzle of cold-pressed olive oil.

Maccheroncini alle canocchie
Maccheroncini with Shrimp

Servings 4
Difficulty *Medium*
Prep Time 25'
Cook Time 12'

12.3 oz (350 g) maccheroncini pasta – 16 shrimp – 3.5 oz (100 g) onion (about 1 1/2 small) – 0.55 lbs (250 g) cherry tomatoes (about 15) – 3 1/2 tbsp (50 ml) brandy – 1 garlic clove – 1 tbsp minced parsley – 5-6 basil leaves – 3 tbsp (40 ml) extra-virgin olive oil – salt and pepper to taste.

Clean the shrimp, slicing the ends of the shell and removing the top part. The slice them into 4-5 pieces.
Wash the tomatoes, cut them into quarters, and remove the seeds.
Chop the onion and garlic and sauté them with 2/3 of the oil over low heat. When they've softened, add the shrimp and brown them on high heat for a few minutes. Add the brandy and let it flambé.
Then add the tomatoes, parsley, and hand-torn basil. Let it simmer for 10 minutes.
Boil the maccheroncini in salted water. Strain the pasta when it's *al dente* and combine it with the shrimp sauce. Drizzle cold-pressed olive oil on top.

Chef's tips
Old Adriatic fishermen recommend that you only buy the shrimp in months with an "R" in the name (except January), because that's when they're best.

Maccheroncini con cipolla di Tropea e verdure
Maccheroncini with Tropea Onion and Vegetables

Servings 4
Difficulty *Low*
Prep Time *30'*
Cook Time *12'*

12.3 oz (350 g) maccheroncini pasta – 0.88 lbs (400 g) eggplant (about 5 cups cubed) – 7 oz (200 g) red bell pepper (about 1 1/3 cups diced) – 7 oz (200 g) green bell pepper (about 1 1/3 cups diced) – 5.3 oz (150 g) Tropea onion (about 2 small onions) – 1.4 oz (40 g) toasted slivered almonds (about 1/3 cup) – 1/3 cup + 1 tbsp (40 g) Pecorino cheese, grated – 1/3 cup + 1 1/2 tbsp (100 ml) extra-virgin olive oil – 1 tbsp minced parsley – salt and pepper to taste.

Mince the parsley and combine it with 2 tablespoons of olive oil in a small bowl.

Wash and clean all the vegetables. Cut the onion into thin wedges, and dice the eggplant and peppers.

Heat 1/4 of the remaining oil in a pan and sauté the onion on low heat. If it starts to overcook, add a few tablespoons of water.

Separately sauté the eggplant and peppers in the last bit of oil.

Mix together all the vegetables and season with salt and pepper.

Boil the maccheroncini in salted water, strain it when it's *al dente*, and combine it with the vegetables. Sprinkle grated Pecorino and toasted, slivered almonds (just toss the almonds in a very hot nonstick pan for a few seconds to toast them) on top.

Chef's tips
If you prefer, the almonds can be replaced with shelled and peeled pistachios or pine nuts, toasted the same way as the almonds.

Maccheroni cacio e uovo
Egg and Cheese Macaroni

Servings 4
Difficulty Low
Prep Time 10'
Cook Time 11'

12.3 oz (350 g) macaroni – 3 eggs – 2 tbsp (30 g) butter – 2/3 cup (60 g) Parmigiano Reggiano cheese, grated – 1 tsp minced parsley – salt to taste.

Boil the macaroni in salted water.
While it cooks, beat the eggs with the grated Parmigiano in a large bowl and melt the butter in a pot. Strain the pasta when it's *al dente* and mix it with the butter. Then combine it with the eggs and Parmigiano and mix well.
Before the eggs congeal, sprinkle the parsley over the macaroni and serve.

Chef's tips
Before adding the egg and cheese mixture to the pasta, temper it with 3-4 tablespoons of pasta water. You should also take the pasta off the burner before adding it. This makes it harder for the eggs to coagulate and results in a creamier consistency.

Malloreddus con fave
"Malloreddus" with Fava Beans and Black Olives, and Gransardo with Tomato Coulis

Servings 4
Difficulty Low
Prep Time 30'
Cook Time 12'

12.3 oz (350 g) *malloredus* pasta – 3.5 oz (100 g) fresh fava beans (about 2/3 cup) – 3.5 oz (100 g) taggiasca olives (about 23 large) – 1.3 lbs (600 g) San Marzano tomatoes (about 9–10) – 5.3 oz (150 g) Gransardo cheese, in flakes – 1 onion – 8 basil leaves – 2 tbsp (30 ml) extra-virgin olive oil – 1 tsp cornstarch – 1 garlic clove – salt and pepper to taste.

Boil the fava beans in salted water for about 2 minutes, then strain them and peel them. Pit the olives and finely chop them. Blanch the tomatoes and remove the skin and seeds. Dice half of them, and purée the rest with the basil, onion, and a pinch of salt and pepper.

Sauté the whole garlic clove in a bit of olive oil (it will be removed before adding the pasta). Add the fava beans, diced tomato, and olives. Heat the tomato purée in a small nonstick pot. When it reaches a boil, turn off the heat and remove the pot from the burner.

Boil the *malloreddus* in salted water and strain them when they're *al dente*. Add the pasta to the pan of vegetables and let everything cook together on high heat for a minute.

Spread some lukewarm *coulis* (tomato purée) on each plate and cover it with a portion of pasta. Top the pasta with Gransardo flakes and a drizzle of cold-pressed olive oil.

Mezze maniche
con melanzane fritte
Mezze Maniche with Fried Eggplant

Servings 4
*Difficulty **Low***
Prep Time 20'
Cook Time 12'

12.3 oz (350 g) mezze maniche pasta – 0.88 lbs (400 g) eggplant (about 5 cups diced) – 2.8 oz (80 g) salted ricotta, in flakes – 1 bunch of basil – olive oil for frying – salt to taste.

Peel the eggplant and cut it into 1/3–1/2 inch (1 cm) cubes. Fry them in a good amount of olive oil and remove them with a perforated spoon, letting the excess oil drip off. Place them on paper towels to dry.

Boil the pasta in salted water. Strain it when it's *al dente* and mix it with the eggplant in a large bowl. Add the basil, roughly chopped, and serve it topped with ricotta flakes.

Mezze maniche con tonno e asparagi
Mezze Maniche with Tuna and Asparagus

Servings 4
Difficulty *Low*
Prep Time 20'
Cook Time 12'

12.3 oz (350 g) mezze maniche rigate pasta – 5.3 oz (150 g) tuna, packed in olive oil – 7 oz (200 g) asparagus – 2 shallots – 2 tbsp minced parsley – 3 tbsp (40 ml) extra-virgin olive oil – 1/3 cup + 1 tbsp (40 g) Parmigiano Reggiano cheese, grated – salt and pepper to taste.

Thinly slice the shallots and sauté them in a bit of oil on low heat. Remove the tougher parts from the asparagus stems, wash them, and slice them into rounds.

When the shallots have softened, add the asparagus and let it brown. Add 1/2 tablespoon of water to help along the cooking process.

As soon as the asparagus is tender to the touch, add the tuna (well drained) and parsley. Season with salt and pepper to taste.

Meanwhile boil the pasta in salted water. Strain it when it's *al dente* and add it to the pan with the sauce. Mix well, sprinkle with Parmigiano and serve.

Chef's tips
The oil-packed tuna should be well drained and added to the sauce at the end. This way it remains flavorful and tender, and it doesn't dry out.

Minestrone alla genovese
Minestrone alla Genovese

Servings 4
Difficulty **Low**
Prep Time **1h**
Cook Time **30'**

3 oz (90 g) leeks (about 1 leek) – 2.5 oz (70 g) celery (about 2 medium stalks) – 0.44 lbs (200 g) potatoes (about 1 medium potato) – 5.3 oz (150 g) zucchini (about 1 small zucchini) – 2.8 oz (80 g) carrots (about 1 1/2 small carrots) – 3.9 oz (110 g) fennel (about 1 1/4 cups sliced) – 3.5 oz (100 g) bell pepper (about 1 1/2 small peppers) – 3.5 oz (100 g) broccoli, no stems (about 1 1/2 cups) – 3.5 oz (100 g) Romanesco broccoli, no stems (about 1 1/2 cups) – 3.5 oz (100 g) cauliflower, no stems (about 1 cup) – 4 Brussels sprouts – 5.3 oz (150 g) cut spaghetti – 1/3 cup (80 ml) extra-virgin olive oil – 5.3 oz (150 g) Parmigiano cheese rind, exterior scraped clean – 8 1/2 cups (2 L) water – salt to taste.
For the pesto: 0.5 oz (15 g) basil leaves (about 30 leaves) – 1/3 cup (30 g) Parmigiano Reggiano cheese, grated – 3 tbsp (20 g) aged Pecorino cheese, grated – 2 tsp (5 g) pine nuts – half a garlic clove – 1/3 cup + 1 1/2 tbsp (100 ml) extra-virgin olive oil (preferably Ligurian) – salt to taste.

Heat the 8 1/2 cups of water and clean and dice all the vegetables. Warm up half the oil in a pot, add the vegetables, and let them cook for 4-5 minutes. Pour in the boiling water and add the Parmigiano rind. Bring the contents of the pot to a boil, turn down the heat, and simmer for at least 15 minutes. Season with salt to taste and add the pasta.

Meanwhile, clean the basil and lay it out on a cloth to dry. Blend it with the oil, garlic, pine nuts, and a pinch of salt. Then add the grated cheeses to the pesto and mix well.

Once the pasta is cooked (it should take about 5-6 minutes), turn off the heat. Let the minestrone cool and transfer it to individual bowls. Serve each portion with 1 tablespoon of pesto, a drizzle of cold-pressed olive oil, and a piece of Parmigiano rind.

Chef's tips
Minestrone is traditionally cooked for a very long time, but try to cook it for less to maintain the textures and vivid colors of the various vegetables. If you want to meld the flavors further, purée a few ladlefuls of the soup and add it back to the rest.

Pastina al sugo di pesce
Pastina in Fish Broth

Servings 4
Difficulty High
Prep Time 40'
Cook Time 30'

0.44 lbs (200 g) musky octopus – 0.88 lbs (400 g) tub gurnard – 0.26 lbs (120 g) mullet – 1.76 oz (50 g) squid rings – 0.44 lbs (200 g) small cuttlefish – 0.22 lbs (100 g) mussels – 0.22 lbs (100 g) clams – 1/3 cup + 1 1/2 tbsp (100 ml) extra-virgin olive oil – 7 oz (200 g) minute pasta – 1.76 oz (50 g) onion (about 1/3 cup chopped) – 4 plum tomatoes, or 12.3 oz (350 g) whole peeled tomatoes – 1 tbsp minced parsley – salt and pepper (or hot red pepper) to taste – 8 slices of rustic bread (optional).

Rinse the clams, flushing out any sand. Thoroughly scrape the mussels clean and remove the beards. Clean the tub gurnard and mullet, fillet them, and cut them into 3/4-1 inch (2-3 cm) diamonds. Clean the cuttlefish and musky octopus, and rinse the squid rings.

Finely chop the onion and sauté it in the oil in a covered saucepan. Meanwhile peel the tomatoes, remove the seeds, and slice them very thinly. When the onion has turned golden brown, add the tomatoes. Let them cook for 5 minutes, then add all the fish. Season with salt and cook for 15-20 minutes, adding a few ladlefuls of hot water as needed.

Separately boil the pastina in salted water and strain it when it's halfway done.

When the fish is ready, add the pastina and let it finish cooking in the fish broth. Serve it very hot with minced parsley, ground black pepper (or hot red pepper flakes), and slices of toasted rustic bread (optional).

Penne agli asparagi
Penne with Asparagus

Servings 4
Difficulty Low
Prep Time 15'
Cook Time 11'

12.3 oz (350 g) penne rigate pasta – 0.55 lbs (250 g) asparagus – 3 1/2 tbsp (50 g) butter – 1/3 cup + 1 tbsp (40 g) Parmigiano Reggiano cheese, grated – 2 garlic cloves – 2 eggs – hot red pepper to taste – salt to taste.

Carefully wash the asparagus and remove the tough parts. Slice the stems into rounds and leave the tips whole. Put them in a pot (terracotta if possible) with the butter, whole garlic clove, and a bit of hot pepper (at your discretion). Stew them for about 10 minutes on medium heat.

Beat the eggs in a bowl with the grated Parmigiano and a pinch of salt.

Boil the pasta in salted water and strain it when it's *al dente*. Remove the garlic and hot pepper from the pot of asparagus, and add the pasta. Then add the egg and cheese mixture, quickly stir it into the pasta, and serve immediately.

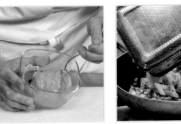

Penne all'arrabbiata
Penne all'Arrabbiata

Servings 4
Difficulty Low
Prep Time 30'
Cook Time 9'

12. 3 oz (350 g) penne pasta – 2 tbsp (0.3 dl) extra-virgin olive oil – 21 oz (600 g) crushed tomatoes or whole peeled tomatoes – hot red pepper to taste – 2 garlic cloves, peeled and sliced – salt to taste.

Sauté the garlic with the olive oil and hot red pepper to taste, but don't let it brown too much. If you're using fresh hot pepper it should be sliced, but if you're using dried hot pepper wear disposable gloves and crush it by hand.

Once the garlic and hot pepper are slightly browned, add the crushed tomatoes (or whole peeled tomatoes, chopped). Season with salt to taste and cook on high heat for 15 minutes, stirring occasionally.

Meanwhile boil the penne in salted water. When it's *al dente*, strain it and combine it with the sauce.

Chef's tips
Penne rigate are recommended for arrabbiata sauce because the ridges hold the sauce better.

Penne di farro
Spelt Penne with Sausage, Scampi, and Cardoons

Servings 4
Difficulty Low
Prep Time 1h
Cook Time 10'

12.3 oz (350 g) spelt flour penne pasta – 12 scampi – 2 fresh pork sausages, about 0.22 lbs (100 g) – 0.55 lbs (250 g) cardoons – 1 garlic clove – 1 lemon – 1 tbsp minced parsley – 3 1/2 tbsp (50 ml) extra-virgin olive oil – salt and pepper to taste.

Cook the sausage in a skillet over medium heat for 10 minutes. Let it cool completely and slice it into thin rounds. Arrange it in a pan lined with parchment paper and bake it in a preheated oven at 325° F (170° C) for 15 minutes, until it's crispy.

Clean the cardoons, removing the fibrous parts, and cube them. Boil them for 5 minutes in salted water with a bit of lemon juice. Strain them and let them cool.

Clean and devein the scampi, removing the heads and shells. Leave the ends on 8 scampi, which will be used whole. Dice the other 4 scampi.

Heat half the oil in a pan with the whole garlic clove. Sauté the whole scampi for a minute on each side. Remove them from the pan, set them aside, and season them with salt and pepper.

Combine the remaining scampi with the cardoons in the same pan. Sauté them for a minute, then add the parsley (set aside a pinch of for later) and season with salt and pepper to taste.

Boil the pasta in salted water and strain it when it's *al dente*. Add it to the pan along with the whole scampi and let everything cook together for a minute, mixing well.

Top it with crispy sausage and a sprinkling of parsley.

Penne nei cestini di Parmigiano
Penne with Lamb and Artichokes in Parmesan Baskets

Servings 4
Difficulty Low
Prep Time 39'
Cook Time 9'

12.3 oz (350 g) smooth penne pasta – 0.66 lbs (300 g) lamb – 4 artichokes – 1/3 cup + 1 tbsp (40 g) Parmigiano Reggiano cheese, grated – 1/3 cup + 1 1/2 tbsp (100 ml) extra-virgin olive oil – 1/3 cup + 1 1/2 tbsp (100 ml) dry white wine – 2/3 cup (150 ml) water – 1 sprig of rosemary – 1 onion – salt and pepper to taste.
For the baskets: 1.76 oz (50 g) Parmigiano Reggiano cheese – 1.76 oz (50 g) Pecorino cheese.

Dice the lamb and mince the onion. Clean the artichokes and slice them. Strip the rosemary from the stem and mince it.

Heat the oil in a pan and sauté the lamb with the onion. Add the artichokes and let them cook for a few minutes. Then add the white wine and let it evaporate completely. Add 2/3 cup (150 ml) of water and let it all stew for 10 minutes, seasoning with salt and pepper to taste.

Boil the pasta in salted water and strain it when it's *al dente*. Combine it with the sauce and minced rosemary, then sprinkle the Parmigiano on top and mix well.

For the baskets: Heat a small nonstick pan. Mix together the grated Parmigiano and Pecorino. When the pan is very hot, spread the cheese evenly on the bottom and let it melt. This should result in a compact, light brown wafer. Place it on an upside down ramekin while it's still hot and carefully mold it around the bottom to create the basket shape. Let it cool there and repeat the process until you have four baskets. Serve the finished pasta inside them.

Penne mare e monti
Surf and Turf Penne

Servings 4
Difficulty Low
Prep Time 30'
Cook Time 10'

12.3 oz (350 g) penne pasta – 1.10 lbs (500 g) clams – 3 1/2 tbsp (50 ml) white wine – 0.66 lbs (300 g) cultivated mushrooms – 3 1/2 tbsp (50 ml) extra-virgin olive oil – garlic cloves – 1 tbsp minced parsley – salt and pepper to taste.

Heat half the oil in a pot and sauté half the minced parsley with 1 whole garlic clove. Wash the clams well and add them along with the white wine. Cover the pot and let the clams cook until they open. Remove some of the shells and the garlic clove. Filter the liquid from the pot.

Clean and slice the mushrooms and mince the other garlic clove. Heat the remaining oil in another pot with the minced garlic and remaining parsley. Add the mushrooms and let them sauté on high heat for a few minutes. Season them with salt and pepper. Add the clams with their liquid and if necessary, let the sauce thicken.

Meanwhile boil the pasta in salted water. Strain it when it's *al dente* and transfer it to the pot of clam sauce. Let everything cook together for a minute, mixing well, and serve.

Penne rigate con salsiccia
Penne Rigate with Sausage, Cabbage, and Smoked Provola

Servings 4
Difficulty *Low*
Prep Time 20'
Cook Time 10'

12.3 oz (350 g) penne rigate – 0.44 lbs (200 g) sausage – 0.33 lbs (150 g) Savoy cabbage – 1 garlic clove – 1 sprig of rosemary, chopped – 3 1/2 tbsp (50 ml) extra-virgin olive oil – 2 oz (60 g) smoked Provola cheese – 1/3 cup (30 g) Parmigiano Reggiano, grated – salt and pepper to taste.

Brown the sausage in a wide, shallow pan with the whole garlic clove and chopped rosemary. Julienne the cabbage and add it to the pan along with 3-4 tablespoons of water. Let it braise on low heat for 5 minutes.
When the sauce is ready, boil the penne in a large pot of salted water. Strain the pasta and toss it with the finished sauce and grated Parmigiano. Top each serving with thin strips of smoked Provola.

Penne saporite al rosmarino
Rosemary Penne

Servings 4
Difficulty Low
Prep Time 20'
Cook Time 11'

12.3 oz (350 g) penne pasta – 3/4 cup + 1 tbsp (80 g) Pecorino cheese, grated – 3.5 oz (100 g) onion (about 1 1/2 small) – 1 oz (30 g) pine nuts (about 4 tbsp) – 1 1/2 tbsp (20 g) butter – 2 sprigs of rosemary – 1 garlic clove – hot red pepper – 3 1/2 tbsp (50 ml) dry white wine – 2 tbsp (30 ml) extra-virgin olive oil – salt to taste.

Heat a few tablespoons of oil and a pat of butter in a pot. Mince the rosemary, pine nuts, onion, and garlic together. Add the mixture to the pot and let it cook on low heat. Season it with salt and add the wine. Turn the heat up high and let the wine evaporate. Then turn the heat down again, add a pinch of hot pepper, and let it cook for another 10 minutes.
Boil the pasta in salted water and strain it when it's *al dente*. Add it to the pot of sauce with a bit of pasta water and let everything cook together for a minute. Sprinkle grated Pecorino on top and serve.

Chef's tips
It's best to mince the rosemary, pine nuts, onion, and garlic with a knife. A food processor would break them down too much and the results would be less than optimal.

Pennette con zucca e pancetta
Pennette with Pumpkin, Pancetta, and Modena Balsamic Vinegar

Servings 4
Difficulty *Low*
Prep Time 40'
Cook Time 10'

14 oz (400 g) pennette pasta – 10.5 oz (300 g) pumpkin (about 2 1/2 cups diced) – 7 oz (200 g) smoked pancetta, sliced 1/8 inch (3 mm) thick – 1 yellow onion – 1 tbsp minced parsley – 1 sprig of rosemary – 1 garlic clove – Modena balsamic vinegar to taste – 1 1/2 tbsp (20 ml) extra-virgin olive oil – 3 cups (0.75 L) water – salt and pepper to taste.

Clean the pumpkin, remove the seeds, and cut it into 1/3-1/2 inch (1 cm) cubes.

Place the pumpkin scraps in a pan with the onion and a pinch of salt. Pour in about 3 cups (750 ml) of water, or enough to cover everything. Bring it to a boil and let the vegetables cook. Then purée them until the texture is very creamy. If it's too dense, add a bit of the water they cooked in. Cut the pancetta into thin strips. Mince the rosemary, parsley, and garlic.

Heat some oil in a pan and sauté the diced pumpkin. Season it with salt and pepper, remove it from the pan, and set it aside. Sauté the pancetta in the same pan. When the fat starts to brown, add the garlic, rosemary, and half the parsley. Let it cook for 2 minutes, then add the pumpkin purée and diced pumpkin.

Boil the pasta in salted water and strain it when it's *al dente*. Add it to the pan of sauce and let everything cook together. Stir quickly, incorporating the diced pumpkin you set aside earlier.

Top each serving with parsley and a few drops of balsamic vinegar.

Pennette lisce con baccalà, olive e uva passa
Pennette with Cod, Olives, and Raisins

Servings 4
Difficulty *Low*
Prep Time 20'
Cook Time 9'

12.3 oz (350 g) pennette lisce pasta – 0.88 lbs (400 g) salt-dried cod, reconstituted – 3.5 oz (100 g) taggiasca olives (about 23 large) – 0.7 oz (20 g) raisins (about 2 tbsp packed) – 3 1/2 tbsp (50 ml) extra-virgin olive oil – 1/2 lemon (peel only) – 1 garlic clove – 1 tbsp minced parsley – salt and pepper to taste.

Soak the raisins in water for about 10 minutes. Remove the skin from the reconstituted cod and cut it into small pieces. Mince the garlic and sauté it in the oil. Then add the olives and half the parsley. After a few seconds, add the cod. Season with salt and pepper to taste and let it cook for 5 minutes.

Strain the raisins and mince them along with the lemon peel and remaining parsley. Boil the pasta in salted water, strain it when it's *al dente*, and set aside 1/4 cup + 1 tablespoon of pasta water.

Add the pasta and pasta water to the pan with the cod. Let it all cook together for a minute, mixing well. Top each serving with the minced raisin mixture.

Pennette rigate con anguilla
Pennette Rigate with Eel, Balsamic Vinegar, and Pecorino Quenelles

Servings 4
Difficulty Low
Prep Time 35'
Cook Time 10'

12.3 oz (350 g) pennette rigate pasta – 0.66 lbs (300 g) eel – 0.44 lbs (200 g) wild cabbage – 3 1/2 tbsp (50 ml) balsamic vinegar – 1 tbsp minced rosemary – 1/3 cup + 1 1/2 tbsp (100 ml) extra-virgin olive oil – salt and pepper to taste.
For the quenelles: 1 cup (100 g) Pecorino cheese, grated – 4 tbsp (30 g) flour – 1 egg – 1 tsp minced parsley.

Dice the eel, fry about 1/3 of it, and keep it warm.

Finely chop the cabbage and heat the oil in a large pan. Sauté the remaining 2/3 of the eel with the rosemary for a few minutes. Then add the cabbage and let it cook for another 7-8 minutes. Pour in the balsamic vinegar and let all the liquid evaporate.

Mix the Pecorino with the egg, flour, and parsley. Shape it into small *quenelles* (oblong balls) and boil them in a small pot for 4 minutes.

Boil the pasta in salted water and strain it when it's *al dente*. Combine it with the sauce and top it with *quenelles* and fried eel.

Interesting Fact
The large female eel is called a "capitone" and can weigh up to 13 pounds (6 kg), while the males don't weigh more than 0.44 pounds (200 g).

Pennette rigate con peperoni arrostiti, pollo e acciughe
Pennette Rigate with Roasted Bell Peppers, Chicken, and Anchovies

Servings 4
Difficulty **Low**
Prep Time 40'
Cook Time 10'

12.3 oz (350 g) pennette rigate pasta – 7 oz (200 g) red bell pepper (about 1 large) – 7 oz (200 g) yellow bell pepper (about 1 large) – 0.66 lbs (300 g) chicken breast – 1.76 oz (50 g) anchovy fillets – 3 1/2 tbsp (50 ml) dry white wine – 3 tbsp (40 ml) extra-virgin olive oil – 3 basil leaves – 1 garlic clove – salt and pepper to taste.

Arrange the peppers in a pan and roast them in the oven at 350° F (180° C) for 15 minutes. When they're done, put them in a container and seal it well with plastic wrap (make sure it's airtight) so they'll be easier to peel. In the meantime, dice the chicken breast. Then peel the peppers, remove the seeds, and cut them into small matchsticks.

Brown the chicken with the oil and the whole garlic clove (to be removed before adding the sauce to the pasta). After a few minutes add the anchovies, basil (cut into strips), and white wine. Let all the liquid evaporate. Add the peppers, season with salt and pepper to taste, and let it all simmer for a minute.

Boil the pasta in salted water and strain it when it's *al dente*. Combine it with the sauce and mix well.

Chef's tips
You can also roast the peppers over the burner on a gas stove, holding them with a large fork and letting them blister over the flame. Placing the roasted peppers in an airtight container makes the cleaning process quicker and easier, because the condensation produced by the high temperature of the pepper helps detach the skin.

Pipe rigate con cavolfiore, prosciutto cotto e Pecorino
Pipe Rigate with Cauliflower, Ham, and Pecorino

Servings 4
Difficulty Low
Prep Time 25'
Cook Time 10'

12.3 oz (350 g) pipe rigate pasta – 0.88 lbs (400 g) cauliflower – 0.44 lbs (200 g) ham, in one slice – 1/3 cup + 1 tbsp (40 g) Pecorino cheese, in flakes – 1 1/2 tbsp (20 g) butter – 3/4 cup + 1 1/2 tbsp (200 ml) heavy cream – fresh thyme to taste – salt and pepper to taste.

Clean the cauliflower and divide it into florets. Boil it in salted water, making sure it stays a bit crunchy.

Cut the prosciutto into strips and sauté it with the butter and whole garlic clove (to be removed before adding the pasta). After a few minutes, add the cauliflower and cream. Season with salt and pepper to taste and let it cook for 5-6 minutes.

Boil the pasta in salted water. Strain it when it's *al dente* and combine it with the sauce. Top it with thyme and Pecorino flakes, and serve.

Chef's tips
Before boiling the cauliflower, dissolve a few tablespoons of flour in the water.

Pipe rigate con fave
Pipe Rigate with Fava Beans and Whelks in Tomato Sauce

Servings 4
Difficulty Medium
Prep Time 45'
Cook Time 10'

12.3 oz (350 g) pipe rigate pasta – 7 oz (200 g) spring onions (about 8 large spring onions) – 10.5 oz (300 g) fava beans – 14.1 oz (400 g) whelks – 5.3 oz (150 g) onion (about 1 cup chopped) – 1.4 oz (40 g) carrots (about 1/3 cup chopped) – 2.5 oz (70 g) celery (about 2/3 cup chopped) – 1 bunch of parsley – 1 garlic clove – 1/3 cup + 1 1/2 tbsp (100 ml) white wine – 1/4 cup (60 ml) extra-virgin olive oil – 7 oz (200 g) tomatoes (about 2 small tomatoes) – hot red pepper (fresh or dried) to taste – salt to taste.

Thoroughly flush out the whelks, rinsing them in cold water several times. Dice the onion, carrots, and celery. Boil the vegetables and whelks in unsalted water for 5 minutes. Strain them, setting aside the water they cooked in, and remove the shells.

Blanch the fava beans in lightly salted water and peel them.

Thinly slice the spring onions and sauté them in half the oil with hot pepper to taste. Add the whelks and the wine. Peel the tomatoes, remove the seeds, and dice them. Let all the liquid evaporate and add the tomatoes to the pan. Add a ladleful of the water you set aside earlier and let it all cook for 25-30 minutes, stirring occasionally. About 5 minutes before you take the sauce off the heat, add the fava beans and season with salt.

Combine the parsley leaves and remaining oil in a food processor and blend well.

Boil the pasta in salted water and strain it when it's *al dente*. Add it to the whelk sauce and stir to combine. Serve it with a drizzle of the blended parsley and olive oil.

Reginette con sugo alla cacciatora
Reginette in Cacciatore Sauce

Servings 4
Difficulty **Medium**
Prep Time
1h and 20'
Cook Time 9'

12.3 oz (350 g) reginette pasta – half a rabbit (about 1.6 lbs/750 g) – 1.76 oz (50 g) black olives, pitted (about 11 large) – 5.3 oz (150 g) onion (about 2 small) – 2.8 oz (80 g) carrots (about 1 1/2 small) – 2.5 oz (70 g) celery (about 2 medium stalks) – 1.4 oz (40 g) Caciocavallo cheese, grated (about 1/3 cup) – 1/3 cup + 1 1/2 tbsp (100 ml) white wine – 17.6 oz (500 g) crushed tomatoes – 1/4 cup (60 ml) extra-virgin olive oil – 1 garlic clove – 1 sprig of rosemary – dried oregano to taste – 1 tsp minced parsley – salt and pepper to taste.

Divide the rabbit into 8 pieces. Season it with salt and pepper and sear it in a pan with the oil. Add the garlic and rosemary. Finely dice the vegetables and add them as well. Let everything brown for 3-4 minutes, then pour in the wine. Let it evaporate and add the crushed tomatoes. If necessary, add more salt and pepper. Let the sauce cook on low heat for at least 40 minutes. If it gets too dry, add a few tablespoons of water.

When the sauce is done, remove all the rabbit meat from the bones and add the meat back to the sauce. If you prefer, you can set a side 1 piece of rabbit per person.

Add the olives, season with oregano, and let the sauce cook for another 10 minutes. Boil the pasta in salted water and strain it when it's *al dente*. Combine it with the sauce and serve each portion with a piece of rabbit (if you chose to set some aside). Top it off with a generous sprinkling of Caciocavallo.

Riccioli di sfoglia con prosciutto, peperoni e piselli
Riccioli di Sfoglia with Prosciutto, Peppers, and Peas

Servings 4
Difficulty *Low*
Prep Time 15'
Cook Time 5'

12.3 oz (350 g) riccioli di sfoglia pasta – 5.3 oz (150 g) prosciutto di Parma, in one slice about 1/8 inch (3 mm) thick – 3.5 oz (100 g) peas (about 2/3 cup) – 7 oz (200 g) red bell pepper, peeled and quartered (about 1 1/2 medium) – 3/4 cup + 1 1/2 tbsp (200 ml) heavy cream – 2 tbsp (30 g) butter – 2/3 cup (60 g) Parmigiano Reggiano cheese, grated – salt and pepper to taste.

Melt the butter over low heat and add the prosciutto, diced very finely (about 1/8 inch or 3 mm). When it's browned, add the pepper (roasted, peeled, and diced). After a few seconds add the cream. Let it simmer over low heat until the sauce reaches a boil. Remove it from the heat, season with salt and pepper to taste, and keep it warm.
Boil the riccioli in salted water and add the peas for the last 3-5 minutes, letting them cook together. Strain them both when the pasta is *al dente*. Combine the pasta and peas with the sauce and stir in the grated Parmigiano. Serve immediately.

Chef's tips
A tasty alternative is to substitute sausage, cut into 1/3-3/4 inch (1-2 cm) pieces, for the prosciutto.

Rigatoni "alla pastora"
Rigatoni alla Pastora

Servings 4
Difficulty Low
Prep Time 15'
Cook Time 11'

12.3 oz (350 g) rigatoni pasta – 0.55 lbs (250 g) ricotta, very fresh – 0.55 lbs (250 g) sausage – 2/3 cup (60 g) Pecorino cheese, grated – fresh thyme to taste – 1/4 cup + 1 tbsp (70 ml) water – salt and pepper to taste.

Remove the sausage from the casing and break it up by hand. Put it in a pan and pour the water over it. Cover the pan and let the sausage cook. When all the fat has dissolved, strain it and set aside both the liquid and the sausage pieces (they can be used for another dish).
Sift the ricotta into a very large bowl. Add the liquid from the sausage, stirring continuously. Then add a pinch of salt and a generous amount of freshly ground pepper.
Boil the pasta in salted water. Strain it when it's *al dente*, keep it fairly moist, and combine it with the ricotta. Add the Pecorino and a few thyme leaves, and mix it all together thoroughly. Serve the pasta immediately, nice and hot.

Chef's tips
The goal of this traditional "poor man's" dish was to use every ingredient to the maximum. Naturally, you can leave the sausage in if you prefer a heartier meal.

Ruote ai peperoni
Ruote with Bell Peppers

Servings 4
Difficulty *Low*
Prep Time 20'
Cook Time 8'

12.3 oz (350 g) ruote pasta – 3 1/2 tbsp (50 ml) extra-virgin olive oil – 1 red bell pepper – 1 yellow bell pepper – 3.5 oz (100 g) onion (about 1 1/2 small) – 1/3 cup + 1 1/2 tbsp (100 ml) heavy cream – vegetable broth as needed (best if fresh) – salt and pepper to taste.
For the vegetable broth: Half a carrot – Half a celery stalk, with a few leaves – Half an onion – 4 1/4 cups (1 L) water – salt to taste.

Start by making the vegetable broth. Wash and peel half a carrot, half an onion, and half a celery stalk with a few leaves still attached. Boil them for at least 30 minutes in 4 1/4 cups (1 L) of water, seasoning with salt to taste. When the broth is done, strain it and use it for the pasta sauce.
Slice the onion and sauté it in the oil. When it's golden brown, add the peppers (cleaned and cut into thin strips).
Let the vegetables cook, adding vegetable broth as necessary. Continue until the peppers are soft, seasoning with salt and pepper to taste. When they're done, stir in the cream.
Boil the pasta in salted water, strain it when it's *al dente*, and combine it with the pepper sauce.

Sedanini rigati con astice, prosciutto croccante e menta
Sedanini Rigati with Lobster, Prosciutto, and Mint

Servings 4
*Difficulty **Low***
Prep Time 20'
Cook Time 12'

12.3 oz (350 g) sedanini rigati pasta – 1 medium lobster, about 1.65–1.75 lbs (750/800 g) – 2.8 oz (80 g) prosciutto (dry-cured) in one piece – 2 shallots – 8 mint leaves – 3 1/2 tbsp (50 ml) extra-virgin olive oil – 1/3 cup + 1 1/2 tbsp (100 ml) white wine – 3/4 cup + 1 1/2 tbsp (200 ml) fish broth (fresh or boullion) – salt and pepper to taste.

Blanch the lobster for 7-8 minutes. Let it cool and remove the meat from the shell. Mince the shallots. Cut the prosciutto into strips and sear it in a very hot nonstick pan.

Sauté the minced shallot in the oil. Add the lobster and let it brown for a minute. Pour in the white wine and let all the liquid evaporate.

Add the fish broth and julienned mint, then let it cook for another couple of minutes. Season it with salt and pepper to taste.

Soil the pasta in salted water and strain it when it's *al dente*. Combine it with the lobster sauce and top each serving with hot, crispy prosciutto strips.

Sedanini rigati con pesto di rucola e salmone
Sedanini Rigati with Arugula Pesto and Salmon

Servings 4
Difficulty **Low**
Prep Time 35'
Cook Time 12'

12.3 oz (350 g) sedanini rigati pasta – 3.5 oz (100 g) arugula (about 5 cups) – 3/4 cup + 1 1/2 tbsp (200 ml) olive oil – 1 garlic clove – 0.7 oz (20 g) pine nuts (about 2 1/2 tbsp) – 1.76 oz (50 g) potatoes (about 1/3 small) – 3 1/2 tbsp (50 ml) vegetable broth (fresh or bouillon cube) – salt and pepper to taste – 7 oz (200 g) salmon – 0.7 oz (20 g) shallot (2 tbsp minced) – 1 tsp minced rosemary – 4.2 oz (120 g) cherry tomatoes (about 7) – 1 tsp (5 ml) vodka.

Boil the potatoes in salted water. Strain them and purée them with the arugula, garlic, pine nuts, vegetable broth, and 2/3 cup (150 ml) of olive oil.
Sauté the shallot in the remaining oil. Slice the salmon into thin strips and add it to the shallot. Pour in the vodka and let it evaporate over high heat. Add the tomatoes (cut into quarters) and the minced rosemary. Let it cook for 4-5 minutes, then combine it with the potato purée.

Boil the pasta in salted water and strain it when it's *al dente*. Combine it with the sauce and mix well. Another option is to add the cooked pasta to the pan with the salmon and let them cook together for a minute, then spread some arugula pesto on each plate and place a portion of pasta on top.

Spaghetti aglio, olio, peperoncino
Spaghetti with Oil, Garlic, and Hot Pepper

Servings 4
Difficulty Low
Prep Time 10'
Cook Time 10'

12.3 oz (350 g) spaghetti – 1 garlic clove – fresh hot red pepper to taste – 1 tsp chopped parsley – 4 1/2 tbsp (70 ml) extra-virgin olive oil – salt to taste.

Boil the spaghetti in a pot of salted water.
Mince and mix the garlic, hot red pepper, and parsley.
Pour the oil into a wide, shallow pan on medium heat. Let it warm up for a few seconds, then add the minced garlic mix. When it starts to brown, add a ladleful of pasta water.
When the spaghetti is *al dente*, strain it well and add it to the pan. Cook for a minute or two, mixing well and letting all the flavors come together. Serve immediately.

Chef's tips
The garlic can be sliced instead of minced so that it's less likely to brown too much and become too strong. This also makes it easier to avoid for those who prefer not to eat it.

Spaghetti ai due formaggi
Two-Cheese Spaghetti

Servings 4
Difficulty **Low**
Prep Time 5'
Cook Time 8'

12.3 oz (350 g) spaghetti – 5.3 oz (150 g) Gorgonzola cheese – 1 cup (100 g) Parmigiano Reggiano cheese, grated – 2 1/2 tbsp (50 ml) heavy cream – 1 1/2 tbsp (20 g) butter – 1 sprig of thyme – salt and pepper to taste.

Boil the spaghetti in a large amount of salted water. Meanwhile melt the Gorgonzola in a saucepan with the butter. Add the cream and 1/2 cup of the grated Parmigiano. Mix well, until the sauce is creamy and consistent. Strip the thyme from the stem and add it at the end.
Strain the spaghetti when it's *al dente*. Mix it with the cheese sauce, adding the remaining Parmigiano and ground pepper to taste.

Chef's tips
For a lighter dish you can replace the cream with milk,
or even pasta water.

Spaghetti al pomodoro
Spaghetti with Tomato Sauce

Servings 4
Difficulty Low
Prep Time 30'
Cook Time 8'

12.3 oz (350 g) spaghetti – 2 tbsp (30 ml) extra-virgin olive oil – 21 oz (600 g) crushed tomatoes or whole peeled tomatoes – 3.5 oz (100 g) onion (about 2/3 cup chopped) – 1 garlic clove – 8 basil leaves – 1/3 cup + 1 tbsp (40 g) Parmigiano Reggiano cheese, grated – salt and pepper to taste.

Mince the onion and sauté it in the oil with the whole garlic clove. When it's turned a nice golden brown color, add the crushed tomatoes (or whole peeled tomatoes, chopped) and season with salt and pepper to taste. Cook the sauce on high heat for about 20 minutes, stirring occasionally. Remove the garlic at the end and add the basil, roughly chopped.
Boil the spaghetti in salted water. When it's *al dente*, strain it thoroughly and toss it with the tomato sauce. Top with grated Parmigiano.

Chef's tips
If the tomatoes are too acidic, you can add a teaspoon of sugar to compensate.

Spaghetti alla bottarga
Spaghetti alla Bottarga

Servings 4
Difficulty Low
Prep Time 5'
Cook Time 10'

12.3 oz (350 g) spaghetti – 1 garlic clove – 2.1 oz (60 g) *bottarga* (cured fish roe) – 1/3 cup + 1 1/2 tbsp (1 dl) extra-virgin olive oil – salt and pepper to taste.

Combine the oil and whole garlic clove in a wide, shallow pan. Cook on low heat to let the oil absorb the garlic flavor. Before the garlic is overly roasted, remove it from the pan and discard it. Grate the *bottarga* and add half of it to the oil. Then add ground pepper to taste.
Boil the spaghetti in salted water. When it's *al dente*, strain it and toss it with the oil and *bottarga* until everything is thoroughly combined. Top each serving with the remaining bottarga, grated or slivered.

Interesting Fact
Cured fish roe (bottarga) can come from tuna or mullet. The internal ovaries or egg masses of the fish are salted with sea salt, pressed, and dried for 60-90 days. The hardened roe is generally sold in small logs. Mullet roe is more of a delicacy and therefore more costly. The color ranges from gold to amber depending on how long it's aged. The flavor is intense and decisive, but also very delicate. Tuna roe is darker in color and has a stronger, more pronounced flavor.

Spaghetti alla carbonara
Spaghetti alla Carbonara

Servings 4
Difficulty **Low**
Prep Time 10'
Cook Time 8'

12.3 oz (350 g) spaghetti – 5.3 oz (150 g) guanciale (cured pig's cheek) or pancetta – 4 egg yolks – 3.5 oz (100 g) Pecorino Romano cheese, grated (about 1 cup) – salt and pepper to taste.

Beat the egg yolks with a pinch of salt and 1 tablespoon of Pecorino.

Slice the guanciale lengthwise. Then slice it crosswise into strips, or dice it into pieces about 1/16 – 1/8 of an inch (2 mm) thick. Lightly sauté the guanciale in a wide, shallow pan on medium heat so the fat dissolves.

Boil the spaghetti in salted water. When it's *al dente*, strain it well.

Add the spaghetti to the pan and toss it with the guanciale for a few seconds, then turn off the heat. Add the beaten yolks and a ladleful of pasta water, and mix it all together for 30 seconds.

Finish by adding the remaining Pecorino. Stir one last time and serve immediately.

Spaghetti alla chitarra allo scoglio
Chitarra Spaghetti with Shellfish

Servings 4
Difficulty Medium
Prep Time 1h
Cook Time 6-7'

For the pasta: 1 1/2 cups (200 g) Italian "00" flour – 2/3 cup (100 g) fine semolina – 2 eggs – 3 1/2 tbsp (50 ml) white wine.

For the sauce: 0.88 lbs (400 g) mussels – 0.88 lbs (400 g) clams – 0.22 lbs (100 g) squid, julienned – 4 small mullet – 4 scampi – 4 small cuttlefish, julienned – 5.3 oz (150 g) cherry tomatoes (about 9) – 2/3 cup (150 ml) white wine – 1 garlic clove – 1 tbsp minced parsley – 1 bunch of basil – 1 sprig of fresh oregano – 1/4 cup + 1 1/2 tbsp (80 ml) extra-virgin olive oil – salt and pepper to taste.

For the fried breadcrumbs: 1 1/3 cups + 1 tbsp (150 g) breadcrumbs – 1 oz (30 g) anchovies, packed in oil – 1 oz (30 g) capers, unsalted (about 3 1/2 tbsp) – 1.76 oz (50 g) Gaeta olives, pitted (about 11 large) – 2 sprigs of fresh oregano – 1 garlic clove – 1 tsp minced parsley – 1 1/2 tbsp (20 ml) extra-virgin olive oil.

Combine the flours and mix in the eggs (adding white wine as needed) until the dough is soft but dense. Cover it with a cloth and let it sit for about 20 minutes. Roll the dough out to a thickness of 1/8 inch (3 mm) and cut it into pieces to fit the *chitarra* (guitar), the tool used for making this type of square spaghetti. Lay the sheet of dough over the strings of the *chitarra* and press down over it with a rolling pin. Lay out the spaghetti on trays lightly floured with semolina, but don't let them overlap too much.

Then make the fried breadcrumbs. Chop all the ingredients and sauté them in the oil. Add the breadcrumbs and let them cook until they're a light hazelnut color. Heat the oil in a pan with the garlic (minced) and parsley, basil (chopped), and oregano (stripped from the stem and chopped). Add the mussels (well-scraped with the beards removed), the clams (flushed and rinsed), and the white wine. Cover the pan and let them cook until they open. Take the clams and mussels out of the pan, remove about 3/4 of the shells, and transfer them to a large bowl. Strain the liquid from the shellfish and pour it back into the pan. Add the squid, cuttlefish, mullet (skinned, gutted, filleted, rinsed, and diced), whole shrimp, and quartered tomatoes to that same pan. Let them cook for a few minutes, then add the mussels and clams. Season with salt and pepper to taste. When it's done, there should still be some liquid in the sauce.

Boil the pasta in salted water and strain it when it's *al dente*. Add it to the pan of sauce and let everything cook together for a minute. Distribute it among individual plates and sprinkle with fried breadcrumbs to taste.

Spaghetti alla mozzarella
Spaghetti with Mozzarella

Servings 4
*Difficulty **Low***
Prep Time 15'
Cook Time 8'

12.3 oz (350 g) spaghetti – 7 tbsp (100 g) butter – 3/4 cup + 1 tbsp (80 g) Parmigiano Reggiano cheese, grated – 5.3 oz (150 g) mozzarella – 2 tbsp (30 ml) milk – oregano to taste – salt to taste.

Boil the spaghetti in lightly salted water and strain it when it's very *al dente*. Combine it with 5 1/2 tablespoons of butter and 1/2 cup of the grated Parmigiano. Grease a large pan and arrange the pasta in a single layer, about 1-1 1/2 inches (3-4 cm) high.
Slice the mozzarella and lay the slices on top of the spaghetti. Drizzle the 2 tablespoons of milk over the mozzarella, then sprinkle it with the remaining Parmigiano.
Bake the spaghetti in a preheated oven at 350° F (180° C) for a few minutes, just until the mozzarella begins to melt. Serve it immediately.

Chef's tips
This dish can also be made ahead of time. Cook the spaghetti a few minutes less than the time indicated on the package instructions. Stir in some oil so it doesn't stick together and let it cool in a large pan. Then continue as you would for the regular recipe and let it bake 4-5 minutes longer.

Spaghetti alle olive taggiasche su tortino di alici fresche
Spaghetti with Taggiasca Olives and Baked Fresh Anchovies

Servings 4
Difficulty Low
Prep Time 45'
Cook Time 8'

12.3 oz (350 g) spaghetti – 3.5 oz (100 g) taggiasca olive pesto (or black olive pesto) – 16 fresh anchovies – 4 tbsp (25 g) toasted breadcrumbs – 1/4 cup (25 g) Cacio-cavallo cheese, grated – 1 tsp minced parsley – 3 1/2 tbsp (50 ml) extra-virgin olive oil – 10 tbsp leaves (30 g) fresh oregano – salt to taste.

Clean the anchovies, removing the heads and innards. Slice them in half lengthwise, open them up, remove the bones, rinse them, and dry them.

Spread a layer of breadcrumbs (toasted in a very hot nonstick pan), parsley, and grated Caciocavallo on the bottom of 4 ramekins. Arrange 4 anchovies in each one, sprinkle them lightly with salt, and bake them at 350° F (180° C) for 10-12 minutes.

Combine 2 tablespoons of olive oil with the fresh oregano in a food processor and blend well.

Boil the spaghetti in salted water and strain it when it's *al dente*. Combine it with the olive pesto and remaining oil.

Serve it over the anchovies, placing a portion of spaghetti in each ramekin, and drizzle it with the blended olive oil and oregano.

Chef's tips
If necessary, you can prepare the anchovies early and refrigerate them, covering the ramekins well with plastic wrap. Put them in the oven 5 minutes before you add the pasta to the water.

Spaghetti alle vongole con pesto rosso e Pecorino
Spaghetti with Clams, Red Pesto, and Pecorino

Servings 4
Difficulty *Low*
Prep Time *30'*
Cook Time *8'*

12.3 oz (350 g) spaghetti – 1.3 lbs (600 g) clams – 2.1 oz (60 g) Pecorino cheese – extra-virgin olive oil to taste – 1/2 garlic clove – 1 tsp minced parsley – red pesto, 1 tsp per person – 3 1/2 tbsp (50 ml) white wine – salt to taste.
For the red pesto: 1.76 oz (50 g) sun-dried tomatoes marinated in oil (about 1 cup drained) – 0.5 oz (15 g) pine nuts (2 tbsp) – 1/4 garlic clove – 2 1/2 tbsp (15 g) Parmigiano Reggiano cheese, grated – 1 tbsp (15 ml) extra-virgin olive oil.

To make the red pesto, combine all the listed ingredients in a tall and narrow container. Blend them with an immersion blender until the sauce is creamy and homogenous.

Heat some oil in a pan and sauté the parsley and garlic, both minced. Add the clams (cleaned and rinsed) and the white wine. Cover the pot and let them clams cook until they open. Then uncover the pot and let the liquid reduce slightly.

Turn off the heat and add the pesto along with 1/3 of the Pecorino.

Boil the pasta in salted water. Strain it when it's *al dente* and toss it in the pan with the clam sauce, letting everything cook together for a minute. Serve it with the remaining Pecorino sprinkled on top.

Spaghetti coi broccoli in tegame
Spaghetti with Broccoli

Servings 4
Difficulty Low
Prep Time 30'
Cook Time 8'

12.3 oz (350 g) spaghetti – 14 oz (400 g) crushed tomatoes – 0.66 lbs (300 g) broccoli – 1.4 oz (40 g) raisins (about 1/4 cup packed) – 1.4 oz (40 g) pine nuts (about 1/3 cup) – 1 tbsp minced parsley – 3 1/2 tbsp (50 ml) extra-virgin olive oil – 1 garlic clove – salt to taste.

Clean the broccoli and divide it into florets, removing the stems. Boil it in salted water and strain it when it's still slightly crunchy. Let it cool just slightly, until it's lukewarm.
Sauté the garlic in the oil. Add the crushed tomatoes and let it cook over medium heat for 10 minutes. Then stir in the raisins and pine nuts, and season with salt.
Boil the spaghetti in salted water and strain it when it's very *al dente*. Transfer it to a preheated bowl and arrange the broccoli on top. Cover the broccoli with tomato sauce and sprinkle the minced parsley on top. Mix the spaghetti with pan-cooked broccoli and serve.

Spaghetti con le cozze
Spaghetti with Mussels

Servings 4
Difficulty Low
Prep Time 30'
Cook Time 8'

12.3 oz (350 g) spaghetti – 2.2 lbs (1 kg) mussels – 2 garlic cloves – 2 tbsp minced parsley – 3 1/2 tbsp (50 ml) extra-virgin olive oil – salt and pepper to taste.

Wash the mussels and scrape them well. Cook them over high heat until they open and remove any empty shells. Filter the liquid from the pot with a fine mesh strainer.

Mince the garlic and parsley and sauté them in the oil. When they start to turn golden brown, add the mussels with the filtered liquid. Season generously with salt and pepper.

Meanwhile boil the spaghetti in salted water and strain it when it's *al dente*. Add it to the mussels, let everything cook together for a minute, and serve it hot.

Chef's tips
Discard any mussels that are already open and any that don't open when you cook them.
Make sure the garlic and parsley don't brown too much when you sauté them. You can also set aside a few tablespoons of olive oil and add them at the end.

Spaghetti con *tartare* di mazzancolle
Spaghetti with Treviso Radicchio and King Prawns Tartar

Servings 4
Difficulty **Low**
Prep Time *20'*
Cook Time *8'*

12.3 oz (350 g) spaghetti.
For the sauce: 3 tbsp (40 ml) extra-virgin olive oil – 2.1 oz (60 g) onion, minced (about 1/3 cup) – 0.66 lbs (300 g) Treviso radicchio – 1 garlic clove, minced – 3 1/2 tbsp (50 ml) white wine – 1 tbsp minced parsley – salt and pepper to taste.
For the tartar: 16 king prawns – 2 tsp (10 ml) extra-virgin olive oil – salt and pepper to taste.

Mince the onion, parsley, and garlic. Clean and rinse the radicchio and cut it into strips. Drizzle some oil into a pan over medium heat and sauté the onion for a couple of minutes. Add the garlic and radicchio and let it cook for another 2 minutes, or until the radicchio has wilted. Season with salt and pepper.

Meanwhile, peel and devein the prawns. Chop them finely, put them in a bowl with a pinch of salt and pepper and a tablespoon of olive oil, and mix well.

Boil the spaghetti in salted water until it's *al dente*. Strain it and immediately combine it with the radicchio, adding the minced parsley and a drizzle of olive oil.

Distribute the spaghetti among individual serving plates and top each one with a spoonful of the prawns tartar. Sprinkle them with ground black pepper and a pinch of minced parsley. Finish with a drizzle of cold-pressed olive oil.

Spaghetti con il rancetto
Spaghetti Rancetto

Servings 4
Difficulty Low
Prep Time 30'
Cook Time 8'

12.3 oz (350 g) spaghetti – 5.3 oz (150 g) guanciale (cured pig's cheek) – 5.3 oz (150 g) onion (about 2 small onions) – 21 oz (600 g) crushed tomatoes – 1/2 cup + 1 1/2 tbsp (60 g) Pecorino cheese, grated – 2 sprigs of marjoram – 3 1/2 tbsp (50 ml) extra-virgin olive oil – salt and pepper to taste.

Mince the onion and dice the guanciale. Sauté them in a pan with the oil, letting them turn golden brown. Add the crushed tomatoes and cook it all on medium heat for 15-20 minutes. Add the marjoram (stripped from the stem and minced) toward the end and season with salt and pepper to taste. Boil the spaghetti in salted water. Strain it when it's *al dente* and combine it with the sauce and grated Pecorino.

Chef's tips
IIf you can't get guanciale, you can substitute diced pancetta. Blanch it in a small pot of unsalted water for 1-2 minutes and strain it with a fine mesh strainer to remove some of the fat.

Spaghetti con scampi e finocchio
Spaghetti with Scampi and Fennel

Servings 4
Difficulty Low
Prep Time 20'
Cook Time 8'

12.3 oz (350 g) spaghetti – 2.2 lbs (1 kg) scampi – 1.1 lbs (500 g) fennel bulbs (about 2) – 7 oz (200 g) cherry tomatoes (about 12) – 1/3 cup + 1 1/2 tbsp (100 ml) heavy cream – 3 tbsp (40 ml) extra-virgin olive oil – salt and pepper to taste.

Clean the scampi, removing the heads and shells (except for the very end). Sauté them in half the oil and set them aside.

Clean, rinse, and julienne the fennel, setting aside the green leaves for later use. Sauté it in the same pan you used for the scampi, adding the remaining oil. Season with salt and pepper to taste and let it cook for a few minutes.

Add the cream and tomatoes (cut in half), and let it cook for about 5 more minutes. About a minute before turning off the heat, add the scampi to warm them up a bit.

Boil the pasta in salted water, strain it when it's *al dente*, and combine it with the sauce. Top it with fennel leaves to taste.

Scampi Ingredients and Directions

Sauce Directions

Spaghetti con uovo e prosciutto
Spaghetti with Eggs and Prosciutto

Servings 4
Difficulty **Low**
Prep Time 20'
Cook Time 8'

12.3 oz (350 g) spaghetti – 4 eggs – 3.5 oz (100 g) prosciutto (dry-cured) – 1 small onion – 2/3 cup (60 g) Parmigiano Reggiano cheese, grated – 3 1/2 tbsp (50 g) butter – 3 1/2 tbsp (50 ml) dry white wine – 1 tsp minced rosemary – salt to taste.

Thinly slice the onion and cut the prosciutto into strips. Sauté both of them in the butter until they start to take on a bit of color. Add the white wine and let it evaporate. Then add the minced rosemary.

In a large bowl combine the eggs with the grated Parmigiano and a pinch of salt, mixing well with a wooden spoon. Meanwhile boil the spaghetti in lightly salted water and strain them when they're *al dente*. Transfer them to the bowl with the eggs and quickly mix everything together. Pour in the hot butter and prosciutto sauce and serve immediately.

Spaghetti integrali con crema di asparagi e caprino
Whole Wheat Spaghetti with Creamy Asparagus and Caprino

Servings 4
Difficulty *Low*
Prep Time 30'
Cook Time 8'

12.3 oz (350 g) whole wheat spaghetti – 0.88 lbs (400 g) asparagus – 2.8 oz (80 g) fresh Caprino cheese – 1 bunch of basil – 1 shallot – fresh mint leaves – 1/2 garlic clove – 2 tbsp (30 ml) extra-virgin olive oil – salt and pepper to taste.

Clean and rinse the asparagus. Remove the tougher parts of the stems and slice them into rounds. Keep the tips separate and boil them in salted water. Set aside 1/4 cup + 1 tablespoon of the water after straining them.

Mince the shallot and sauté it in the oil with the whole garlic clove. When they've turned golden brown, add the sliced stems and season with salt and pepper. Then add a few hand-torn mint and basil leaves. Add the water you set aside earlier and let it cook for 10 minutes. Then purée everything.

Boil the spaghetti in salted water and strain them when they are *al dente*. Combine them with the purée and asparagus tips, and let it all cook together for a minute. Distribute it among the serving plates and top each one with a *quenelle* (spoonful) of fresh Caprino.

Spaghetti tagliati con broccoli alla romana
Cut Spaghetti with Broccoli alla Romana

Servings 4
Difficulty **Medium**
Prep Time 40'
Cook Time 6'

12.3 oz (350 g) cut spaghetti – 1.1 lbs (500 g) broccoli – 2.1 oz (60 g) prosciutto (dry-cured), in one slice – 2.1 oz (60 g) pork rinds – 1 1/2 tbsp (20 ml) extra-virgin olive oil – 3.5 oz (100 g) onion (about 1 1/2 small onions) – 1 garlic clove – 1/2 cup + 1 1/2 tbsp (60 g) Pecorino Romano cheese, grated – 4 1/4 cups (1 L) water – salt and pepper to taste.

Divide the broccoli into florets, wash it thoroughly, and cook it in lightly salted water on medium heat. When it's done, remove the pot from the heat.

Slice the onion, crush the garlic, and cut the prosciutto into small strips. Sauté the onion and garlic in the oil until they turn golden brown, then add the prosciutto to the pot. Mix well and add the water.

Meanwhile clean the pork rinds very carefully, removing any hairs and slicing them thinly. Blanch them in unsalted water, then add them to the pot with the prosciutto and water. Bring it to a boil, add a pinch of salt and pepper, and let it cook for about 5 minutes. Add the spaghetti and let it cook in the soup. A few minutes before you turn off the heat, add the broccoli florets with some of the water they cooked in (the soup should be slightly dense).

Serve with grated Pecorino and a generous sprinkling of pepper.

Spaghettini con i totanetti
Spaghettini with Squid

Servings 4
*Difficulty **Low***
Prep Time 10'
Cook Time 5'

12.3 oz (350 g) spaghettini – 1.1 lbs (500 g) small squid – 1/3 cup + 1 1/2 tbsp (100 ml) extra-virgin olive oil – 1 garlic clove, minced – 1 tbsp minced parsley – 3 1/2 tbsp (50 ml) dry white wine – 0.08 oz (2.5 g) cuttlefish ink – salt to taste.

Clean the squid and cut them into rounds. Sauté them in the oil with the garlic and parsley. Add the white wine and let it evaporate. Then add the cuttlefish ink, season with salt to taste, and let it finish cooking (should take about 10 minutes in total).
Boil the pasta and strain it when it's *al dente*. Combine it with the squid and serve very hot.

Strozzapreti con capesante e pesto
Strozzapreti with Scallops and Pesto

Servings 4
Difficulty Low
Prep Time 40'
Cook Time 10'

12.3 oz (350 g) strozzapreti pasta – 4 large scallops – 1 1/2 tbsp (20 ml) extra-virgin olive oil – 1 tbsp minced parsley.

For the fish sauce: 3.5 oz (100 g) white fish (hake) – 2.8 oz (80 g) carrots (about 1 1/2 small) – 2.5 oz (70 g) celery (about 2 medium) – 5.3 oz (150 g) onion (about 2 small) – 4 tbsp (30 g) flour – 2 tbsp (30 g) butter – 1 1/4 cups (1 L) water – salt and pepper to taste.

Per il pesto: 1 oz (30 g) basil leaves (about 1 1/4 cups) – 2/3 cup (60 g) Parmigiano Reggiano cheese, grated – 1/3 cup + 1 tbsp (40 g) aged Pecorino cheese, grated – 0.35 oz (10 g) pine nuts (about 1 tbsp) – 3/4 cup + 1 1/2 tbsp (200 ml) extra-virgin olive oil – 1 garlic clove – salt to taste.

Blend the basil, pine nuts, peeled garlic, and oil in a food processor. Then add the two grated cheeses and mix well. Season the pesto with salt to taste and refrigerate it.

Boil the vegetables and fish in 1 1/4 cups of water for at least 20 minutes. When the broth is done, strain it and set is aside for later use.

Start the cream sauce by melting the butter in a pot. Add the flour, whisking continuously, and let it cook for 1-2 minutes. Season with salt and pepper, then add 2 cups (500 ml) of fish broth. Let it cook until the sauce is smooth and creamy.

Clean and cube the scallops, and sauté them in the oil. Boil the pasta in salted water and strain it a few minutes earlier than the time indicated on the package instructions. Combine it with the pesto, scallops, and a few ladlefuls of cream sauce.

Transfer the pasta to a greased baking dish and bake it at 350° F (180° C) for 10 minutes. Sprinkle with minced parsley and serve.

Tortiglioni al ragù e melanzane
Tortiglioni with Ragù and Eggplant

Servings 4
Difficulty *Medium*
Prep Time
2h and 25'
Cook Time 12'

12.3 oz (350 g) tortiglioni pasta – 0.66 lbs (300 g) bottom round of veal – 1.76 lbs (800 g) eggplant (about 1 1/2) – 3.5 oz (100 g) white button mushrooms – 1.76 oz (50 g) prosciutto (dry-cured) – 2.8 oz (80 g) chicken giblets – 35 oz (1 kg) crushed tomatoes – 3 1/2 tbsp (50 ml) dry white wine – 2.6 oz (75 g) onion (about 1 small) 1 bunch of basil – 1 cup + 3 tbsp (120 g) Parmigiano Reggiano cheese, grated – 3 1/2 tbsp (50 ml) extra-virgin olive oil – additional extra-virgin olive oil for frying – salt and pepper to taste.

Sauté the finely chopped prosciutto and sliced onion in 1 tablespoon of oil. Add the meat and let it brown on high heat with the onion. Pour in the wine and let it evaporate completely. Then add the tomatoes along with enough water to cover the meat. Season with salt and pepper to taste and cover the pot. Let it cook on medium heat for about 2 hours.

Wash the eggplant and cut it into 1/3-1/2 inch (1 cm) cubes. Fry the cubes in a large amount of oil, letting any excess oil drip off as you remove them. Salt the fried eggplant generously, wrap it in paper towels, and set it aside.

Wash the basil leaves and boil them for 30 seconds. Immediately transfer them to a bowl of ice water to cool, then blend them with 1/4 cup + 1 tablespoon of oil in a food processor.

As soon as the veal is cooked, strain it and dice it. Filter the sauce with a fine mesh strainer, collecting the liquid in another pot. Add the diced meat to the filtered liquid along with the diced chicken livers and the mushrooms. Let it all simmer together for 5 minutes.

Boil the rigatoni in lightly salted water. Strain the pasta when it's *al dente* and combine it with the meat sauce. Top it with fried eggplant and a sprinkling of grated Parmigiano, and garnish it with the basil oil.

Tortiglioni integrali con carciofi
Whole Wheat Tortiglioni with Artichokes, Prosciutto, and Tuscan Pecorino

Servings 4
Difficulty Low
Prep Time 40'
Cook Time 12'

12.3 oz (350 g) whole wheat tortiglioni pasta – 4 artichokes – 5.3 oz (150 g) sliced prosciutto – 2.8 oz (80 g) Pecorino Toscano cheese, in flakes – 3 1/2 tbsp (50 ml) extra-virgin olive oil – 1 sprig of rosemary – 1 garlic clove – 1 onion, sliced – salt and pepper to taste.

Remove the pointed tips from the artichokes and set aside the outer leaves. Cut the hearts in half and remove any tough or stringy parts. Thinly slice the remaining artichoke heart pieces.

Place a pan over medium heat and add a dash of oil. Let it warm up for a few seconds, then sauté the onion slices. When the onion begins to soften, add the artichoke leaves and pour in enough water to cover everything. Let it braise for about 30 minutes. When the leaves are nice and soft, purée them and pass them through a fine mesh strainer.

Cut the prosciutto into strips and chop the rosemary leaves and garlic.

Brown the sliced artichoke hearts with a dash of oil on medium heat. Add the prosciutto, rosemary, garlic, and salt and pepper to taste. Cook for another 2 minutes, adding the strained artichoke purée toward the end.

Boil the tortiglioni in a large pot of salted water. When they're *al dente*, strain them and combine them with all the other ingredients in the pan. Let everything cook together for a minute, then transfer to serving plates. Top with pecorino flakes and a dash of olive oil.

Troccoli al ragù lucano
Troccoli with Gran Ragù Lucano

Servings 4
Difficulty Medium
Prep Time
1h and 15'
Cook Time 12'

12.3 oz (350 g) troccoli pasta – 2.6 oz (75 g) pork, finely diced – 3.5 oz (100 g) veal, finely diced – 4.4 oz (125 g) lamb, finely diced – 2.5 oz (70 g) fresh pork sausage – 1.76 oz (50 g) *lardo battuto* (cured pork fat pounded to a cream with herbs and spices) – 17.6 oz (500 g) whole peeled tomatoes – 2 1/2 tbsp (40 g) tomato paste – 3.5 oz (100 g) onion, minced (about 2/3 cup) – 1 tbsp minced parsley – 1/3 cup + 1 1/2 tbsp (100 ml) red wine – 1/3 cup + 1 tbsp (40 g) Parmigiano Reggiano cheese, grated – hot pepper and horseradish to taste (optional) – salt to taste.

Sauté the pounded pork fat with the onion and minced parsley. As soon as the onion is golden brown, add the ground meats and the sausage (broken up). Add the red wine last.

When everything is uniformly browned (add a bit of water if it dries out too much), add the tomato paste. Ten minutes later, add the whole peeled tomatoes. Bring it to a boil, then turn down the heat and let it cook for 1 hour. Season with salt to taste.

Boil the pasta in salted water, strain it when it's *al dente*, and combine it with the ragù.

You can add a piece of dried hot pepper and some grated horseradish at your discretion, as well as grated Parmigiano to taste.

Vermicelli all'abruzzese
Vermicelli all'Abruzzese

Servings 4
Difficulty *Low*
Prep Time 30'
Cook Time 9'

12.3 oz (350 g) vermicelli pasta – 5.3 oz (150 g) guanciale (cured pig's cheek) or pancetta, in one slice – 3.5 oz (100 g) onion (about 1 1/2 small) – 1/2 cup (50 g) Pecorino cheese, grated – 1/3 cup + 1 1/2 tbsp (100 ml) extra-virgin olive oil – 1 tsp minced parsley – salt and pepper to taste.

Dice the guanciale (or pancetta) and chop up the onion.

Boil the pasta in salted water.

Sauté the onion and guanciale in 3/4 of the oil until they're uniformly golden brown. Add a ladleful of pasta water and let the sauce thicken over high heat. Season with lots of freshly ground pepper.

Strain the pasta when it's *al dente* and add it to the sauce. Add the minced parsley, grated Parmigiano, and a drizzle of cold-pressed olive oil to bring it all together. Mix well to coat the pasta thoroughly.

Chef's tips
For a thicker sauce, you can add 1 teaspoon of flour to the cooked onion and guanciale, mixing well before adding the pasta water.

Vermicelli con pomodoro, spada, olive nere e finocchio selvatico
Vermicelli with Tomato, Swordfish, Black Olives, and Wild Fennel

Servings 4
Difficulty Low
Prep Time 15'
Cook Time 9'

12.3 oz (350 g) vermicelli pasta – 0.33 lbs (150 g) cherry tomatoes on the vine (about 9 tomatoes) – 0.35 lbs (160 g) swordfish – 3.5 oz (100 g) black olives, pitted (about 23 large) – 2.8 oz (80 g) onion (about 1 small) – 3 1/2 tbsp (50 ml) white wine – 3 1/2 tbsp (50 ml) extra-virgin olive oil – 1 tbsp minced parsley – wild fennel to taste – salt and pepper to taste.

Wash the tomatoes, remove the seeds, and dice them. Then dice the fish, finely chop the olives, and julienne the onion.

Sauté the onion in the oil. Add the fish and let it brown, then season with salt and pepper. Pour in the white wine and let it evaporate. Once the liquid has evaporated, add the tomato and let it cook for a few more minutes. Add more salt and pepper if necessary.

Boil the pasta in salted water and strain it when it's *al dente*. Combine it with the sauce and top it with minced parsley and wild fennel.

Vermicelli con vongole in bianco
Vermicelli in White Clam Sauce

Servings 4
Difficulty *Low*
Prep Time 20'
Cook Time 13'

12.3 oz (350 g) vermicelli pasta – 2.2 lbs (1 kg) clams – 1/3 cup + 1 1/2 tbsp (100 ml) extra-virgin olive oil – 1 tbsp minced parsley – 1 garlic clove – salt and pepper to taste.

Carefully wash the clams and arrange them in a large pan with 1 tablespoon of olive oil. Cover the pan and let them cook until they open (about 2-3 minutes). Remove it from the heat and remove some of the shells. Strain the liquid from the pan, pour it back in with the clams, and set it all aside. Pour the olive oil into another pan and sauté the garlic, finely chopped. When it starts to turn golden brown, add the clams with their liquid and let it come to a boil.
Meanwhile boil the vermicelli in salted water. Strain them when they're *al dente*, but leave a fair amount of pasta water with them. Combine them with the clam sauce and finish with a generous sprinkling of ground pepper and a handful of minced parsley.

Chef's tips
Make the clam sauce while the pasta cooks, which will produce a more fragrant result. This recipe works well with other shellfish too, particularly cockles, tellin clams, and razor clams.

Ziti spezzati ai formaggi
Broken Ziti with Cheese

Servings 4
Difficulty Low
Prep Time 10'
Cook Time 10'

12.3 oz (350 g) ziti – 3.5 oz (100 g) mozzarella, cut into strips – 3.2 oz (90 g) Edamer cheese, cut into strips – 2/3 cup (150 g) melted butter – 1 cup (100 g) Parmigiano Reggiano cheese, grated.

Use a serrated knife to make 2 small crosswise incisions on each piece of pasta, just deep enough so it will break apart cleanly. Break each one into 3 pieces.
Boil the ziti in salted water, strain it when it's *al dente*, and transfer it to a preheated bowl. Add the 3 cheeses and the melted butter, and mix well. Serve immediately, before the cheese starts to melt.

Chef's tips
You can use other cheeses based on personal preference. And you can chop them in a food processor instead of slicing them by hand.

BAKED PASTA

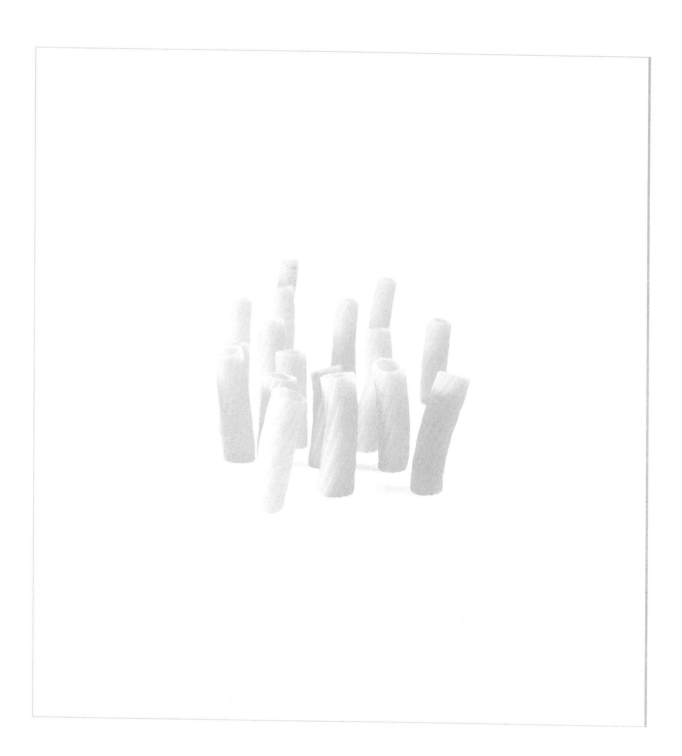

Modern *lasagna* may well be the namesake of the most famous pasta in antiquity, *lagana*. These sheets of dough were already known and used in ancient Rome, where they were cooked in a sauce. Today they're boiled separately, then baked with all the sauce and filling. They even appear in Petronius's *Satyricon*, where the wealthy Trimalchio serves layers of dough spread with *garum*, a fermented fish sauce mixed with spices, during a lavish banquet. The modern version has certainly undergone some changes, but the familiar image of "lasagna" is always there, regardless of the era. Layers of lasagna with cheese spread between them were popular in Italy, Spain, and France during the Middle Ages. The definitive step toward modern lasagna, which calls for a base of meat sauce combined with a béchamel sauce (made of milk, butter, and flour), occurred in the 17th century. Though the famous sauce is attributed to the Marquis Louis de Bechamel, it appears that it was already known in the Medici courts of 16th century Italy.

More recent Italian lore suggests that *cannelloni*, another type of baked pasta, was "invented" in Amalfi as a result of a longstanding

COMPETITION BETWEEN TWO RESTAURANTS AND THEIR RESPECTIVE CHEFS. LASAGNA, MADE FROM ROLLED OUT DOUGH, AND CANNELLONI, MADE WITH A PASTA MACHINE, ARE AMONG THE MOST TRADITIONAL ITALIAN BAKED PASTAS. WITH A THOUSAND DIFFERENT FILLINGS ORIGINATING IN VARIOUS REGIONS OF ITALY, THEY FULLY REPRESENT THE TRADITIONAL HOLIDAY FIRST COURSE.

THESE FILLINGS ARE BASED ON TRADITIONS, SEASONS, AND CONVENTIONS. MEAT, VEGETABLES, CHEESES, AND COLD CUTS ARE MIXED WITH TOMATO, CREAM, OR BÉCHAMEL SAUCES. TOGETHER THEY FORM THE RICH AND TENDER HEART OF THESE DELICIOUS AND WELL-LOVED DISHES.

SEMOLINA PASTAS ARE ALSO AT HOME IN BAKING DISHES. IN FACT, MANY SHORT PASTAS SEEM TO EXIST FOR THE VERY PURPOSE OF "CATCHING" THE SAUCE AND ENHANCING IT IN THE HEAT OF THE OVEN AS IT BAKES INTO A GOLDEN AND BUBBLING CRUST: BAKED *MACARONI*, STUFFED SHELLS, *MEZZE MANICHE*, AND *TORTIGLIONI*, FLAVORED WITH WONDERFUL ITALIAN CHEESES OR EVEN TASTIER *RAGÙ*, EMERGE TRIUMPHANT FROM THE OVEN.

Cannelloni con speck e radicchio
Cannelloni with Speck and Radicchio

Servings 4
Difficulty **Medium**
Prep Time 55'
Cook Time 20'

For the pasta: 1 2/3 cups (200 g) Italian "00" flour – 2 eggs.
For the filling: 14 oz (400 g) ricotta – 1.1 lbs (500 g) red radicchio – 1 (3.5 oz/100 g) slice of speck ham – 2 1/2 tbsp (40 ml) extra-virgin olive oil – 3/4 cup + 2 1/2 tbsp (90 g) Parmigiano Reggiano cheese, grated – 1 tbsp minced parsley – salt and pepper to taste.
For the Béchamel Sauce: 2 1/2 tbsp (35 g) butter – 1/4 cup (30 g) Italian "00" flour – 2 cups (500 ml) milk – salt to taste – nutmeg to taste.

Pour the flour onto a work surface or into a bowl and create a well in the center. Break the eggs and pour them into the well. Start working them into the flour with a fork, then use your fingers and palms to continue mixing until a smooth and consistent dough forms. Wrap it in plastic and refrigerate it for 30 minutes.
Finely chop the radicchio, then wash it and drain it thoroughly.
Pour the oil into a pan and let it heat up for a few seconds. Add the radicchio and season with salt and pepper. Cover the pan and let it cook until the radicchio becomes slightly crispy. Once it's cooled, add the ricotta, the speck (finely diced), and 2/3 of the Parmigiano.
Preheat the oven to 350° F (180° C).
Start heating the milk for the béchamel sauce. Heat the butter separately in a deep pot, and when it's melted, add the flour. Cook for 3–4 minutes on low heat, whisking continuously. Slowly add the hot milk and season with a pinch of salt and nutmeg. Continue cooking until the sauce is dense and creamy, stirring continuously to avoid lumps.
Take the dough out of the refrigerator and cut it into 3/4-1 inch (2-3 cm) slices. With a rolling pin or pasta machine, flatten each slice into a very thin sheet about 3-4 inches (8-10 cm) wide. Cut each sheet into 3 x 4 inch (10 x 8 cm) rectangles and boil them in salted water for 5 minutes. Remove them with a perforated spoon and lay them out on a cloth to cool and dry, making sure they don't overlap.
Place a line of filling down the center of each rectangle and roll them up. Butter a baking dish and lay the cannelloni inside, one right next to the other, with no space in between. Cover them with an even layer of béchamel, sprinkle the remaining Parmigiano on top, and dot the surface with butter.

Cannelloni gratinati
Baked Cannelloni

Servings 4
Difficulty *Medium*
Prep Time 60'
Cook Time 20'

For the pasta: 1 2/3 cups (200 g) Italian "00" flour – 2 eggs.
For the filling: 2 1/2 tbsp (40 ml) extra-virgin olive oil – 1 oz (30 g) carrots (1/4 cup, chopped) – 0.7 oz (20 g) celery (just under 1/4 cup, chopped) – 1.4 oz (40 g) onion (1/4 cup, chopped) – 0.55 lbs (250 g) beef – 7 oz (200 g) spinach, cooked (a little over 1 cup cooked) – 1/4 cup (60 ml) dry white wine – 1/3 cup (80 g) butter – 1 1/3 cups (120 g) Parmigiano Reggiano cheese, grated – 1 egg – nutmeg to taste – salt and pepper to taste.
For the Béchamel Sauce: 2 1/2 tbsp (35 g) butter – 1/4 cup (30 g) Italian "00" flour – 2 cups (500 ml) milk – salt to taste – nutmeg to taste.

Pour the flour onto a work surface or into a bowl and create a well in the center. Break the eggs into the well and start incorporating them into the flour with a fork. Then use your fingers and palms to continue mixing until a smooth, consistent dough forms. Wrap it in plastic and refrigerate the dough for about 30 minutes. Mince the vegetables and sauté them in the oil. Chop the beef into small pieces and add it to the vegetables. When it's thoroughly browned, pour in the white wine and let it cook until the liquid is absorbed. Then add the already cooked spinach and a pinch of salt and pepper to taste. Cook for 15-20 minutes.

Let the mixture cool and blend it in a food processor. Then add the egg, half Parmigiano, and a pinch of nutmeg. Heat the milk for the béchamel sauce. Heat the butter separately, and when it is melted, add the flour and let the mixture cook on low heat for 3-4 minutes, whisking continuously. Then slowly add the hot milk and season with salt and nutmeg to taste. Let the mixture cook until the sauce is dense and creamy.

Remove the pasta dough from the refrigerator and cut it into slices 3/4-1 inch (2–3 cm) wide. Flatten each slice with a pasta machine or rolling pin until you have very thin sheets about 3-4 inches (8-10 cm) wide. Cut each sheet of dough into 3 x 4 inch (10 x 8 cm) rectangles and boil them in salted water for 2-3 minutes. Remove them from the pot and lay them out on a cloth to cool and dry.

Place a line of filling down the center of each rectangle and roll them up. Butter a baking dish and lay the cannelloni inside, leaving no space between them. Pour an even layer of béchamel sauce on top. Then sprinkle the remaining Parmigiano and dot the surface with butter. Bake in a preheated oven (375° F/190° C) for 15-20 minutes. When the cannelloni are cooked, remove them from the oven and serve.

Conchiglioni ripieni di pollo e spinaci
Conchiglioni Stuffed with Chicken and Spinach

Servings 4
Difficulty Low
Prep Time 45'
Cook Time 10'

10.5 oz (300 g) conchiglioni (jumbo shells) – 8.8 oz (250 g) chicken breast – 5.3 oz (150 g) spinach, cooked (about 3/4 cup + 1 tbsp) – 1.76 oz (50 g) onion (about 1/3 cup chopped) – 1 tbsp (15 g) butter – 1 cup + 4 tbsp (120 g) Parmigiano Reggiano cheese, grated – 1 1/4 cups (30 cl) extra-virgin olive oil – 1 egg yolk – nutmeg to taste – salt and pepper to taste.
For the Béchamel Sauce: 2 1/2 tbsp (35 g) butter – 1/4 cup (30 g) Italian "00" flour – 2 cups (500 ml) milk – salt to taste – nutmeg to taste.

Boil the conchiglioni in salted water and strain them 2 minutes before they should be done (refer to package directions for cooking time). Let them cool briefly.

Mince the onion and sauté it in a bit of oil. Dice the chicken breast and add it to the onion, browning them together. When the chicken is a nice golden brown, add the cooked spinach and season with salt and pepper. Continue to cook it on medium heat for 10 minutes.

Let the stuffing cool, then blend it with the egg yolk, half the Parmigiano, and a pinch of nutmeg in a food processor.

Preheat the oven to 375° F (190° C).

Start heating the milk for the béchamel sauce. Heat the butter separately in a deep pot, and when it's melted add the flour. Let it cook for 3-4 minutes on low heat, whisking continuously. Slowly add the hot milk, and season with salt and a pinch of ground nutmeg. Let it cook until the sauce is dense and creamy, stirring continuously to avoid lumps.

Butter a baking dish and line it with a light layer of béchamel. Use a pastry bag to pipe the filling into the shells and lay them in the baking dish. When it's full, cover them with an even layer of béchamel. Sprinkle the remaining Parmigiano on top and dot the surface with butter. Bake the shells for 10 minutes.

Farfalle gratinate dell'ortolano
Baked Farfalle with Vegetables

Servings 4
Difficulty Low
Prep Time 40'
Cook Time 15-20'

12.3 oz (350 g) farfalle pasta – 1.76 oz (50 g) carrots (about 1 small carrot) – 1.76 oz (50 g) red and yellow bell pepper (about 1 small pepper) – 1.76 lbs (800 g) eggplant (about 1 1/2 eggplants) – 3.5 oz (100 g) tomatoes (about 1 small tomato) – 1.76 oz (50 g) red turnips (about 1 small turnip) – 1/3 cup (40 g) flour – 3 tbsp (40 g) butter – 1/2 cup (50 g) Parmigiano Reggiano cheese, grated – 1/2 cup (50 g) Pecorino cheese, grated – 2 cups (500 ml) milk – 1 tsp chives – 2 tbsp (30 ml) extra-virgin olive oil – vegetable oil for frying – nutmeg to taste – salt and pepper to taste.

Clean and julienne all the vegetables, then drizzle some extra-virgin olive oil in a pan and sauté them with the chives.

Start making a béchamel sauce by melting the butter in a deep pot. Add the flour and let it cook for 3-4 minutes on low heat, whisking continuously. Then slowly add the heated milk and season with a pinch of nutmeg. Continue cooking until the sauce is dense and creamy.

Peel and clean the eggplant. Cut 1/8-inch (3 mm) slices, using a mandoline slicing tool if you have one. Put the slices in a strainer, sprinkle them with salt, and let them sit for 20 minutes. Then heat a good amount of vegetable oil in a pan and fry them.

Boil the pasta in a large pot of salted water and strain it 1-2 minutes before it's done (refer to package directions for cooking time). Mix the farfalle with the vegetables, béchamel, and grated cheeses. Line a baking dish with fried eggplant slices and fill it with pasta. If there's any grated cheese left over, sprinkle it on top. Bake it in a preheated oven (365° F/185° C) for 15-20 minutes, until the surface is bubbling and golden.

Garganelli incassati
Garganelli Incassati

Servings 4
Difficulty High
Prep Time
1h and 30'
Cook Time 15'

7 oz (200 g) egg garganelli pasta – 3.5 oz (100 g) prosciutto (dry-cured), in one piece – 2/3 cup (150 ml) heavy cream – 3 1/2 tbsp (50 g) butter – 0.88 oz (25 g) black truffles – 1/3 cup + 1 tbsp (40 g) Parmigiano Reggiano cheese, grated – 1 tbsp minced parsley – salt and pepper to taste.
For the pâte brisée: 3 cups + 3 tbsp (400 g) flour – 1 2/3 tsp (10 g) salt – 3/4 cup + 1 1/2 tbsp (200 ml) water – 1 egg yolk.
For the fonduea: 1 tbsp (15 g) butter – 2 tbsp (15 g) flour – 1 cup (250 ml) milk – 1.76 oz (50 g) Fontina cheese – 1 egg yolk.

Mix the flour and other pâte brisée ingredients on a work surface until the dough comes together, being careful not to overwork it. Wrap it in plastic and refrigerate it for about 1 hour.

Cut the prosciutto into small strips and sauté it in the butter. When it's golden brown add the chopped truffles, followed immediately by the cream and parsley. Bring it all to a boil and let it cook for a few minutes. Season with salt and pepper to taste.

Preheat oven to 350° F (180° C).

Boil the pasta in salted water and strain it 2 minutes early, referring to the package directions for cooking time. Combine the garganelli with the sauce and Parmigiano cheese.

Take the dough from the refrigerator and roll out two discs, each 1/8 inch (4 mm) thick. Lay one of them in a 10-11 inch (26-28 cm) round cake pan, lining the bottom and sides. Pour the pasta inside and cover it with the other piece of dough, sealing the edges well. Beat the egg yolk with a tiny bit of water and brush it over the top.

Bake it for about 10-15 minutes, until the surface is golden brown.

Meanwhile make the fondue. Melt the butter in a pot, mix in the flour, and let it cook for 3-4 minutes. Then add the hot milk and let it continue to cook until the sauce has thickened. Add the Fontina and wait for it to melt completely before stirring in the egg yolk. Remove the pan from the oven and arrange a layer of fondue and a slice of "garganelli incassati" ("boxed up" garganelli) on each plate.

Lasagne al radicchio rosso e mascarpone
Radicchio and Mascarpone Lasagna

Servings 4
Difficulty *Medium*
Prep Time *1h*
Cook Time *20'*

For the pasta: 2 1/3 cups (300 g) Italian "00" flour – 3 eggs.
For the filling: 1.1 lbs (500 g) Treviso radicchio – 7 oz (200 g) white spring onions (about 13 medium spring onions) – 1.1 lbs (500 g) mascarpone – 3/4 cup + 1 1/2 tbsp (200 ml) red wine – 1/3 cup (30 g) Parmigiano Reggiano cheese, grated – 1 1/2 tbsp (20 g) butter – 1 sprig of thyme – 1 tbsp minced parsley – 1/3 cup + 1 1/2 tbsp (100 ml) extra-virgin olive oil – salt to taste.

Mix together the flour and eggs until a smooth and consistent dough forms. Wrap it in plastic and let it sit for 30 minutes. Roll it out to 1/32 inch (1 mm) thick and cut it into rectangles that will fit in the pan you are using for the lasagna.

Boil the rectangles of pasta in salted water for 1 minute. Then strain them and quickly run cold water over them to stop the cooking process. Lay them out on a cloth to dry.

Wash the radicchio and cut it into strips, and slice the spring onions into thin rounds. Stew them together in half the oil over medium heat. Add the red wine and let it evaporate, seasoning with salt to taste. Remove the thyme from the stem and add it to the pan at the very end, after it's all cooked for about 15 minutes.

Butter a baking dish and line the bottom with the first layer of pasta. Then alternate layers of radicchio and mascarpone, separated by layers of pasta. Continue in that order until the filling ingredients have run out, and finish with a layer of pasta. Lightly butter the top and sprinkle it generously with grated Parmigiano.

Cover the baking dish with aluminum foil, being careful not to let it touch the surface of the lasagna. Bake it in a preheated oven at 300° F (150° C) for about 20 minutes.

When the surface is golden and bubbling, remove the lasagna from the oven. Garnish it with a mixture of the minced parsley and remaining oil.

Lasagne alla bolognese
Lasagna Bolognese

Servings 4/6
Difficulty High
Prep Time 2h
Cook Time 23-30'

For the green pasta: 1 2/3 cups (200 g) Italian "00" flour – 1 egg – 2.1 oz (60 g) spinach, cooked and squeezed dry (about 1/3 cup).
For the béchamel sauce: 2 cups (500 ml) milk – 2 1/2 tbsp (35 g) butter – 1/4 cup (30 g) Italian "00" flour – salt – grated nutmeg.
For the ragù: 2 tbsp (30 ml) extra-virgin olive oil – 1 oz (30 g) celery (about 2 small stalks) – 1.76 oz (50 g) carrots (about 1 small) – 2.1 oz (60 g) onion (about 1 small) – 0.7 oz (20 g) pancetta – 0.22 lbs (100 g) ground pork – 0.26 lbs (120 g) ground beef – 1/4 cup + 1 1/2 tbsp (80 ml) red wine – 3 1/2 tbsp (60 g) tomato paste – 2 cups (0.5 L) water – 1 bay leaf – salt – pepper.
For the topping: 3/4 cup + 1 tbsp (80 g) Parmigiano Reggiano cheese, grated – 1 1/2 tbsp (20 g) butter.

Purée the spinach and mix it with the flour and eggs until a smooth and consistent dough forms. Wrap it in plastic and refrigerate it for about 30 minutes.

Chop the vegetables and sauté them over medium heat with the bay leaf and a bit of oil. When they're golden brown, add the ground beef, pork, and chopped pancetta. Turn the heat up and let them cook. As soon as the meat is browned, season it with salt and pepper and pour in the red wine. Let the wine evaporate, then add the tomato paste. Add enough water to cover everything and let it cook over low heat for at least 30 minutes. Preheat oven to 350° F (180° C).

Take the dough out of the refrigerator and roll it out into sheets, about 1/32-1/16 inch (1.5 mm) thick. Cut it into 3 x 4 inch (8 x 10 cm) rectangles and boil them in salted water, a few at a time, for about 15 seconds. Strain them, let them cool, and lay them out on a cloth.

Heat the milk for the béchamel sauce. Heat the butter separately, and when it's melted, add the flour. Cook for 3-4 minutes on low heat, whisking. Add the hot milk and season with a pinch of salt and nutmeg. Continue cooking until the sauce is dense and creamy, stirring continuously to avoid lumps.

Grease a baking dish and line it with the first layer of pasta. Cover that with a layer of ragù, followed by a layer of béchamel, then Parmigiano. Continue in that order. Finish with a layer of béchamel and Parmigiano. Bake the lasagna for 20-30 minutes. Let it cool for 10 minutes, then bring it to the table.

Lasagne alla cacciatora
Lasagna Cacciatore

Servings 4/6
Difficulty *Medium*
Prep Time
1h and 30'
Cook Time 10'

For the green pasta: 1 cup + 3 tbsp (150 g) Italian "00" flour – 1.2 oz (35 g) spinach (boiled, squeezed dry, and chopped), about 3 tbsp – 1 egg.
For the yellow pasta: 1 2/3 cups (200 g) flour – 2 eggs.
For the ragù: Half a rabbit, deboned (about 0.88–1.1 lbs/400-500 g) – 1.1 lbs (500 g) tomatoes (about 4 medium) – 2.1 oz (60 g) pancetta – 2.6 oz (75 g) onion, finely chopped (just under 1/2 cup) – 3 1/2 tbsp (50 ml) Marsala – 1 garlic clove – 1 sprig of rosemary – 1 bunch of sage – 1 tbsp minced parsley – tbsp (30 ml) oil – 1/3 cup + 1 tbsp (40 g) Parmigiano Reggiano cheese, grated – salt and pepper to taste.
For the béchamel sauce: 3/4 cup + 1 1/2 tbsp (200 ml) milk – 1 tbsp (15 g) butter – 2 tbsp (15 g) Italian "00" flour – nutmeg to taste – salt to taste.
For the filling: 1 1/2 tbsp (20 g) butter – 1/3 cup (30 g) Parmigiano Reggiano cheese, grated.

Pour the flour and create a well in the center. Break the eggs and drop them into the well. Mix them into the flour until a soft and homogenous dough forms. Wrap it in plastic and let it sit for about 30 minutes before rolling it out. Do the same for the green pasta, adding the spinach along with the eggs. Preheat oven to 375° F (190° C). Meanwhile make the béchamel sauce. Heat the butter in a pot, and when it's melted add the flour. Cook for 3-4 minutes on low heat, whisking continuously. Slowly add the hot milk and season with a pinch of salt and nutmeg. Continue cooking until the sauce is dense and creamy, stirring to avoid lumps.
Use a pasta machine or rolling pin to roll both pieces of dough out to a thickness of about 1/32 inch (1 mm) and cut it into 2 3/4-3 inch (7-8 cm) squares.
Heat the oil and chopped pancetta in a pan. Add the onion, garlic, sage, and rosemary. When it starts to turn golden brown, add the rabbit (diced) and brown it for a few minutes. Add the Marsala and let it evaporate, then add the crushed tomatoes. Season with salt and pepper to taste and let it all cook on low heat for about 20 minutes. Remove the herbs when it's done.
Boil the pasta squares in salted water for a couple of minutes. Strain them, let them cool, and lay them out on a cloth to dry. Grease individual ramekins. Alternate layers of green and yellow pasta with layers of ragù and béchamel. Finish with grated Parmigano and dot the surface with butter. Bake them for about 10 minutes.

Lasagne con asparagi e baccalà
Cod and Asparagus Lasagna

Servings 4
*Difficulty **Medium***
Prep Time 1h
Cook Time 20'

For the pasta: 2 1/3 cups (300 g) Italian "00" flour – 3 eggs.
For the béchamel sauce: 3 tbsp (45 g) butter – 1/4 cup + 1 tbsp (40 g) Italian "00" flour – 2 cups (0.5 L) milk – salt to taste.
For the filling: 0.66 lbs (300 g) asparagus – 0.55 lbs (250 g) salt-dried cod, reconstituted – 1 oz (30 g) shallot (about 3 tbsp chopped) – 1 garlic clove – 3 tsp (40 ml) extra-virgin olive oil – 3 1/2 tbsp (50 ml) vegetable broth – salt and pepper.

Pour the flour onto a cutting board or marble counter and create a well in the center. Break the eggs and drop them into the well. Start working them into the flour with a fork, then use your fingers and palms to knead the dough until it's smooth and consistent. Wrap it in plastic and refrigerate it for 30 minutes.
Roll the dough out to 1/32 inch (1 mm) thick and cut it into 4 x 4 3/4 inch (10 x 12 cm) rectangles. Boil the pasta in salted water and strain it when it's al dente. Cool it off immediately by putting it in a bowl of salted ice water. Then lay the rectangles out on cloths to dry.
Preheat oven to 350° F (180° C).
Start heating the milk for the béchamel sauce. Heat the butter separately in a deep pot, and when it's melted, add the flour. Cook for 3-4 minutes on low heat, whisking continuously. Slowly add the hot milk and season with salt to taste. Continue cooking until the sauce is dense and creamy, stirring continuously to avoid lumps. If it's too dense, add a bit of milk. If it's too thin, let it cook a few more minutes.
Mince the shallot and sauté it in the oil with the whole garlic clove. Clean the asparagus and cut them into 1/3-3/4 inch (1-2 cm) pieces. Add them to the pan and let them brown a bit, then add the chopped up cod and season with salt and pepper to taste. Add a ladleful of broth and let the sauce cook for about 10 minutes.
Grease a baking dish and arrange layers of pasta followed by layers of the cod and asparagus sauce. Top each layer of sauce with a few tablespoons of béchamel and sprinkle it with Parmigiano.
Bake the lasagna for about 20 minutes. Let it cool for 5-10 minutes and serve.

Lasagne con funghi
Mushroom Lasagna

Servings 4
Difficulty Medium
Prep Time 1h
Cook Time 10'

For the pasta: 1 2/3 cups (200 g) flour – 2 eggs.
For the filling: 0.4 lbs (180 g) ground beef – 1 (0.22lbs/100 g) slice of prosciutto (dry-cured) – 1.76 oz (50 g) dried mushrooms – 3.5 oz (100 g) onion (about 2/3 cup chopped) – 2.8 (80 g) carrots (about 2/3 cup chopped) – 2.5 oz (70 g) celery (about 2/3 cup chopped) – 3/4 cup + 1 tbsp (80 g) Parmigiano Reggiano cheese, grated – 5 1/2 tbsp (80 g) butter – 3 1/2 tbsp (50 ml) milk – 2/3 cup (150 ml) water – 1 tbsp minced parsley – salt to taste.

Mix the flour and eggs until a smooth and consistent dough forms. Wrap it in plastic and let it sit for 30 minutes. Roll it out to a thickness of 1/32 inch (1 mm) and cut it into 3-inch (7-8 cm) squares. Boil them in salted water for 1 minute, 5-6 squares at a time. Remove them with a perforated spoon and lay them out on a damp cloth that's been soaked in cold water and squeezed thoroughly, making sure they don't overlap.

Chop the onion, carrot, and half a stalk of celery. Reconstitute the dried mushrooms by soaking them in cold water for 15 minutes, then squeeze out any excess water and chop them up.

Melt a pat of butter in a saucepan and sauté the chopped vegetables for about 5 minutes. Add the ground beef and parsley, letting it brown for another 3-4 minutes. Add a few tablespoons of milk, followed by the mushrooms. Mix well, season with salt to taste, and pour in 2/3 cup (150 ml) of water. Turn down the heat to the lowest setting and let it cook for 30 minutes.

Cut the prosciutto into thin strips. Grease a wide, shallow baking dish with the butter and line the bottom with lasagna squares. Spread a few tablespoons of the meat and mushroom mixture over the pasta and add a few strips of prosciutto. Dot it with butter and sprinkle it with Parmigiano. Add another layer of pasta and continue in the same order until all the ingredients have run out, alternating lasagna squares with the meat and mushroom mixture and finishing with a layer of pasta. Pour lots of melted butter on top and sprinkle it with grated Parmigiano.

Bake the lasagna in a preheated oven at 375° F (190° C) for 10 minutes. When the surface is golden and bubbling, remove the pan from the oven. Let it cool for 10 minutes and serve.

Lasagne con ricotta
Ricotta Lasagna

Servings 4
Difficulty Low
Prep Time 45'
Cook Time 10'

For the pasta: 2 1/3 cups (300 g) Italian "00" flour – 3 eggs.
For the filling: 2 tbsp minced parsley – 3/4 cup + 1 tbsp (80 g) Parmigiano Reggiano cheese, grated – 1 1/2 tbsp (20 g) butter – 1.1 lbs (500 g) ricotta.
For the Béchamel Sauce: 3 tbsp (40 g) butter – 1/4 cup (35 g) Italian "00" flour – 2 cups (5 dl) hot milk – salt to taste.

Mix the flour and eggs until a smooth and consistent dough forms. Wrap it in plastic and let it sit for at least 30 minutes. Roll the dough out to a thickness of 1/32 inch (1 mm) and cut it into 4-inch (10 cm) squares.

Start the béchamel sauce by melting the butter in a pot. Add the flour and let it cook on low heat for 3-4 minutes, whisking continuously. Slowly add the hot milk and let the mixture continue to cook until a dense and creamy sauce forms. Season it with a pinch of salt, the minced parsley, and half the grated Parmigiano. While sauce is still hot, add the ricotta, stirring vigorously to temper it with the béchamel.

When the sauce is done, boil the pasta in salted water for 1 minute, 5-6 squares at a time. Remove them with a perforated spoon and lay them out on a damp cloth that's been soaked in cold water and squeezed thoroughly, making sure they don't overlap.

Grease a baking dish with 1 tablespoon (10 g) of butter. Line the bottom with pasta squares, cover them with a layer of the ricotta mixture, and sprinkle some Parmigiano on top. Continue layering pasta, ricotta, and Parmigiano until all the ingredients run out. Finish with a layer of pasta and dot the surface with another tablespoon (10 g) of butter. Sprinkle the remaining Parmigiano on top.

Bake the lasagna in a preheated oven at 350° F (180° C) until the surface is crispy, then remove it from the oven and serve.

Lasagne con salmone e spinaci
Salmon and Spinach Lasagna

Servings 4
Difficulty Medium
Prep Time 1h
Cook Time 20'

For the pasta: 2 1/3 cups (300 g) Italian "00" flour – 3 eggs.
For the purée: 3 tbsp (45 g) butter – 1/4 cup + 1 tbsp (40 g) flour – 2 cups (0.5 L) vegetable broth – salt to taste.
For the filling: 0.55 lbs (250 g) salmon fillet – 0.66 lbs (300 g) fresh spinach (about 10 cups) – 1 oz (30 g) fresh ginger – 1/3 cup + 1 1/2 tbsp (1 dl) extra-virgin olive oil – 1 garlic clove – salt and pepper to taste.

Pour the flour onto a cutting board or marble counter and create a well in the center. Break the eggs and drop them into the well. Start working them into the flour with a fork, then use your fingers and palms to knead the dough until it's smooth and consistent. Wrap it in plastic and refrigerate it for 30 minutes.

Roll the dough out to 1/32 inch (1 mm) thick and cut it into 4 x 4 3/4 inch (10 x 12 cm) rectangles. Boil the pasta in salted water and strain it when it's *al dente*. Cool it off immediately by putting it in a bowl of salted ice water. Then lay the rectangles out on cloths to dry.

Preheat oven to 350° F (180° C).

Now make the sauce. Melt the butter in a deep pot, being careful not to let it burn. Add the flour, whisking continuously. Then start pouring in the broth, still whisking to avoid lumps. Bring it to a boil and maintain it for 1 minute to thicken the sauce slightly.

Sauté the whole garlic clove in half the oil. Add a teaspoon of grated ginger along with the spinach (washed and strained). Season with salt and sauté it for a few seconds, but don't let it cook too much. Remove the skin and any bones from the salmon. Dice it and sauté it in the remaining oil. Season it with salt and pepper to taste.

Spread some sauce in a greased baking dish and cover it with a layer of pasta. Cover it with a few spoonfuls of sauce, salmon pieces, and spinach. Continue in this order until all the ingredients have run out. Bake the lasagna for about 20 minutes. Let it cool for 5-10 minutes and serve.

Lasagne del norcino
Norcino Lasagna

Servings 4
*Difficulty **Medium***
*Prep Time **2h***
*Cook Time **20'***

For the pasta: 2 1/3 cups (300 g) Italian "00" flour – 3 eggs.
For the béchamel sauce: 5 tbsp (70 g) butter – 1/2 cup + 1 tbsp (70 g) Italian "00" flour – 4 1/4 cups (1 L) milk – nutmeg to taste – salt to taste.
For the filling: – 0.22 lbs (100 g) sausage – 0.22 lbs (100 g) pancetta, in one piece – 0.22 lbs (100 g) pork – 1.76 oz (50 g) pork rinds – 8.8 oz (250 g) crushed tomatoes – 5.3 oz (150 g) onion (about 2 small) – 1 sprig of rosemary – 1 garlic clove – 1/3 cup + 1 1/2 tbsp (1 dl) white wine – salt and pepper.

Pour the flour and create a well in the center. Break the eggs and pour them into the well. Start working them into the flour with a fork, then use your fingers and palms to knead the dough until it's smooth and consistent. Wrap it in plastic and refrigerate it for about 30 minutes. Roll the dough out to 1/32 inch (1 mm) thick and cut it into 4 x 4 3/4 inch (10 x 12 cm) rectangles. Boil the pasta in salted water and strain it when it's *al dente*. Cool it off by putting it in a bowl of salted ice water. Then lay the rectangles out on cloths to dry. Preheat oven to 350° F (180° C).

Start heating the milk for the béchamel sauce. Heat the butter separately, and when it's melted, add the flour. Cook for 3-4 minutes on low heat, whisking. Slowly add the hot milk and season with a pinch of salt and nutmeg. Continue cooking until the sauce is dense and creamy, stirring continuously to avoid lumps. If it gets too dense, add a bit of milk. If it's too thin, let it cook for a few more minutes.

Chop the onion, garlic, and rosemary. Sauté them in a saucepan and add the chopped meat, diced pancetta, and broken up sausage. Brown everything together for a few minutes, then add the white wine. Once it's evaporated, add the crushed tomatoes and let it cook for about 20 minutes. Season with salt and pepper to taste.

Grease a baking dish and spread a layer of béchamel on the bottom. Cover it with a layer of pasta, then continue in the following order: béchamel, meat sauce, Parmigiano. There should be enough of everything to make 4 layers.

Bake the lasagna for 20 minutes. Sprinkle each serving with finely chopped pork rinds.

Lasagne di pesce
Seafood Lasagna

Servings 4
*Difficulty **Medium***
Prep Time
1h and 30'
Cook Time 20'

For the pasta: 2 1/3 cups (300 g) Italian "00" flour – 3 eggs.
For the cream: 3 tbsp (45 g) butter – 1/4 cup + 1 tbsp (40 g) flour – 2 cups (0.5 L) fish broth – 1 parsley stalk – salt to taste.
For the filling: 0.77 lbs (350 g) angler – 0.66 lbs (300 g) clams – 0.25 lbs (120 g) cherry tomatoes (about 7) – 8 shrimp – 1 bunch of parsley – 1 garlic clove – hot red pepper to taste – 1/3 cup + 1 1/2 tbsp (1 dl) white wine – 3 1/2 tbsp (0.5 dl) extra-virgin olive oil – salt and pepper to taste.

Pour the flour and create a well in the center. Break the eggs and drop then into the well. Mix the ingredients together until a smooth and consistent dough forms. Wrap it in plastic and let it sit for about 30 minutes. Roll it out to a thickness of about 1/32 inch (1 mm) and cut it into 4 x 4 3/4 inch (10 x 12 cm) rectangles. Boil them in salted water, strain them, and cool by putting them in a bowl of salted ice water. Then lay them out on a cloth to dry.

Put the mussels in a pot with half the oil, the whole garlic clove, minced parsley, white wine, and a piece of hot red pepper. Cook them on high heat until they open. Remove the shells and strain the liquid from the pot.

Preheat oven to 350° F (180° C). Fillet the angler and clean the shrimp. Make the fish broth by putting all the discarded parts in a pot with 4 1/4 cups (1 L) of cold water and the parsley stalk. Bring it to a boil and let it simmer for about 20 minutes. Then strain the broth and use it for the lasagna.

Wash the tomatoes, cut them into quarters, and remove the seeds. Sauté them over very high heat with a bit of oil, then set them aside. Dice the angler and the shrimp. Sauté them for a few seconds, then add the tomatoes and season with salt and pepper. Add the minced parsley and the clams.

Now make the cream sauce. Melt the butter in a deep pot, making sure it doesn't burn. Add the flour, whisking continuously. Pour in the hot broth and the liquid from the clams. Keep whisking to prevent lumps. Bring it to a boil and maintain it for 1 minute to thicken the sauce. Spread a layer of sauce in a greased baking dish. Add a layer of pasta, then another of sauce, then the fish. Continue in this order. Bake the lasagna for about 20 minutes. Let it cool for 5-10 minutes and serve. Garnish each plate with cream sauce to taste

Lasagne integrali con verdure
Whole Wheat Lasagna with Winter Vegetables and Montasio

Servings 4/5
*Difficulty **Medium***
*Prep Time **1h***
Cook Time 20'

For the pasta: 1 2/3 cups (200 g) Italian "00" flour – 3/4 cup + 1 1/2 tbsp (100 g) whole wheat flour – 3 eggs – salt to taste.

For the béchamel sauce: 1/3 cup (50 g) Italian "00" flour – 3 1/2 tbsp (50 g) butter – 2 cups (0.5 L) milk – salt and pepper to taste.

For the filling: 7 oz (200 g) red onion (about 2 medium) – 7 oz (200 g) broccoli – 7 oz (200 g) pumpkin (about 1 3/4 cups cubed) – 5.3 oz (150 g) cultivated mushrooms – 3.5 oz (100 g) chard (about 3 cups) – 1.76 oz (50 g) sun-dried tomatoes (just under 1 cup) – 0.88 lbs (400 g) Montasio cheese – 1 tsp minced savory – 1/4 cup (60 ml) extra-virgin olive oil – 1 cup (100 g) Parmigiano Reggiano cheese, grated – salt and pepper to taste.

Combine the flours and create a well in the center. Break the eggs and drop them into the well. Mix everything together until a smooth and consistent dough forms. Wrap it in plastic and let it sit for 30 minute. Roll it out to 1/32 inch (1 mm) thick and cut it into rectangles, about 4 x 8 inches (10 x 20 cm). Boil the rectangles in salted water and cool them in a bowl of ice water. Lay them out on a cloth to dry.

Wash the chard and blanch it in salted water. Strain it and put it in ice water to preserve the bright green color. Do the same for the broccoli. Clean and julienne the onion. Sauté it in half the oil over medium heat. When it's softened, turn up the heat and add the pumpkin (already cleaned and cubed). Wait a few minutes and add the broccoli and chard, roughly chopped. Chop the sun-dried tomatoes and add them at the end. Clean and slice the mushrooms. Sauté them with the savory and remaining oil. Add them to the other vegetables and season with salt and pepper. Preheat oven to 400° F (200° C).

Meanwhile make the béchamel sauce. Melt the butter, add the flour, whisking. Add the hot milk, still whisking to avoid lumps. Bring it to a boil and maintain it for a few minutes to thicken the sauce. Add salt and pepper to taste.

Grease a baking dish and alternate layers of pasta with layers of vegetables, about 3 tablespoons of béchamel, a sprinkling of Montasio and a sprinkling of Parmigiano. Continue until all the ingredients have run out. Finish with a layer of béchamel and Parmigiano.

Bake the lasagna for about 20 minutes. Let it cool for 5 minutes and serve.

Mezze maniche ripiene al formaggio ai porcini
Mezze Maniche Stuffed with Porcini Mushrooms and Cheese

Servings 4
Difficulty Low
Prep Time 40'
Cook Time 10'

7 oz (200 g) mezze maniche pasta – 1.76 oz (50 g) fresh ricotta – 1.76 oz (50 g) Caprino cheese – 1.76 oz (50 g) Robiola cheese – 1/3 cup + 1 tbsp (40 g) Parmigiano Reggiano cheese, grated – 5.3 oz (150 g) fresh porcini mushrooms – 1 egg yolk – 1 tbsp catmint – 2 tbsp (30 ml) extra-virgin olive oil – salt and pepper to taste.

Boil the pasta in salted water and strain it 1 minute before it's done according to the cooking time on the package instructions. Stir in a bit of olive oil so it doesn't stick together.

Carefully clean the mushrooms with a damp cloth. Dice them and sauté them in a bit of oil, but don't let them soften too much. Season them with salt and pepper and let them cool.

Combine the cheeses in a large bowl and mix well. Add a pinch of salt and pepper, half the Parmigiano, and the egg yolk. Stir in the mushrooms and adjust the seasoning if necessary.

Fill the mezze maniche with the mushroom and cheese mixture. Line a pan with parchment paper and arrange the pasta neatly inside. Sprinkle the remaining Parmigiano on top and bake it at 350° F (180° C) for about 10 minutes, until a crispy golden crust forms.

Mince the catmint and mix it with the oil in a small cup. Top each portion of stuffed pasta with the herbed oil.

Pasta e patate al forno
Oven-Baked Pasta and Potatoes

Servings 4
Difficulty Medium
Prep Time 40'
Cook Time 10-15'

7 oz (200 g) ziti or penne pasta – 7 oz (200 g) potatoes (about 1 medium) – 7 oz (200 g) fresh tomatoes (about 1 1/2 medium) – 5.3 oz (150 g) Calabrian salami or sopressata – 2.8 oz (80 g) Caciocavallo cheese – 7 oz (200 g) green bell pepper (about 1 1/2 medium) – 2.8 oz (80 g) onion (about 1 small) – 8 basil leaves – 3 1/2 tbsp (50 ml) extra-virgin olive oil – salt to taste.

Wash and peel the tomatoes, then remove the seeds and chop them finely. Slice the onion and tear up the basil leaves by hand. Remove the seeds from the pepper and dice it. Sauté the tomato and onion in the oil for a few minutes. Add the pepper and basil with a pinch of salt, and let everything continue to cook.

Preheat oven to 350° F (180° C).

Peel and slice the potatoes. Boil them in a pot of salted water and strain them when they're very *al dente*. Do the same for the pasta, separately.

Thinly slice the salami and cheese. Line a baking dish with parchment paper and arrange a layer of potatoes on the bottom. Cover them with a layer of sauce. Layer part of the salami and cheese over the sauce. Add a layer of pasta next, followed by another layer of sauce, then some salami and cheese.

When you've used up all the ingredients, bake the pasta until the surface is golden and bubbling.

Maccheroni al forno
Baked Macaroni

Servings 4
Difficulty Low
Prep Time 1h
Cook Time 10'

10.5 oz (300 g) ridged macaroni.
For the filling: 3/4 cup + 1 tbsp (80 g) Pecorino cheese, semi-aged – 0.66 lbs (300 g) ground veal – 3 tbsp (40 g) butter – 1 2/3 cups (400 ml) beef broth – 1/3 cup + 1 1/2 tbsp (100 ml) heavy cream – 5.3 oz (150 g) onion (about 2 small) – salt and pepper.
For the filling: 0.33 lbs (150 g) ham – 0.33 lbs (150 g) turkey breast – 0.33 lbs (150 g) chicken livers – 1/3 cup (75 ml) heavy cream – 1 small black truffle.

Chop the onion and sauté it on low heat with 2 tablespoons of butter and the ground beef. Brown it for 5 minutes, then add a ladleful of broth. Let it cook for another 20 minutes and season with salt and pepper to taste.

Preheat oven to 350° F (180° C).

Finely chop the ham, turkey, and chicken livers in a food processor. Add the cream and a pinch of salt and pepper. Mix well and add the truffle, finely diced (about 1/16 inch or 2 mm).

Boil the pasta in salted water. When it's very *al dente*, strain it and quickly run cold water over it. Strain it again, very thoroughly.

Use a pastry bag to fill each piece of pasta with the ham and turkey mixture. Grease a baking dish and arrange a layer of pasta on the bottom. Cover it with a layer of sauce and sprinkle it with a bit of finely diced Pecorino. Repeat the process in that order until all the ingredients run out.

Pour the heavy cream over the top, then dot the surface with the remaining butter and grated Pecorino. Bake it for about 10 minutes, or until a crispy crust forms on top. Remove it from the oven and serve it immediately.

Rosette di baccalà
Cod Rosettes with Parsley and Lemon Sauce

Servings 4
Difficulty Medium
Prep Time 1h
Cook Time 10'

For the pasta: 2 1/3 cups (300 g) Italian "00" flour – 3 eggs.
For the filling: 0.66 lbs (300 g) unsalted dried cod – 3.5 oz (100 g) potatoes, boiled (about 1/2 small) – 3 1/2 tbsp (50 ml) white wine – 1 garlic clove – salt and pepper to taste – 2/3 cup (150 ml) vegetable broth .
For the sauce: 1 bunch of parsley – extra-virgin olive oil as needed – cornstarch as needed – 1 lemon – salt and pepper to taste.
For the topping: 1 1/2 tbsp (20 g) butter.

Pour the flour onto a work surface and create a well in the center. Add the eggs and mix until a smooth and consistent dough forms. Wrap it in plastic and let it sit for 30 minutes.

Sauté the garlic in a bit of oil and add the cod, sliced into steaks. Pour in the wine and let it evaporate. Add the vegetable broth and let the cod finish cooking. Season it with salt and pepper to taste.

Transfer the cod to a bowl, add the potatoes, and stir them together with a spoon until the mixture is consistent.

Roll the dough out to about 1/16-1/32 inch (1.5 mm) thick and cut it 6 x 10 inch (15 x 25 cm) rectangles. Boil them in salted water for a minute and transfer them to a bowl of salted ice water to cool. Then lay them out to dry on a cloth.

Use a spatula to spread the filling on each rectangle. Roll them up like spring rolls and cut them crosswise into rounds, about 1-1 1/2 inches (3-4 cm) wide.

Arrange them in a greased pan, top them with flakes of butter, and bake them at 350° F (180° C) for 10 minutes.

Sauté the whole garlic clove (to be removed later) and minced parsley in the oil for 2 minutes. Add the vegetable broth and cornstarch. Let the sauce thicken to the desired consistency, adding the lemon juice and grated zest at the end. Season it with a pinch of salt and pepper.

Top each serving of rosettes with a drizzle of parsley-lemon sauce.

Schiaffoni ripieni di ricotta
Schiaffoni Stuffed with Ricotta, Zucchini, and Prosciutto

Servings 4
Difficulty Low
Prep Time 50'
Cook Time 10'

7 oz (200 g) schiaffoni pasta – 14 oz (400 g) ricotta – 7 oz (200 g) zucchini (about 1 medium) – 3.5 oz (100 g) prosciutto, in one piece – 3 tbsp (40 ml) extra-virgin olive oil – 3/4 cup + 2 1/2 tbsp (90 g) Parmigiano Reggiano cheese, grated – 1 tbsp (15 g) butter – salt and pepper to taste.
For the béchamel sauce: 2 1/2 tbsp (35 g) butter – 1/4 cup (30 g) Italian "00" flour – 2 cups (500 ml) milk– nutmeg to taste – salt to taste.

Boil the pasta in salted water and strain it a couple of minutes before it's done according to the time indicated on the package instructions. Quickly run cold water over it and strain it again, very thoroughly. Stir in a bit of olive oil so it doesn't stick together.

Clean the zucchini and dice them very finely, about 1/16 inch (2 mm). Do the same for the prosciutto.

Preheat oven to 375° F (190° C).Heat the oil in a pan and quickly cook the zucchini on high heat until it's very crispy. Let it cool, then mix it with the ricotta, diced prosciutto, and 2/3 of the grated Parmigiano.

Start heating the milk for the béchamel sauce. Heat the butter separately in a deep pot, and when it's melted, add the flour. Cook for 3-4 minutes on low heat, whisking continuously. Slowly add the hot milk and season with a pinch of salt and nutmeg. Continue cooking until the sauce is dense and creamy, stirring continuously to avoid lumps.

Use a pastry bag to pipe the filling into the schiaffoni. Grease a baking dish and spread béchamel sauce over the bottom and sides. Fill it with pasta and pour the remaining béchamel on top. Sprinkle it with the remaining Parmigiano and a few flakes of butter.

Bake the schiaffoni for about 10 minutes.

Timballo tradizionale di maccheroni
Traditional Baked Macaroni

For the pastry dough: 1 cup + 1 1/2 tbsp (250 g) butter, softened – 3/4 cup + 2 1/2 tbsp (180 g) sugar – 4 cups (500 g) flour – 2 eggs – salt to taste.
For the filling: 5.3 oz (150 g) macaroni – 2.1 oz (60 g) tomato paste (about 3 1/2 tbsp) – 3.5 oz (100 g) ground pork – 4.2 oz (120 g) ground beef – 1.76 oz (50 g) chicken livers – 1 oz (30 g) celery (about 1/3 cup chopped) – 1.76 oz (50 g) carrots (just over 1/3 cup chopped) – 2 oz (60 g) onion (just over 1/3 cup chopped) – 0.7 oz (20 g) pancetta – 1/4 cup + 1 1/2 tbsp (80 ml) red wine – 2 cups (500 ml) water – 1 bay leaf – 2 tbsp (30 ml) extra-virgin olive oil – 1/2 cup (50 g) Parmigiano Reggiano cheese, grated – salt and pepper to taste. (+ 1 egg for the egg wash)

Mix the sugar with the softened butter. Add the eggs and mix well, then add the flour and a pinch of salt. Mix it all together but don't overwork the dough. Wrap it in plastic and refrigerate it for at least 1 hour.

Chop the onions, carrots, and celery. Drizzle some oil in a saucepan and sauté the vegetables with the bay leaf on medium heat. When they've turned golden brown add the ground meats, chopped pancetta, and chicken livers (cleaned and diced). Turn up the heat and let them brown. As soon as they're well browned, season with salt and pepper and add the red wine. Let the liquid evaporate completely, then turn down the heat and add the tomato paste. Add just enough water to cover everything and simmer on low heat for at least 30 minutes.

Roll half the dough out on a floured surface until it's 1/8 inch (4 mm) thick. Lay it in a 10–11 inch (26-28 cm) round cake pan, covering the bottom and sides. Roll the rest of the dough out into a disc, the same thickness as the other half, which will be the top crust of the "pie".

Boil the pasta in salted water and strain it when it's very *al dente* (a few minutes earlier than the cooking time indicated on the package directions). Combine it with the sauce and grated cheese, and pour it into the dough-lined pan. Lay the disc of dough on top and seal the edges well.

Beat the egg and brush it over the top. Bake at 350° F (180° C) for about 20 minutes, until the top is crispy and golden.

Tortiglioni gratinati al formaggio
Baked Cheese Tortiglioni with Porcini Mushrooms and Anchovy Sauce

Servings 4
*Difficulty **Low***
Prep Time 20'
Cook Time 15'

12.3 oz (350 g) tortiglioni pasta – 3.5 oz (100 g) Asiago cheese – 1.76 oz (50 g) Caprino cheese – 1 oz (30 g) Parmigiano Reggiano cheese – 3.5 oz (100 g) fresh porcini mushrooms – 1 oz (30 g) anchovies, packed in salt – 5 tbsp (20 g) parsley – 1/4 cup (60 ml) extra-virgin olive oil – 1 garlic clove.
For the béchamel sauce: 3 cups (750 ml) milk – 1/3 cup (45 g) Italian "00" flour – 3 tbsp (45 g) butter – nutmeg to taste – salt to taste.

Heat the milk for the béchamel sauce. Melt the butter separately in a deep pot, then add the flour and let it cook for 3-4 minutes on low heat, whisking continuously. Slowly pour in the hot milk, seasoning with salt and a bit of grated nutmeg. Let the sauce cook until it's dense and creamy, stirring continuously to avoid lumps. When it's reached the right consistency, add the cheeses and let them melt.

Boil the pasta in salted water. Strain it 2 minutes earlier than the cooking time indicated on the package and combine it with the béchamel. Butter a baking dish and spread the pasta inside. Bake it in a preheated oven at 350° F (180° C) for 15 minutes. Take it out of the oven and set it aside for 10 minutes.

Wash and slice the mushrooms. Drizzle some olive oil in a pan and sauté them on high heat for a few seconds, then season them with salt and pepper. Rinse the anchovies and remove any bones, then blend them in a food processor with the garlic and extra-virgin olive oil.

After the pasta has cooled for 10 minutes, place a portion on each serving plate. Garnish it with mushrooms and drizzle the anchovy sauce on top.

PASTA
SALADS

In every culture, there are numerous dishes, often with remote origins, that pair cooked grains with various other types of food. The most popular combination is surely that of grains and vegetables, but there are also many other additions like meat, fish, shellfish, legumes, and cheeses.

Couscous is a very popular dish in the Arab world, but it's also a deeply rooted Sicilian tradition that has now been adopted by mainland Italy as well. These grains of durum wheat semolina, steamed and fluffed like rice, may have inspired the idea to use not only grains, but also various shapes and sizes of pasta, as the basis for summer dishes with a wide variety of additional ingredients.

For example, you can start with a very basic and very Italian pasta salad comprised of cherry tomatoes and mozzarella garnished with fragrant basil leaves. Staying on the Mediterranean track, you can then create other blends with fish, or classic fresh summer vegetables like bell peppers, eggplant, olives, and capers.

PASTA SALAD IS SYNONYMOUS WITH LIGHT FARE. WHITE MEATS LIKE CHICKEN AND TURKEY, PERHAPS SEASONED WITH EXOTIC CURRY, ALSO WORK PERFECTLY, WHETHER THEY'RE COMBINED WITH THE CELEBRATED AND HIGHLY REFINED TRADITIONAL BALSAMIC VINEGAR FROM MODENA, OR ACCOMPANIED BY SURPRISE ELEMENTS LIKE RAISINS AND ALMONDS. FRUIT CAN ALSO BE A PART OF THESE DELICATE AND APPETIZING DISHES. FOR EXAMPLE, PAIRING FRESH CHEESES WITH PEARS (OR GREEN APPLES) ISN'T THE LATEST DISCOVERY OF SOME MODERN CHEF, BUT A CUSTOM DOCUMENTED IN RENAISSANCE COURTS.

CONSIDERING THE POPULARITY OF ONE-PLATE MEALS TODAY, PASTA SALAD RECIPES ARE PERFECT FOR A SEASON WHERE THE HEAT CURBS YOUR DESIRE TO EAT HEAVIER FOODS, BUT DOES NOTHING TO DIMINISH THE PLEASURE OF SAMPLING VIVID COLORS WITH YOUR EYES OR THE ENJOYMENT OF A WIDE RANGE OF FRESH AND APPETIZING FLAVORS WITH YOUR PALATE.

Insalata di castellane
Castellane Pasta Salad
with Salmon, Fennel, and Lemon

Servings 4
Difficulty *Low*
Prep Time 25'
Cook Time 10'

12.3 oz (350 g) castellane pasta – 0.66 lbs (300 g) salmon fillet – 1 fennel bulb – 2 lemons – 1/3 cup (80 ml) extra-virgin olive oil – 1 tbsp chives, minced – salt to taste – black pepper.

Boil the pasta in salted water. When it's very *al dente*, strain it and quickly run cold water over it to cool it off. Strain it again, very thoroughly. Transfer it to a large bowl and mix in a bit of olive oil so it doesn't stick together.

Grate the lemon zest, being careful not to include the white part. Slice the lemons in half and juice them. Slice the fennel very thinly and season it with a pinch of salt, ground pepper, and half the lemon juice. Remove the skin and any bones from the salmon fillet, then cut it into 3/4 inch (2 cm) cubes. Cook it over high heat on a flat griddle or nonstick pan with a bit of oil. Season it with salt and pepper and set it aside.

Mix the remaining lemon juice with the oil and a pinch of salt and pepper. Add the lemon zest and the minced chives. Combine all the ingredients with the pasta, mix well, and top it with the herbed lemon oil.

Insalata di cellentani con tonno e peperoni
Cellentani Pasta Salad with Tuna and Peppers

Servings 4
*Difficulty **Low***
Prep Time 45'
Cook Time 8'

12.3 oz (350 g) cellentani pasta – 0.66 lbs (300 g) fresh tuna – 2/3 cup (150 ml) extra-virgin olive oil – 0.55 lbs (250 g) red bell pepper (about 2 medium) – 0.55 lbs (250 g) yellow bell pepper (about 2 medium) – 1.4 oz (40 g) capers (about 4 1/2 tbsp) – 1 tsp minced parsley – 1 garlic clove – 2 sprigs of fresh thyme – salt and pepper to taste.

Remove the skin and any bones from the tuna. Let it marinate with the thyme sprig and a bit of olive oil for 15 minutes. Grill it on a flat griddle, seasoning lightly with salt and pepper. Let it cool a bit and slice it against the grain, into pieces about 1/8 inch (3-4 mm) thick.

Boil the pasta in salted water. When it's very *al dente*, strain it and quickly run cold water over it to cool it off. Strain it again, very thoroughly. Transfer it to a large bowl and mix in a bit of olive oil so it doesn't stick together.

Wash the peppers and bake them in a preheated oven at 350° F (180° C) for about 20 minutes. Peel them, remove the seeds, and cut them into diamonds. Flavor them with the garlic (thinly sliced), thyme (stripped from the stem), and a drizzle of olive oil. Purée the capers with the oil.

In a large bowl combine the pasta with the peppers and a teaspoon of minced parsley. If necessary, add a bit of olive oil and a pinch of salt and pepper. Distribute it among the serving plates and top each one with a slice of tuna. Finish with a drizzle of caper oil.

Insalata di conchiglie
Conchiglie Pasta Salad with King Prawns, Cherry Tomatoes, and Tropea Onion

Servings 4
Difficulty Low
Prep Time 1h
Cook Time 10'

12.7 oz (360 g) conchiglie pasta – 3.5 oz (100 g) cherry tomatoes (about 6) – 12 king prawns – 1 small Tropea onion – hot red pepper (fresh or dried) to taste – 4-5 basil leaves – 1 garlic clove – 1/3 cup + 1 1/2 tbsp (100 ml) extra-virgin olive oil – salt to taste – sugar to taste.

Boil the pasta in salted water. When it's very *al dente*, strain it and quickly run cold water over it to cool it off. Strain it again, very thoroughly. Transfer it to a large bowl and mix in a bit of olive oil so it doesn't stick together.

Wash the tomatoes, cut them in half, and arrange them in a pan. Sprinkle them with a handful of salt and a pinch of sugar. Drizzle them with olive oil and bake them at 200° F (100° C) for about 45 minutes.

Clean the prawns. Sauté the garlic with the oil and a few thin slices of fresh hot pepper. When the garlic is well browned, add the prawns and sauté them as well, but don't let them overcook.

Clean and dice the onion. Stew it in a separate pan on low heat with a bit of oil. If necessary, add a bit of water.

Add the tomatoes, prawns, and onion to the pasta. Mix well, adding some extra virgin olive oil and fresh basil (cut into strips). Season with salt and pepper to taste and serve.

Insalata di *cous cous* con cozze, vongole e gamberi
Couscous Salad with Mussels, Clams, and Shrimp

Servings 4
Difficulty Low
Prep Time 50'

10.5 oz (300 g) precooked couscous – 0.55 lbs (250 g) mussels – 0.55 lbs (250 g) clams – 8 shrimp – 2.8 oz (80 g) carrots (about 1 1/2 small) – 2.5 oz (70 g) celery (about 2 medium stalks) – 1/3 cup + 1 1/2 tbsp (100 ml) extra-virgin olive oil – 1 tsp minced parsley – 1 tbsp minced chives – 1 garlic clove – hot red pepper to taste – salt and pepper to taste.

Sauté the garlic and hot pepper in 1 tablespoon of olive oil. Add the mussels and clams, well cleaned and rinsed. Let them cook over high heat until they open, then remove the shells.
Clean and shell the shrimp, and heat 2 tablespoons of oil in another pan. Sauté the shrimp briefly and season them with salt and pepper.
Finely dice the carrots and celery, and sauté them in a bit of oil. Season them lightly with salt.
Pour the couscous into a deep pot. Boil enough water for that amount of couscous (the ratio should be 1:1). Pour the water over the couscous and mix well with a wooden fork so the grains don't clump. Cover the pot with plastic wrap, sealing it completely, and let it sit for about 30 minutes.
Carefully fluff the couscous with a fork. Stir in the shrimp, diced vegetables, 1 teaspoon of minced parsley, and the chives. Season it with salt and pepper to taste, and drizzle in some cold-pressed olive oil. Top each serving with mussels and clams.

Insalata di *cous cous* vegetariana
Vegetarian Couscous Salad

Servings 4
Difficulty Low
Prep Time 40'

10.5 oz (300 g) precooked couscous – 3.5 oz (100 g) red onion (about 1 1/2 small) – 1.76 oz (50 g) peas (about 1/3 cup) – 1.76 oz (50 g) yellow bell pepper (about 1/4 large) – 3.5 oz (100 g) carrots (about 2 small) – 3.5 oz (100 g) zucchini (about 1/2 medium) – 3.5 oz (100 g) tomatoes (about 1 small) – 1/3 cup (80 ml) extra-virgin olive oil – 1 1/4 cups (300 ml) vegetable broth or water – parsley to taste – oregano (preferably fresh) to taste – 1-2 tsp poppy seed – salt to taste.

Boil enough vegetable broth (or water) for the couscous (the ratio should be 1:1). Put the couscous in a deep pot and pour the boiling broth over it. Mix well with a wooden fork and cover the pot with plastic wrap, sealing it completely. Let it sit for 30 minutes, then fluff it thoroughly with a fork.

Clean all the vegetables, except the tomato and peas. Dice them into pieces about 1/16-1/8 inch (2-3 mm). Sauté all the vegetables separately in extra-virgin olive oil, making sure they turn crispy. Blanch the peas. Peel the tomato, remove the seeds, and dice it.

Combine the vegetables with the couscous (make sure it doesn't clump). Add the poppy seed and oregano. Drizzle with olive oil, season with salt to taste, and serve.

Insalata di ditalini
Ditalini Pasta Salad with Green Apple, Raisins, Almonds, and Speck Ham

Servings 4
Difficulty Low
Prep Time 20'
Cook Time 10'

12.3 oz (350 g) ditalini pasta – 2 green apples – 2.6 oz (75 g) raisins (about 1/2 cup packed) – 3.5 oz (100 g) almonds, shelled and peeled (about 3/4 cup whole) – 2.8 oz (80 g) speck ham – 1/3 cup (80 ml) extra-virgin olive oil – 1 lemon – salt and pepper to taste.

Boil the pasta in salted water. When it's very *al dente*, strain it and quickly run cold water over it to cool it off. Strain it again, very thoroughly. Transfer it to a large bowl and mix in a bit of olive oil so it doesn't stick together.

Wash the apples and remove the cores, but don't peel them. Cut them into 1/3-1/2 inch (1 cm) cubes and put them in a bowl of cold water with the juice of half a lemon.

Soak the raisins in another bowl of water for about 10 minutes. Meanwhile cut the speck into diamonds. Drizzle some oil in a nonstick pan and sauté the speck until it's crispy.

Slice the almonds and toast them in the oven or toss them in a hot nonstick pan for a few seconds. Strain the raisins and apples and set them out to dry on a cloth or paper towels.

Whisk the remaining lemon juice with the oil and a pinch of salt and pepper. Combine all the ingredients with the pasta, mixing well, and drizzle the lemon oil on top.

Insalata di farfalle
Farfalle Pasta Salad with Avocado, Tomatoes, Corn, and Mozzarella

Servings 4
Difficulty Low
Prep Time 25'
Cook Time 12'

12.3 oz (350 g) farfalle pasta – 7 oz (200 g) cherry tomatoes (about 12) – 8.8 oz (250 g) mini mozzarella balls – 5.3 oz (150 g) canned corn – 1.76 oz (50 g) onion (about 3/4 small) – 1 avocado – 6 basil leaves – 1/3 cup + 1 1/2 tbsp (100 ml) extra-virgin olive oil – 1/2 garlic clove – 1 lemon – salt and pepper to taste.

Boil the pasta in salted water. When it's very *al dente*, strain it and quickly run cold water over it to cool it off. Strain it again, very thoroughly. Transfer it to a large bowl and mix in a bit of olive oil so it doesn't stick together.

Use a potato peeler to grate strips of lemon zest, being careful not to include the white part. Then cut the lemon in half and juice it.

Pit and peel the avocado. In a food processor, combine it with the oil, garlic, onion, 3 basil leaves, lemon juice, and a generous pinch of salt and pepper. Blend until the mixture is creamy and homogenous.

Cut the mozzarella balls into quarters. Do the same for the tomatoes and remove the seeds.

Combine the pasta with the tomatoes, mozzarella, lemon peel (cut into thin strips), and corn (thoroughly strained). Add the avocado dressing and mix well.

Insalata di farfalle con pollo al curry
Farfalle Pasta Salad with Curry Chicken

Servings 4
Difficulty Low
Prep Time 35'
Cook Time 10'

12.3 oz (350 g) farfalle pasta – 0.66 lbs (300 g) chicken breast – 2 tbsp (30 ml) extra-virgin olive oil – 6 1/2 tbsp (100 g) mayonnaise – 1 tsp curry – coconut milk (or vegetable broth) as needed – 2.1 oz (60 g) peas (about 1/3–1/2 cup) – salt to taste.

Dice the chicken breast and sprinkle it with a pinch of curry. Sauté it in a bit of oil until it is cooked, and season it with salt.

Boil the pasta in salted water. When it's very *al dente*, strain it and quickly run cold water over it to cool it off. Strain it again, very thoroughly. Transfer it to a large bowl and mix in a bit of olive oil so it doesn't stick together.

Boil the peas in salted water, strain them, and let them cool.

Dilute the remaining curry with 1-2 tablespoons of coconut milk (or vegetable broth) and mix it with the mayonnaise. If necessary, add a bit more coconut milk – the mayonnaise should have the consistency of heavy cream.

Stir the mayonnaise into the pasta. Then add the chicken and peas. Garnish according to preference and serve.

Insalata di fiocchi rigati con robiola, pere e rucola
Fiocchi Rigati Pasta Salad with Robiola, Pears, and Arugula

Servings 4
Difficulty Low
Prep Time 15'
Cook Time 10'

12.7 oz (360 g) fiocchi rigati pasta – 3.5 oz (100 g) fresh Robiola cheese – 1.5 lbs (700 g) pears (about 4 medium) – 1/3 cup (80 ml) extra-virgin olive oil – 3.5 oz (100 g) arugula (about 5 cups) – balsamic vinegar to taste – salt and pepper to taste.

Boil the pasta in salted water. When it's very *al dente*, strain it and quickly run cold water over it to cool it off. Strain it again, very thoroughly. Transfer it to a large bowl and mix in a bit of olive oil so it doesn't stick together.

Wash the arugula and let it dry thoroughly. Peel the pears, slice them in half, remove the cores, and dice them.

Carefully mix the Robiola with the pasta. Then add the pears and season with oil and salt.

Distribute it among the serving plates and top each portion with arugula. Then add a drizzle of cold-pressed olive oil, a few drops of balsamic vinegar, and sprinkle with ground black pepper.

Chef's tips
An excellent summer alternative is to replace the pears with fresh figs, peeled and cut into quarters.

Insalata di fusilli
Fusilli Salad with Green Beans, Peppers, and Chicken in Anchovy Dressing

Servings 4
Difficulty Low
Prep Time 30'
Cook Time 13'

12.3 oz (350 g) fusilli pasta – 8.8 oz (250 g) chicken breast – 8.8 oz (250 g) red bell pepper (about 1 1/2 large peppers) – 8.8 oz (250 g) yellow bell pepper (about 1 1/2 large peppers) – 3.5 oz (100 g) green beans (about 18 beans) – 1 oz (30 g) anchovies, packed in oil – 5 basil leaves – 3/4 cup + 1 1/2 tbsp (200 ml) extra-virgin olive oil – 1 garlic clove – salt to taste.

Boil the pasta in salted water. Strain it when it's very *al dente* and quickly cool it off by running cold water over it. Strain it again, very thoroughly. Transfer it to a large bowl and stir in a bit of olive oil so it doesn't stick together.

Wash the peppers and roast them in a hot oven or on a grill. Then peel them, remove the seeds, and cut them into strips about 1/8-1/4 inch (0.5 cm) wide.

Cut the chicken breast into strips and sauté it in a bit of oil. Season it with a pinch of salt.

Clean the green beans, wash them, and cut them into pieces about 1 inch (3 cm) long. Boil them in lightly salted water.

Make the dressing by blending the anchovies, garlic, basil, and oil in a food processor.

Combine the roasted peppers, chicken, and green beans with the pasta. Add the anchovy dressing, mix well, and serve.

Insalata di gemelli con tacchino
Gemelli Pasta Salad with Turkey, Hazelnuts, and Scamorza

Servings 4
Difficulty Low
Prep Time 35'
Cook Time 10'

12.3 oz (350 g) gemelli pasta – 7 oz (200 g) turkey breast – 7 oz (200 g) carrots (about 3 medium carrots) – 2.8 oz (80 g) toasted hazelnuts (about 3/4 cup coarsely ground) – 2.8 oz (80 g) smoked scamorza cheese – 1 garlic clove – 2 sprigs of thyme – 1 sprig of rosemary – 1 bunch of sage – 1/4 cup + 1 1/2 tbsp (80 ml) extra-virgin olive oil – salt and pepper to taste.

Chop the herbs and combine them with 3 1/2 tablespoons (50 ml) of oil.

Thinly slice the turkey breast. Drizzle some oil in a pan and brown the turkey for a few minutes, then season with salt and pepper. Let it cool and combine it with the herb-flavored olive oil, setting aside a few tablespoons for later. Let the turkey marinate.

Boil the pasta in salted water. When it's very *al dente*, strain it and quickly cool it off by running cold water over it. Then strain it again, very thoroughly. Transfer it to a large bowl and stir in a bit of olive oil so it doesn't stick together.

Peel and wash the carrots and cut them into strips. Add them to the pasta along with the turkey and season with salt and pepper. Toast the hazelnuts in a very hot nonstick pan for a few minutes, then roughly crush them. Cut the scamorza into strips and stir the cheese and nuts into the pasta salad.

Distribute it among serving plates and top it with the remaining herb-flavored olive oil.

Insalata di gnocchi di semola con capesante e porcini
Semolina Gnocchi Salad with Scallops and Porcini Mushrooms

Servings 4
Difficulty *Low*
Prep Time 20'
Cook Time 14'

12.3 oz (350 g) semolina gnocchi – 8 scallops – 7 oz (200 g) porcini mushrooms – 1 garlic clove – 1 tsp minced parsley – 1 tsp minced chives – 1 sprig of thyme – 1/4 cup + 1 1/2 tbsp (80 ml) extra-virgin olive oil – salt to taste.

Boil the pasta in salted water. When it's very *al dente*, strain it and quickly run cold water over it to cool it off. Strain it again, very thoroughly. Transfer it to a large bowl and mix in a bit of olive oil so it doesn't stick together.

Remove any dirt from the mushrooms and clean them thoroughly with a damp cloth. Cut them into 1/3–3/4 inch (1-2 cm) cubes.

Sauté the whole garlic clove and thyme sprig in the olive oil. Add the mushrooms and let it all cook on high heat. Season with salt and pepper and let the mushrooms cook for a few minutes, making sure they don't get too soft.

Clean the scallops. Drizzle some olive oil in a pan and brown them for 1-2 minutes on each side. Season them lightly with salt and pepper.

Mix the pasta with the mushrooms and scallops (whole or chopped, according to preference). Add a pinch of parsley and chives, and finish with a drizzle of cold-pressed olive oil.

Chef's tips
If you're using frozen porcini mushrooms it's best to slice them before they've completely thawed, while they're still a little hard. Be careful not to overcook them or they'll fall apart.

Insalata di mezze penne con baccalà, fave e olive
Mezze Penne Pasta Salad with Cod, Fava Beans, and Olives

Servings 4
Difficulty *Low*
Prep Time 40'
Cook Time 11'

12.3 oz (350 g) mezze penne pasta – 7 oz (200 g) fava beans, fresh or frozen (about 1 1/3 cups) – 0.55 lbs (250 g) salt-dried cod, reconstituted – 1.76 oz (50 g) black olives (about 11 large olives) – 6.3 oz (180 g) tomatoes, very ripe (about 1 1/2 medium tomatoes) – 1 bunch of basil – vegetable broth as needed – 1/3 cup + 1 1/2 tbsp (100 ml) extra-virgin olive oil – 1 garlic clove – salt and pepper to taste.

Boil the pasta in salted water. Strain it when it's very *al dente* and quickly run cold water over it. Then strain it again, very thoroughly. Pour it into a large bowl and stir in a bit of olive oil so it doesn't stick together.

Use an immersion blender to mix half the oil with the basil, then pass the mixture through a fine mesh strainer.

Sauté the whole garlic clove in half the remaining oil. Add the reconstituted cod, chopped into small pieces. Season with salt and pepper to taste and let the fish cook quickly, making sure it doesn't fall apart. If necessary, add some vegetable broth.

Cut an X into the bottom of the tomatoes and boil them for 20 minutes. Let them cool, peel them, remove the seeds, and dice them.

Boil the fava beans in lightly salted water, let them cool, and peel them. Season them with salt, pepper, and the remaining oil.

Add the fava beans, olives, tomatoes, and cod to the pasta. Mix well and season with salt and pepper. Distribute the pasta salad among individual bowls and top each serving with basil oil.

Insalata di pipe rigate alla greca
Greek Pasta Salad

Servings 4
Difficulty *Low*
Prep Time 15'
Cook Time 10'

12.3 oz (350 g) pipe rigate pasta – 2 tomatoes – 7 oz (200 g) feta cheese – 2.1 oz (60 g) kalamata olives (about 13-14 large olives) – 2.8 oz (80 g) cucumber (about 1/4 large cucumber) – oregano (fresh or dried) to taste – 1/3 cup + 1 1/2 tbsp (100 ml) extra-virgin olive oil – salt to taste.

Boil the pasta in salted water and strain it when it's very *al dente*. Quickly cool it off by running cold water over it and strain it again, very thoroughly. Transfer the pasta to a large bowl and mix in a bit of olive oil so it doesn't stick together.
Wash and dice the tomatoes, and cut them into 3/4-inch (2 cm) cubes. Peel the cucumber, remove the seeds, and cut it into medium-sized cubes. Do the same for the feta, making sure to wet the knife before each cut so the cheese doesn't crumble.
Add the tomatoes, cucumber, and feta to the pasta and mix well. Season with oregano to taste, add plenty of olive oil, and garnish with olives.

Chef's tips
For a stronger flavor, you can also add half a red onion, thinly sliced.

250

Insalata di ruote margherita
Wagon Wheel Pasta Salad

Servings 4
Difficulty *Low*
Prep Time 15'
Cook Time 8'

12.3 oz (350 g) wagon wheel pasta – 8.8 oz (250 g) buffalo mozzarella – 14 oz (400 g) tomatoes (about 3 medium tomatoes) – 4-5 basil leaves – 1/4 cup + 1 1/2 tbsp (80 ml) extra-virgin olive oil – salt to taste.

Boil the pasta in salted water. Strain it when it's still very *al dente* and quickly run it under cold water to cool it off. Then carefully strain it again. Transfer it to a large bowl and stir in some olive oil so it doesn't stick together.

Wash the tomatoes, remove the seeds, and cut them into 1/3-1/2 inch (1 cm) cubes. Dice the mozzarella, add it to the pasta along with the tomatoes, and mix well.

Season it with the basil (torn up by hand) and a pinch of salt. Stir in the rest of the extra-virgin olive oil and serve.

Chef's tips
For a slightly different presentation, you can use cherry tomatoes and mini mozzarella balls, either whole or cut in half.

Insalata di spaccatelle e prosciutto crudo
Spaccatelle Salad with Prosciutto

Servings 4
Difficulty *Low*
Prep Time 15'
Cook Time 9'

12.3 oz (350 g) spaccatelle pasta – 7 oz (200 g) prosciutto (dry-cured), in one slice – 7 oz (200 g) pickled vegetables – 4 tbsp (60 g) mayonnaise – 3 tsp (15 g) mustard – 1 tsp minced parsley – half a lemon – 3 1/2 tbsp (50 ml) extra-virgin olive oil – salt and pepper to taste.

Combine the mustard and mayonnaise in a bowl. Add a drizzle of olive oil and sprinkle with ground pepper. Dice the prosciutto and chop up the pickled vegetables, making sure they're well strained and all excess brine has been eliminated.

Peel the lemon, and divide the segments. Use a very sharp knife to remove the rind, including all the white part, and dice it very finely.

Boil the pasta in salted water and strain it when it's very *al dente*. Quickly run it under cold water to cool it off. Strain it again, very thoroughly.

Transfer the pasta to a large bowl and mix it with the mustard dressing, prosciutto, vegetables, parsley, and lemon. Season with salt and pepper to taste, stir again to combine everything, and top it off with a drizzle of cold-pressed olive oil.

Chef's tips
You can also use a prosciutto end for this recipe, completely removing the rind and veins of fat.

Tagliolini freddi estivi
Summer Tagliolini Salad

Servings 4
Difficulty Low
Prep Time 45'
Cook Time 3-4'

For the pasta: 2 1/3 cups (300 g) all-purpose flour – 3 eggs.
For the filling: 5.3 oz (150 g) zucchini (about 1 medium) – 4.4 oz (125 g) red bell pepper (about 2 small) – 4.4 oz (125 g) yellow bell pepper (about 2 small) – 2.8 oz (80 g) carrots (about 1 1/2 small) – 5.3 oz (150 g) cucumber (about 1/2 medium) – 1/3 cup + 1 tbsp (90 ml) extra-virgin olive oil – 1 pinch of salt.
For the sauce: 0.5–0.7 oz (15-20 g) shallot (about 1 1/2-2 tbsp chopped) – 2-3 mint leaves – 2 tsp (10 ml) extra-virgin olive oil – 3.5 oz (100 g) plain yogurt – salt and pepper to taste.

Pour the flour onto a work surface and create a well in the center. Mix in the eggs until a firm and consistent dough forms. Wrap it in plastic and let it sit for 30 minutes. Then roll it out to a thickness of 1/32 inch (1 mm). Fold it over onto itself several times and slice it into strips about 1/8 inch (3-4 mm) wide.

Clean and dice all the vegetables and put them in a large bowl. Stir in the olive oil and season them with salt and pepper.

Boil the tagliolini in lightly salted water and strain them when they're very *al dente*. Add them to the bowl of vegetables and mix well to combine all the flavors.

Mix the yogurt with the hand-torn mint leaves and minced shallot. Season with salt, pepper, and a drizzle of cold-pressed olive oil.

Serve this dish warm or cold, with the yogurt sauce on the side.

Non-PASTA PASTA

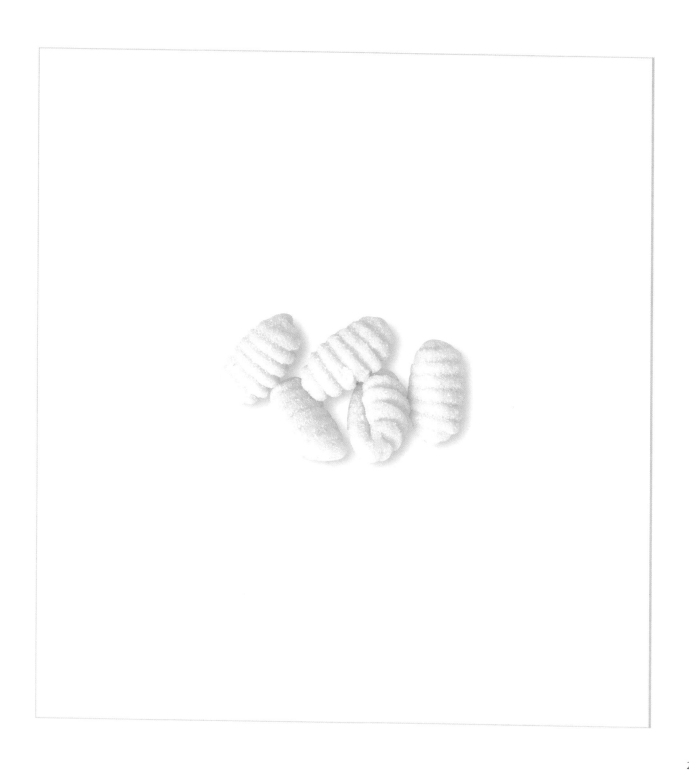

ITALIAN GASTRONOMY PROVIDES A WIDE RANGE OF RECIPES THAT IN-VOLVE ADDING A SMALL AMOUNT OF FLOUR TO MANY DIFFERENT INGRE-DIENTS, AND MOST OF THEM ORIGINATE FROM HIGHLY LOCAL TRADITIONS IN THE NORTHERN REGIONS OF ITALY. TO BE HONEST, THE PRODUCTS OF THESE RECIPES CANNOT TECHNICALLY BE DEFINED AS "PASTA". BUT, OVER TIME, TRADITION HAS RIGHTFULLY PLACED THEM AMONG THE MOST POPULAR AND BEST LOVED FIRST COURSES.

FOR EXAMPLE, BASIC *GNOCCHI* DOUGH IS MADE FROM BOILED POTATOES AND FLOUR. DIFFERENT INGREDIENTS CAN BE ADDED, LIKE SPINACH, PUMPKIN, MUSH-ROOMS, ETC. OTHER RECIPES MIGHT USE CORNMEAL INSTEAD OF WHEAT FLOUR, LIKE *GNOCCHI DI POLENTA*. THEN THERE ARE BREAD-BASED RECIPES, LIKE *CANE-DERLI* FROM TRENTINO OR *GNOCCHI DI PANE* FROM TRIESTE. STILL OTHERS USE CHEESE AS THE MAIN INGREDIENT, LIKE *GNOCCHI DI RICOTTA*. SEMOLINA IS USED FOR *GNOCCHI ALLA ROMANA*, WHILE CHEESE AND EGGS ARE THE BASIS FOR *PAS-SATELLI* (SERVED IN BEEF BROTH).

TUSCAN *GNUDI* CAN BE CONSIDERED A TYPE OF *GNOCCHETTI DI RICOTTA*, WHICH CAN BE TRACED TO VARIOUS ITALIAN REGIONS AND IS A CATEGORY UNTO ITSELF.

THESE "MINI MEATBALLS" ARE MADE FROM EGGS, PARMESAN CHEESE, HERBS, AND OFTEN VARIOUS SPICES. THEY ARE ESSENTIALLY "NAKED" RAVIOLI: PASTA-LESS FILLING SHAPED INTO A BALL, BOILED, AND COATED IN A SIMPLE SAUCE OF BUTTER AND GRATED CHEESE. THIS DISH IS EVEN MENTIONED IN THE *CHRONICLE* OF SALIMBENE DA PARMA, A 13TH CENTURY FRIAR.

CANEDERLI AND *GNOCCHI DI PANE* ARE A DELICIOUS EXAMPLE OF EFFICIENT USES FOR LEFTOVERS, ONCE VERY POPULAR BY VIRTUE OF CUSTOMS AND COMMON SENSE. ALL YOU HAVE TO DO IS MOISTEN SOME STALE BREAD WITH MILK AND FLAVOR IT WITH A FEW PIECES OF HUMBLE *PANCETTA* TO CREATE A NEW AND DELECTABLE DISH.

THESE RECIPES PRECEDED THE WIDESPREAD POPULARITY OF PASTA, WENT ON TO KEEP IT COMPANY, AND CONTINUE TO CONTRIBUTE TO THE CENTURIES-OLD TRADITION OF THE CLASSIC ITALIAN *PRIMO PIATTO* (FIRST COURSE).

Canederli al formaggio
Cheese Dumplings

Servings 4
Difficulty **Low**
Prep Time 30'
Cook Time 20'

0.88 lbs (400 g) stale bread (about 9 1/2 cups diced or 15 large slices) – 6 1/3 cups (1.5 L) beef broth – 3 tbsp (40 g) butter – 8.8 oz (250 g) semi-aged cheese (like Asiago or Montasio) – 1/3 cup (30 g) Parmigiano Reggiano cheese, grated – 1 onion – 3 eggs – 1 tbsp minced chives – 2 tbsp (30 ml) heavy cream – 1 1/2-3 tbsp (20-40 ml) milk – salt – butter to taste (optional).

Melt half the butter in a nonstick pan and toast the diced bread in it. When it's golden brown, put it in a bowl and set it aside.

Thinly slice the onion and sauté it in the remaining butter, being careful not to let it burn. Then add it to the bowl of bread.

Finely chop the cheese (you can mix various types, especially if you have leftovers in the refrigerator) and add it to the bread and onion. Add the grated Parmigiano, chives, and enough cream to bring it all together. Then add the eggs and enough milk to create a dough that's soft, but not too wet.

Shape the dough into small balls, about 1 1/2-2 inches (4-5 cm) in diameter. Meanwhile heat the broth. When it reaches a boil, add the balls of dough and let them cook for about 20 minutes.

If you prefer to leave them in the broth, serve the dumplings immediately in individual bowls. If you prefer them without broth, remove them with a perforated spoon and toss them in melted butter.

Canederli tirolesi
Tyrolean Dumplings

Servings 4
Difficulty Low
Prep Time 20'
Cook Time 15'

1.1 lbs (500 g) stale white bread (about 25 medium slices or 8 cups cubed) – 1 1/4 cups (300 ml) milk – 2/3 cup (150 g) butter – 1 cup + 3 tbsp (150 g) flour – 5 eggs – 2 tbsp minced parsley – 6 1/3 cups (1.5 L) beef broth – nutmeg to taste – salt to taste.

Remove the crust and cut the bread into small cubes. Put it in a large bowl and add the other ingredients in the following order, quickly stirring to combine after each addition. First add the butter, softened to room temperature, then slowly add the milk. Sift the flour in next, followed by all the eggs and the parsley. Finish it off with a pinch of salt and a generous sprinkling of nutmeg.

Shape the mixture into egg-sized balls and boil them in salted water for about 15 minutes. Heat the beef broth while they cook. Remove the dumplings with a perforated spoon and transfer them to deep bowls. Cover them partway with broth and serve.

Cous cous con ragù d'agnello
Couscous with Lamb Ragù and Vegetables

Servings 4
Difficulty Low
Prep Time 1h
Cook Time 2h

1 3/4 cups + 1 tbsp (300 g) durum wheat semolina for couscous (or precooked couscous) – 7 oz (200 g) crushed tomatoes – 0.66 lbs (300 g) lamb – 8.8 oz (250 g) bell pepper (about 1 2/3 cups chopped) – 5 oz (140 g) celery (about 1 1/3 cups chopped) – 5.3 oz (150 g) onion (about 1 cup chopped) – 5.3 oz (150 g) carrots (just over 1 cup chopped) – 3 1/2 tbsp (50 ml) extra-virgin olive oil – 1 garlic clove – 1 bay leaf – broth (beef or vegetable) to taste – salt and pepper to taste.

Make the couscous by putting the semolina in a bowl and slowly pouring in water, a little at a time. Mix it with your fingers until the flour forms tiny clumps. Add a few tablespoons of olive oil and rub the flour between your hands until uniform granules of couscous form.

Add 1 tablespoon of oil to a pot of water and bring it to a boil. Put the couscous in a strainer and place it over the pot. Cover the strainer with the pot lid and let the couscous steam for about 2 hours, fluffing with a fork occasionally to keep it from sticking together.

You can skip this long preparation process by using precooked couscous. Combine it with water or broth in a 1:1 ratio and mix thoroughly. Seal the container well with plastic wrap and let it sit for 30 minutes.

Make the ragù in the meantime. Finely dice all the vegetables and cut the lamb into 1/3-1/2 inch (1 cm) cubes. Drizzle some extra-virgin olive oil into a saucepan and add the lamb, garlic, bay leaf, and vegetables. Brown it all on medium heat for a few minutes. Add the crushed tomatoes and a ladleful of broth. Let it cook for at least 40 minutes, adding more broth (or hot water) if necessary.

Fluff the couscous with a fork again, combine it with the ragù, and serve.

Gnocchetti di burro
Butter Gnocchetti

Servings 4
Difficulty **Low**
Prep Time
2h and 20'
Cook Time 5-6'

7 tbsp (100 g) butter – 3/4 cup (100 g) Italian "00" flour – 3 eggs – 3/4 cup + 1 1/2 tbsp (200 ml) cold beef broth – 3/4 cup + 1 tbsp (80 g) Grana Padano cheese, grated – 4 1/4 cups (1 L) beef broth to cook the gnocchetti.

Heat the butter in a pan until it's melted, then add the flour. Stir in the cold broth until it's very dense, like a thick pureé. Let it cool, then add the grated cheese and the eggs (one at a time, stirring with a spoon). Refrigerate the dough for 2 hours.

Take it out and use 2 teaspoons or a pastry bag to shape it into gnocchetti. Drop them directly into the broth and let them cook for 5-6 minutes on low heat. Serve the gnocchetti in the broth they cooked in.

Gnocchetti di patate in brodo
Potato Gnocchetti in Broth

Servings 4
Difficulty Medium
Prep Time
1h and 20'
Cook Time 2-3'

6 1/3 cups (1.5 L) beef broth – 0.77 lbs (350 g) potatoes – 2 1/2 tbsp (35 g) butter – 2 1/2 tbsp (20 g) all-purpose flour – 1/2 cup (50 g) Parmigiano Reggiano cheese, grated – 3 egg yolks – a pinch of nutmeg – flour as needed.

Boil the potatoes in lightly salted water and peel them. Put them in a large bowl and mash them while they're still hot. Mix in the butter and 1/3 of the Parmigiano, and season with a big pinch of salt and nutmeg. Add the egg yolks and mix thoroughly until a consistent dough forms.

Flour your hands and use your palms to roll the dough into thin cylinders. Let them sit on a lightly floured surface for about 30 minutes, then slice them crosswise into small gnocchetti. Bring the beef broth to a boil and drop the gnocchetti into the pot. As soon the broth comes back to a boil, remove the pot from the heat and serve the gnocchetti immediately. Serve the remaining Parmigiano on the side.

Gnocchetti di spinaci
Spinach Gnocchetti with Prosciutto and Cream Sauce

Servings 4
Difficulty Low
Prep Time 25'
Cook Time 5'

For the gnocchi: 10.5 oz (300 g) spinach (cooked, squeezed dry, and chopped), about 1 1/2 cups cooked – 1 cup + 3 tbsp (150 g) all-purpose flour – 1 tbsp (15 ml) milk.
For the topping: 3.5 oz (100 g) prosciutto (dry-cured), thinly sliced – 1/3 cup + 1 1/2 tbsp (100 ml) white wine – 1 egg yolk – 3 tbsp (40 g) butter – 2/3 cup (150 ml) heavy cream – 1/3 cup + 1 tbsp (40 g) Parmigiano Reggiano cheese, grated – nutmeg to taste – salt and pepper to taste.

Combine the spinach, flour, and milk. Mix until a relatively consistent dough forms.
To make the sauce, melt the butter in a nonstick pan. Cut the prosciutto into strips and sauté it in the butter. When it's golden brown, add the white wine and let it evaporate. Then add the cream and let the sauce thicken on low heat. As soon as it starts to thicken, mix in the egg yolk. Add a pinch of nutmeg, salt, and pepper. Let it cook for about 2-3 more minutes.
Bring a pot of salted water to a boil. Use a pastry bag to form the gnocchetti, squeezing small pieces of the spinach dough directly into the boiling water. After 2-3 minutes (or when they float to the surface), strain them and add them to the pan of sauce. Mix well and serve them hot with a generous sprinkling of grated Parmigiano.

Gnocchi alla romana
Gnocchi alla Romana
with Oxtail Ragù

Servings 4
Difficulty *Medium*
Prep Time
1h and 30'
Cook Time 15'

For the gnocchi: 2 cups (500 ml) milk – 3/4 cup (125 g) semolina – 1 cup (100 g) Parmigiano Reggiano cheese, grated – salt and pepper.
For the ragù: 1.3 lbs (600 g) oxtail – 2.6 oz (75 g) onions (about 1 small) – 1.2 oz (35 g) celery (about 2 small stalks) – 1.4 oz (40 g) carrots (about 1 small) – 1.4 oz (40 g) fat from dry-cured prosciutto – 1 cup (250 ml) red wine – 1 tsp minced parsley – 1 bay leaf – 2 cups (500 ml) beef broth – salt and pepper to taste.

Heat the milk with a pinch of salt. As soon as it reaches a boil, whisk in the semolina and let it cook for 5-7 minutes. Grease a marble work surface and roll the dough out to a thickness of 1/2-2/3 inch (1.5 cm). When it's cooled, use a round pastry cutter to stamp out 1 1/2-2 inch (4-6 cm) discs.
Arrange the discs in a buttered baking dish, overlapping them slightly. Sprinkle grated Parmigiano on top and bake them in a preheated oven at 350° F (180° C) for about 15 minutes.
Cut the oxtail into steaks and cook them in the oil until they're uniformly browned. Dice the celery, carrots, and onion, and mince the prosciutto fat. Sauté them with the bay leaf in a saucepan on low heat.
When they're golden brown, remove 1/3 of the vegetables and set them aside. Add the oxtail steaks and let them cook with the vegetables for a few minutes. Season with salt and pepper, then add the red wine and broth to cover everything. Cover the saucepan and let the ragù cook for 1 hour. If necessary, add more broth.
When it's done, remove the oxtail from the liquid and let it cool. Remove the meat from the bones and dice it. Add the meat back to the ragù along with the vegetables you set aside earlier. Add salt to taste and let the liquid thicken if necessary. To serve, spread some ragù on each plate and lay the baked gnocchi on top.

Gnocchi alla sorrentina
Gnocchi alla Sorrentina

Servings 4
Difficulty Low
Prep Time 50'
Cook Time 5'

1.3 lbs (600 g) white potatoes – about 1 1/2 cups (180-200 g) Italian "00" flour – 12.3 oz (350 g) tomato sauce – 4-5 basil leaves – 8.8 oz (250 g) *"fior di latte"* mozzarella – 1 egg – 1 cup (100 g) Parmigiano Reggiano cheese, grated.

Wash the potatoes and boil them in lightly salted water. When they're well cooked, peel them and mash them, then let them cool. Pour the flour onto a work surface and create a well in the center. Add the potatoes, eggs, and a pinch of salt. Mix it all together and roll the dough into long cylinders. Slice the cylinders crosswise to make the classic gnocchi shape.

Boil the gnocchi in salted water and strain them as soon as they start floating to the surface. Mix them with a dense tomato sauce and lots of grated Parmigiano in a baking dish. Cover them with a layer of thin mozzarella slices, another layer of sauce, Parmigiano, and basil. Preheat the oven to 425° F (220° C) and bake them for a few minutes, just until the cheese melts. Serve immediately.

Chef's tips
The gnocchi can be made ahead of time and frozen. It's best to let them freeze on floured trays first. Once they're frozen, put them in a plastic freezer bag and seal it well, keeping them at -0.4°F (-18°C). Boil them straight from the freezer, but only put a few portions in the pot at a time so the frozen gnocchi don't cool the water too much.

Gnocchi di castagne
Chestnut Gnocchi

Servings 4
Difficulty **Low**
Prep Time 30'
Cook Time 10'

about 2 3/4 cups (300 g) chestnut flour – 1 cup + 3 tbsp (150 g) all-purpose flour – 3/4 cup + 3–4 tbsp (220-230 ml) warm water – 1 cup + 3 tbsp (120 g) Pecorino cheese, grated – 1/4 cup (60 ml) extra-virgin olive oil – a pinch of salt.

Sift both flours and mix them together. Pour them onto a work surface and create a well in the center. Add the warm water and a pinch of salt. Mix it all together until the dough is smooth and dense.

Roll it out to a thickness of about 1/8 inch (3 mm) and let it dry for about 20 minutes. Cut it onto 1 1/2 inch (4 cm) diamonds and sprinkle them generously with all-purpose flour. Drop them into a pot of boiling water and let them cook for 10 minutes.

Remove them from the pot with a perforated spoon. Arrange them in layers on a serving plate, spreading extra-virgin olive oil and grated Pecorino between them.

Gnocchi di fagioli borlotti
Borlotti Bean Gnocchi with Florentine Tripe and Parmesan Wafers

Servings 4
Difficulty High
Prep Time 1h
Cook Time 6-7'

For the gnocchi: 14 oz (400 g) beans, cooked and puréed – 1/2 cup (60 g) Italian "00" flour – 1 egg yolk.

For the tripe: 1.1 lbs (500 g) tripe – 10.5 oz (300 g) crushed tomatoes – 2.5 oz (70 g) celery (about 2 medium stalks) – 2.8 oz (80 g) carrots (1 1/2 small) – 5.3 oz (150 g) onion (about 2 small) – 1 bay leaf – 1 sprig of rosemary – 3 1/2 tbsp (50 ml) extra-virgin olive oil – 1/3 cup + 1 tbsp (40 g) Parmigiano Reggiano cheese, grated – salt and pepper to taste.

For the Parmesan wafers: 1 cup (100 g) Parmigiano Reggiano cheese, grated.

For the topping: 3 tbsp (40 g) butter – 1/3 cup (30 g) Parmigiano Reggiano cheese, grated – 1 tsp minced parsley.

Mix the beans (already strained and puréed) with the flour and egg yolk until a consistent dough forms. Shape it into long ropes about 1/3-1/2 inch (1 cm) thick and cut them crosswise into 3/4-inch (2 cm) pieces.

Cut the tripe into strips 1/8 inch (4-5 mm) wide. Dry sauté it in a pan on medium heat to dry it out. Finely chop the onion, carrot and celery. Sauté them in the oil with the bay leaf and rosemary. Add the tripe and crushed tomato and season with salt and pepper. Let it cook for 40 minutes, adding the Parmigiano at the end.

To make the wafers, heat a small nonstick pan. Spread 1/4 of the Parmigiano on the bottom and let it melt. When it's completely melted, slide a spatula underneath and flip it over to finish the cooking process. Lay it on a piece of parchment paper to cool. Repeat the same steps to make 3 more wafers.

Boil the gnocchi in salted water for 6-7 minutes. Strain them and mix them with the butter (already melted), Parmigiano, and parsley.

Distribute the gnocchi among four individual plates, accompanying each serving with a portion of hot tripe and a parmesan wafer.

Gnocchi di farina giganti
Giant Gnocchi

Servings 4
Difficulty **Low**
Prep Time 45'
Cook Time 15'

For the pasta: 2 cups (250 g) Italian "00" flour – 1 1/3 cups + 2 1/2 tbsp (350 ml) water – salt to taste.
For the filling: 1 oz (30 g) prosciutto (dry-cured), diced – 5.3 oz (150 g) ricotta – 0.5 oz (15 g) Caciocavallo, diced (about 1/8 cup) – 2 oz (60 g) mozzarella, diced (about 2/3 cup) – 1/3 cup (30 g) Parmigiano Reggiano cheese, grated – 1 egg yolk – salt and pepper to taste.
For the topping: 7 oz (200 g) tomato sauce – 1 1/2 tbsp (20 g) butter – 1/2 cup (50 g) Parmigiano Reggiano cheese, grated.

Heat the water with a pinch of salt. As soon as it reaches a boil, remove it from the heat and add 1 1/4 cups (160 g) of flour all at once. Quickly stir it with a wooden spoon and put the pot back on the stove. Continue stirring and let it cook for 4-5 minutes, being carefully not to let the dough stick to the bottom of the pot.
Turn the dough onto a work surface and stretch it out a bit. Let it cool for about 5 minutes, then work in the rest of the flour. When the dough is smooth and well kneaded, shape it into a ball. Cover it with a cloth that's been folded over twice (so there are four layers) and let it sit for a good 15 minutes.
Preheat oven to 350° F (180° C).
Put the ricotta in a bowl and stir it vigorously with a wooden spoon. Add the egg yolk, grated Parmigiano, prosciutto, Caciocavallo, and mozzarella. Season with salt and pepper to taste and mix well.
Divide the dough into pieces the size of a large egg. Stretch and flatten each piece in the palm of your hand until it's very thin. Place some filling in the center and roll the dough up to seal it in, shaping it back into a large egg. Continue to do the same for each piece, flouring your hands often so the dough doesn't stick. Place the finished gnocchi on a lightly floured surface. Heat a large pot of water. When it reaches a boil, add some salt and drop in the gnocchi one at a time. As soon as they float to the surface, remove them with a perforated spoon. Butter a pan and lay the gnocchi inside in a single row. Cover them with lots of tomato sauce and grated Parmigiano, then dot the surface with a few pieces of butter. Bake them for 10-15 minutes so the gnocchi can thoroughly absorb the flavors and the surface turns to a nice, bubbling, golden brown.

Gnocchi di pane
Gnocchi with Red Wine and Spare Rib Ragù

Servings 4
Difficulty Low
Prep Time
1h and 10'
Cook Time 10'

For the gnocchi: 3/4 cup + 3 tbsp (100 g) breadcrumbs – 1 2/3 cups (200 g) Italian "00" flour – 2/3 cup (150 ml) warm water – salt to taste.

For the topping: 1 lb (450 g) pork ribs – 1 oz (30 g) pounded lard – 5.3 oz (150 g) onion (about 2 small) – 2.8 oz (80 g) carrots (about 1 1/2 small) – 2.5 oz (70 g) celery (about 2 medium stalks) – 1.76 oz (50 g) pumpkin (about 1/2 cup cubed) – 1 1/4 cups (3 dl) red wine – 2 cups (500 ml) beef broth – bay leaves, rosemary, and savory to taste – 1/2 cup (50 g) Parmigiano Reggiano cheese, grated – 3 tbsp (40 ml) extra-virgin olive oil – salt and pepper to taste.

Combine the flour and breadcrumbs. Pour them onto a work surface and create a well in the center. Pour the warm water into the center with a pinch of salt. Mix it all together until a consistent dough forms, then wrap it in plastic and let it sit for 30 minutes. Shape the dough into long ropes 1/3-1/2 inch (1 cm) wide, and cut them crosswise into pieces 1/3-1/2 inch (1 cm) long.

Clean and dice the celery, carrot, and onion. Stew them with the lard and half the oil in a saucepan. Then add the cubed pumpkin.

Sear the ribs in a separate pan until they're uniformly browned, then add them to the vegetables. Add the wine and let it evaporate. Pour in enough broth to completely cover the ribs. Cover the pan and let it cook on low heat for about 1 1/2 hours, seasoning with salt and pepper. If necessary, add more broth. Once the ribs are cooked, remove the meat from the bone. Chop it up and add it back to the sauce.

Boil the gnocchi in salted water for about 8 minutes. Remove them with a perforated spoon as soon as they float to the top and add them right to the sauce. Add the grated Parmigiano and cold-pressed olive oil, stirring for a few minutes to bring the flavors together.

Gnocchi di patate al nero di seppia con frutti di mare
Potato Gnocchi with Cuttlefish Ink and Seafood

Servings 4
Difficulty Medium
Prep Time 1h
Cook Time 4'

For the gnocchi: 1 lbs (500 g) potatoes (about 1 1/2 large) – 1 cup (125 g) Italian "00" flour – 1 egg – 0.18 oz (5 g) cuttlefish ink – salt to taste.
For the topping: 0.8 lbs (360 g) tomatoes, very ripe (about 3 medium) – 0.44 lbs (200 g) squid – 4 musky octopus (about 0.22 lbs/100 g) – 12 shrimp (about 0.55 lbs/250 g) – 4 small cuttlefish (about 0.22 lbs/100 g) – 0.44 lbs (200 g) clams – 0.44 lbs (200 g) mussels – 3 1/2 tbsp (50 ml) extra-virgin olive oil – 1 garlic clove – 1 tbsp minced parsley – salt to taste.

Wash the potatoes and place them (unpeeled) in a pot of cold water. Bring it to a boil and add a handful of coarse salt. When the potatoes are cooked, strain them and peel them. Mash them on a flat surface with a potato masher. Mix in the flour, egg, cuttlefish ink, and a pinch of salt.

From small cylinders, 3/4 inch (2 cm) wide. Cut them crosswise into 3/4-inch pieces and place them on a lightly floured surface.

Flush out the clams. Scrape the mussels and eliminate the beards. Shell and devein the shrimp, and finely dice them. Clean the cuttlefish and squid, removing the "beak" (the cartilaginous section). Then rinse them and julienne them. Separate the musky octopus heads from the tentacles and rinse them thoroughly.

Heat the oil in a pan, add the garlic, and sauté it until it turns golden brown. Add all the cleaned and rinsed seafood. Cook it on high heat for a few minutes, then add the parsley and tomato (peeled and diced, with seeds removed). Let everything cook for another 5 minutes and season with salt to taste.

Boil the gnocchi in salted water and remove them with a perforated spoon as soon as they float to the surface. Combine them with the seafood sauce and drizzle them with cold-pressed olive oil.

Gnocchi di patate alla bava
Potato Gnocchi alla Bava

Servings 4
Difficulty Low
Prep Time 40'
Cook Time 4'

For the gnocchi: 1.1 lbs (500 g) potatoes (about 2–3 medium) – 1 cup (125 g) Italian "00" flour – 1 egg – salt to taste.
For the topping: 2 tbsp (30 g) butter – 5.3 oz (150 g) Fontina cheese – 1/3 cup + 1 1/2 tbsp (100 ml) milk.

Wash the potatoes and place them (unpeeled) in a large pot of cold water. Heat the water and add a handful of coarse salt when it reaches a boil. Strain the potatoes as soon as they're cooked (you can use a skewer to test them – if it pierces easily the potatoes are done). Peel them and mash them with a potato masher on a flat work surface.

Mix the potatoes with the flour, egg, and a pinch of salt until a dense dough forms. If it's too soft and wet, add some more flour. Shape the dough into small cylinders 3/4 inch (2 cm) in diameter, and cut them crosswise into 3/4 inch (2 cm) pieces. Roll each one over the tines of a fork, exerting slight pressure with your fingers.

Melt the butter in a pan, being careful not to let it burn. Remove the rind from the Fontina, slice it thinly, and add it to the butter. When the cheese has melted, add the milk.

Meanwhile boil the gnocchi in salted water. As soon as they float to the surface, remove them with a perforated spoon and place them directly in the pan of fondue. Let them cook with the cheese for a minute and serve.

Gnocchi di patate con fave
Potato Gnocchi with Fava Beans, Prosciutto, and Pecorino

Servings 4
Difficulty Low
Prep Time 40'
Cook Time 4'

For the gnocchi: 1.1 lbs (500 g) potatoes (about 2-3 medium) – 1 cup (125 g) Italian "00" flour – 1 egg – salt to taste.

For the topping: 0.88 lbs (400 g) fresh fava beans (about 2 2/3 cups) – 1.76 oz (50 g) yellow onion (about 1 small) – 1 garlic clove – 2.1 oz (60 g) prosciutto di Parma, in one slice – (4 g) basil (about 8 leaves) – 3 1/2 tbsp (50 ml) extra-virgin olive oil – 0.88 lbs (400 g) firm red tomatoes – 0.66 lbs (300 g) Pecorino cheese, in flakes – 8 fresh mint leaves (to taste) – white pepper to taste – salt to taste.

Wash the potatoes and place them (unpeeled) in a large pot of cold water. Heat the water and add a handful of coarse salt when it reaches a boil. Strain the potatoes as soon as they're cooked (you can use a skewer to test them – if it pierces easily the potatoes are done). Peel them and mash them with a potato masher on a flat work surface.

Mix the potatoes with the flour, egg, and a pinch of salt until a dense dough forms. If it's too soft and wet, add some more flour. Shape the dough into small cylinders 3/4 inch (2 cm) in diameter, and cut them crosswise into 3/4 inch (2 cm) pieces. Roll each one over the tines of a fork, exerting slight pressure with your fingers.

Blanch the fava beans in boiling water. Strain them, let them cool, and peel them. Cut an X into the skin on the bottom of each tomato. Drop them in boiling water for 2-3 minutes. Strain them, let them cool, peel them, remove the seeds, and dice them.

Mince the onion and sauté it on medium heat with the oil, whole garlic clove (to be removed later), hand-torn basil, prosciutto cut into strips, and the fava beans. When everything is well browned, add the tomatoes and season with salt and pepper to taste. Let the sauce cook on high heat for a minute. Meanwhile boil the gnocchi in salted water. As soon as they float to the surface, remove them with a perforated spoon and place them directly in the pan with the sauce. Let everything cook together for a few seconds.

Distribute the gnocchi among serving plates and cover them with a generous portion of Pecorino flakes. Drizzle cold-pressed olive oil on top and sprinkle with hand-torn mint leaves to taste.

Gnocchi di patate e castagne
Chestnut and Potato Gnocchi with Lentils and Cotechino Sausage in a Lambrusco Reduction Sauce

Servings 4
Difficulty *Medium*
Prep Time
1h and 15'
Cook Time 3-4'

For the gnocchi: 3.5 oz (100 g) chestnuts, boiled – 0.66 lbs (300 g) potatoes, boiled (about 1- 2 medium) – 1 1/4 cups (160 g) Italian "00" flour – 1 egg – salt to taste.
For the topping: 0.66 lbs (300 g) Cotechino sausage, already cooked – 5.3 oz (150 g) lentils (about 3/4 cup) – 1 oz (30 g) celery, finely diced (about 1/4 cup) – 1 oz (30 g) carrots, finely diced (about 1/4 cup) – 1 oz (30 g) onion, finely diced (about 3 tbsp) – rosemary and bay leaves to taste – 3 1/2 tbsp (50 ml) extra-virgin olive oil.
For the reduction: 3/4 cup + 1 1/2 tbsp (200 ml) Lambrusco – 2 tbsp (25 g) sugar.

Mash the potatoes and chestnuts with a potato masher. Pour the flour onto a work surface and create a well in the center. Add the mashed potatoes and chestnuts, the egg, and a pinch of salt. Mix well and shape the resulting dough into long ropes about 3/4 inch (2 cm) wide. To make the individual gnocchi, cut the ropes crosswise into 3/4 inch (2 cm) pieces.

Combine the Lambrusco with the sugar in a saucepan over medium heat and let it reduce until it reaches a syrupy consistency.

Boil the lentils for the sauce (after soaking them in cold water for 12 hours and straining them thoroughly) in unsalted water. Sauté the vegetables, rosemary, and bay leaves in the oil. Cube the cooked Cotechino sausage and add it to the vegetables once they've reached a nice golden brown. Continue cooking everything for a few more minutes to let the flavors come together, then add the lentils. If necessary, add a few drops of water as well.

Boil the gnocchi in salted water and remove them with a perforated spoon as soon as they float to the surface.

Combine the gnocchi with the Cotechino sausage sauce and garnish each plate with a drizzle of the Lambrusco reduction.

Gnocchi di patate e grano saraceno allo speck
Potato and Buckwheat Gnocchi with Speck Ham

Servings 4
Difficulty **Low**
Prep Time 50'
Cook Time 5'

1.1 lbs (500 g) potatoes (about 2–3 medium) – 3/4 cup + 1 tbsp (100 g) all-purpose flour – 1 1/4 cup (150 g) buckwheat flour – 3.5 oz (100 g) speck ham, in one slice – 1 tsp minced parsley – 1 tsp minced rosemary – 1 tsp minced thyme – 5 1/2 tbsp (80 g) butter – salt to taste.

Boil the potatoes in lightly salted water. Peel them while they're still hot and mash them with a potato masher. Mix the potatoes with the two flours and shape the resulting dough into gnocchi.

Boil the gnocchi in salted water and remove them with a perforated spoon as soon as they float to the surface.

Melt the butter in a large pan and add the diced speck, but don't let it brown too much. Pour the gnocchi directly into the pan and cook them with the butter and speck for a few seconds. Top each serving with a generous sprinkling of minced herbs.

Gnocchi di polenta
Polenta Gnocchi in Roe Deer, Porcini Mushroom, and Beet Ragù

Servings 4
Difficulty Medium
Prep Time
1h and 30'
Cook Time 4-5'

For the gnocchi: 3/4 cup (125 g) instant polenta – 2/3 cup (75 g) all-purpose flour – 1 cup (250 ml) water – 1 egg – 1/4 cup (25 g) Parmigiano Reggiano cheese, grated.
For the topping: 0.66 lbs (300 g) roe deer – 0.7 oz (20 g) pounded lard – 4.2 oz (120 g) porcini mushrooms – 2.1 oz (60 g) beets, cooked (about 1) – 2.6 oz (75 g) onion (about 1 small) – 2.5 oz (70 g) celery (about 2 medium stalks) – 2.8 oz (80 g) carrots (about 1 1/2 small) – 2 sprigs of thyme – 1 tbsp minced parsley – 1 bay leaf – 1 garlic clove – 3 1/2 tbsp (50 ml) red wine – 3 1/2 tbsp (50 g) butter – 1/2 cup (50 g) Parmigiano Reggiano cheese, grated – salt and pepper to taste.

Heat a pot of water on the stove. Just before it reaches a boil, add a generous amount of salt and slowly pour in the polenta, whisking continuously to avoid lumps. This should result in a dense, fully cooked polenta (if you don't use instant polenta, the process takes a good half hour). When it's done, let the polenta cool but don't let it set too much. Then add the egg, flour, and cheese to the lukewarm polenta. Mix well and shape the resulting dough into gnocchi (any shape and size you prefer).
Dice the onion, celery, and carrots. Sauté them over low heat with the lard, garlic, bay leaf, and half the butter. Dice the deer meat and add it to the vegetables, letting it brown on high heat. Then add the red wine. Once it's evaporated, add enough water to cover the meat. Season with salt and pepper and let it finish cooking.
Wipe the mushrooms clean with a damp cloth. Dice them, keeping the caps separate from the stems. Sauté the stems first, then the heads, seasoning with thyme (stripped from the stem) and a pinch of salt and pepper.
Boil the gnocchi in salted water and strain them as soon as they float to the surface. Combine them with the mushrooms, adding a pat of butter and the grated Parmigiano. Let it all cook together for a minute.
Spread some ragù in each plate and top it with gnocchi, cubed beets, and parsley.

Gnocchi di prugne alla triestina
Trieste-Style Prune Gnocchi

Servings 4
Difficulty **Medium**
Prep Time 40'
Cook Time 4'

For the gnocchi: 1.1 lbs (500 g) potatoes (about 2–3 medium) – 1 cup (125 g) Italian "00" flour – 1 egg – 20 prunes – salt.
For the topping: 1/3 cup (50 g) breadcrumbs – 3 1/2 tbsp (45 g) sugar – 5 1/2 tbsp (80 g) butter – ground cinnamon to taste.

Boil the potatoes (unpeeled) in salted water. When they're cooked, strain them and peel them. Mash them with a potato masher and transfer the purée to a work surface. Mix the mashed potatoes with the flour, egg, and a pinch of salt. Pinch off pieces of dough and shape them into large gnocchi, placing a pitted prune in the center of each one. Melt the butter in a nonstick pan, then add the breadcrumbs. Let them brown, adding sugar and cinnamon to taste.

Boil the gnocchi in salted water and remove them with a perforated spoon as soon as they float to the surface. Top them with the cinnamon butter.

Gnocchi di ricotta al pesto di rucola
Ricotta Gnocchi with Arugula Pesto

Servings 4
*Difficulty **Low***
*Prep Time **40'***
*Cook Time **2'***

For the gnocchi: 14 oz (400 g) ricotta – about 1 cup (120 g) Italian "00" flour – 1/3 cup + 1 tbsp (40 g) Parmigiano Reggiano cheese, grated – 1 egg – nutmeg to taste – salt and pepper to taste.

For the pesto: 4.2 oz (120 g) arugula (about 6 cups) – 6.3 oz (180 g) tomatoes, very ripe (about 2 small) – 0.35 oz (10 g) almonds, shelled and peeled (about 8–9) – 1/4 cup (25 g) Parmigiano Reggiano cheese, grated – 1/4 cup + 1 tbsp (70 ml) extra-virgin olive oil – 1/4 a garlic clove – salt and pepper to taste.

Sift the ricotta into a large bowl. Mix it with the flour, egg, and Parmigiano. Season with salt, pepper, and ground nutmeg. Transfer the resulting dough to a work surface and roll it out to a thickness of 1/3-1/2 inch (1 cm). Cut it into small diamonds.

Wash the arugula and combine it with the other ingredients in a food processor. Pulse until the mixture is homogenous and has reached the right consistency. Be careful not to let the pesto get hot. Wash the tomatoes and cut an X into the bottom of each one. Boil them for about 10 seconds, then submerge them in ice water. Peel them, remove the seeds and liquid, and dice them. Combine them with the pesto in a bowl.

Boil the gnocchi in salted water and strain them as soon as they float to the surface. Combine them with the pesto and tomatoes. Mix well and serve, garnishing with fried arugula leaves to taste.

Gnocchi di spinaci al Parmigiano Reggiano
Spinach Gnocchi with Parmigiano-Reggiano

Servings 4
Difficulty **Medium**
Prep Time 25'
Cook Time 5'

10.5 oz (300 g) spinach, cooked and squeezed dry (about 1 2/3 cups cooked) – 10.5 oz (300 g) ricotta – 1 1/2 cups (150 g) Parmigiano Reggiano cheese, grated – 1 cup + 3 tbsp (150 g) Italian "00" flour – 2 eggs – 5 1/2 tbsp (80 g) butter – nutmeg to taste – salt to taste.

Pass the spinach through a vegetable mill, then combine it with the ricotta, eggs, flour, 1 cup of Parmigiano, and a pinch of salt and nutmeg. Mix it all together very thoroughly until the dough is thick and consistent.

Form long cylinders about 1/2-2/3 inch (1.5 cm) thick, then cut them crosswise into 3/4-inch (2 cm) gnocchi and boil them in salted water for a few minutes. Strain the gnocchi and mix them with the melted butter and the remaining Parmigiano. As an alternative, you can mix them with tomato sauce or meat sauce.

Gnocchi di zucca
Pumpkin Gnocchi

Servings 4
Difficulty Low
Prep Time 40'
Cook Time 3-4'

0.88 lbs (400 g) pumpkin, cooked – 1 2/3 cups (100 g) fresh breadcrumbs – 3/4 cup + 1 tbsp (100 g) all-purpose flour – 1 egg – 5 1/2 tbsp (80 g) butter – 1 cup (100 g) Parmigiano Reggiano, freshly grated – 3 sage leaves – 1 sprig of rosemary – nutmeg to taste – salt and pepper to taste.

Pass the pumpkin through a vegetable mill and combine it with the flour, breadcrumbs, egg, and a tablespoon of Parmigiano in a large bowl. Season with nutmeg, salt, and pepper to taste.

Shape the dough into cylinders 3/4 inch (2 cm) thick, and slice them crosswise into 3/4 inch pieces.

Melt the butter with the sage and rosemary (to be removed before using the butter).

Boil the gnocchi in salted water for a few minutes. Strain them when they float to the top and transfer them to a preheated casserole dish. Sprinkle them generously with Parmigiano and drizzle them with the herb butter. Serve immediately.

Chef's tips
The best way to cook the pumpkin for this recipe is to slice it, 1-1 1/2 inches (3-4 cm) thick, with the rind still on. Line a pan with coarse salt and lay the pumpkin slices on top. Bake it at 350-375° F (180-190° C) until it's very soft (test it with a toothpick).

Gnocchi gratinati all'antica
Baked Gnocchi

Servings 4
Difficulty Low
Prep Time 40'
Cook Time 10'

1/2 cup + 2 tbsp (85 g) all-purpose flour – 3/4 cup (85 g) Gruyere cheese – 2/3 cup + 1 tbsp (170 ml) milk – 5 tbsp (70 g) butter – 2 eggs – breadcrumbs as needed – nutmeg to taste – salt to taste.

Combine the milk, 4 tablespoons of butter, and a pinch of salt in a saucepan. As soon as it reaches a boil, remove it from the heat and slowly add the flour, mixing well. Put it back on the burner over high heat and mix until the dough no longer sticks to the bottom or sides of the pan. Take it off the heat again and add the eggs one at a time. Then add 1/2 cup (60 g) of grated Gruyere and a pinch of nutmeg.

Bring a large pot of water to a boil. Use two spoons to shape the dough into quenelles. Add some salt to the water and drop in the gnocchi as you shape them. Continue until you've used all the dough, then turn down the heat and let them simmer for about 15 minutes.

Strain them and lay them out on a kitchen towel. Grease a baking dish and arrange the gnocchi inside. Sprinkle them with a 1:1 mixture of grated Gruyere and breadcrumbs. Melt the remaining butter and drizzle it on top. Bake the gnocchi in a preheated oven at 375° F (190° C) for 10 minutes.

Passatelli al nero di seppia
Black Passatelli with Tub Gurnard and Oregano Pesto

Servings 4
Difficulty Medium
Prep Time
1h and 30'
Cook Time 4-5'

For the passatelli: 1 1/2 cups (150 g) Parmigiano Reggiano cheese, grated – 0.35 oz (10 g) cuttlefish ink – 1 cup (150 g) breadcrumbs – 3 eggs – nutmeg to taste.
For the pesto: 3 tbsp (15 g) fresh oregano – 1.76 oz (50 g) pine nuts (1/3 cup + 2 tsp) – 1 garlic clove – 1/3 cup (30 g) Parmigiano Reggiano cheese, grated – 1/3 cup + 1 1/2 tbsp (100 ml) extra-virgin olive oil.
For the ragù: 1.1 lbs (500 g) tub gurnard – 3.17 oz (90 g) carrots (about 2 small carrots) – 2.5 oz (70 g) celery (about 2 medium stalks) – 6 oz (170 g) zucchini (about 1 medium zucchini) – 1 oz (30 g) shallots (about 1 medium shallot) – 1/2 tbsp (50 ml) extra-virgin olive oil – tbsp (30 ml) white wine – salt and pepper to taste.

Mix together all the passatelli ingredients and wrap the dough in plastic. Refrigerate it for 1 hour. Combine the oregano, pine nuts, garlic, and oil, and blend them together with an immersion blender. Add the grated cheese at the end, mix well, and refrigerate the pesto.

Mince all the vegetables, including the shallot. Drizzle some olive oil in a pan and sauté them together for a few minutes. Clean, rinse, fillet, and skin the fish. Dice it and add it to the pan. Cook everything together for 5-6 minutes, then add the wine and let it evaporate completely. Season with salt and pepper to taste.

Pass the passatelli dough through a potato masher with wide holes, letting the pasta drop directly into boiling salted water. Turn down the heat and let it cook until it floats to the surface. Strain the passatelli and combine it with the tub gurnard ragù.

Serve with pesto to taste.

Passatelli al profumo di limone
Lemon Passatelli with Carpet Shell Clams and Tomato Confit

Servings 4
Difficulty Low
Prep Time 50'
Cook Time 3-4'

For the passatelli: 2 eggs – 1 1/3 cups (200 g) breadcrumbs – 1 1/2 cups (140 g) Parmigiano Reggiano cheese, grated – 1 tbsp (15 g) butter – 1/4 cup (35 g) Italian "00" flour – zest of 1 lemon.
For the topping: 1.3 lbs (600 g) carpet shell clams – 7 oz (200 g) cherry tomatoes (about 12) – 3 1/2 tbsp (50 ml) white wine – 2 garlic cloves – 1 tsp minced parsley – thyme to taste – 1/4 cup (60 ml) extra-virgin olive oil – salt and pepper to taste.

Mix together the eggs, breadcrumbs, Parmigiano, butter, flour, salt, and lemon zest for the passatelli. Cut the tomatoes in half and gently hollow them out. Mince the garlic and herbs and mix them together with a bit of olive oil. Spread the mixture inside the tomatoes and bake then in a preheated oven at 175° F (80° C) for about 2 hours.

Pour half the oil in to a pan with the clams, the other garlic clove, and the white wine. Cover the pan and let the clams cook for a few minutes until they open. Remove the shells from half of them and strain the liquid they cooked in.

Pass the passatelli dough through the proper utensil, letting them fall directly into boiling salted water.

Once they're cooked, toss them in a pan with the remaining oil, tomatoes, clams, and the liquid from the clams. Transfer them to plates and serve.

Passatelli alla marchigiana
Marche-Style Passatelli

Servings 4
Difficulty **Low**
Prep Time 40'
Cook Time 3-4'

6 1/3 cups (1.5 L) beef broth – 1 2/3 cups (100 g) breadcrumbs – 2 large eggs – 6 1/2 tbsp (50 g) flour – 3/4 cup + 1 tbsp (80 g) Parmigiano Reggiano cheese, grated – 2 tbsp (30 g) ox marrow or butter (optional) – 2/3 cup (40 g) breadcrumbs fresh – salt, pepper, and nutmeg to taste – grated zest of half a lemon (optional).

Combine all the ingredients except for the broth and mix them until a soft dough forms. Season it with salt, pepper, and ground nutmeg to taste. Wrap it in plastic and refrigerate it for 30 minutes.

Heat the broth, and when it reaches a boil pass the dough through a potato masher with large holes (or a passatelli iron). Use a knife to cut them as they reach a length of 1-1 1/2 inches (3-4 cm) and let them fall directly into the broth. Continue until all the dough has been used.

Turn the heat down to the lowest setting and let the passatelli simmer for 3-4 minutes. Serve them in individual soup bowls with the hot broth.

Perle di ricotta ed erbe
Herbed Ricotta Gnocchi with Squash Blossoms, Zucchini, and Black Truffles

Servings 4
Difficulty Low
Prep Time 30'
Cook Time 3-4'

For the gnocchi: 1.1 lbs (500 g) fresh ricotta – 1 cup (125 g) flour – 1 cup (100 g) Parmigiano Reggiano cheese – 1 egg – 2.8 oz (80 g) fresh herbs, finely chopped and mixed (parsley, thyme, sage, chives, and fresh oregano), about 1 1/2 cups.
For the topping: 8.8 oz (250 g) zucchini (about 2 small zucchini) – 12 squash blossoms (about 3.5 oz/100 g) – 4 spring onions – 1 small truffle – 2-3 fresh mint leaves – 3 1/2 tbsp (50 g) butter – 3 1/2 tbsp (50 ml) extra-virgin olive oil – salt and pepper to taste.

Sieve the ricotta into a large mixing bowl. Add all the other gnocchi ingredients and mix well. Form tiny balls, about 3/4 inch (2 cm) in diameter.

Wash and dice the zucchini, and mince the spring onions.

Heat the oil and butter in a pan and sauté the spring onions. Add the zucchini and cook on high heat for a few more minutes. Wash and julienne the squash blossoms, and add them to the pan. When it's all cooked, purée 1/3 of the mixture. Add the purée back to the rest of the sauce and season with salt and pepper.

Boil the gnocchi in salted water. Once they begin floating to the surface, let them cook for 1 more minute. Then strain them and pour them directly into the pan with the sauce. Stir to combine and top each serving with grated truffle.

Strangolapreti del Trentino
Strangolapreti del Trentino

Servings 4
Difficulty **Low**
Prep Time 25'
Cook Time 5'

4 stale bread rolls (about 0.55 lbs/250 g) – 2/3 cup (150 ml) milk – 0.88 lbs (400 g) beet greens – 2 eggs – 2/3 cup (80 g) flour.
For the topping: 1 cup (100 g) Parmigiano Reggiano cheese, grated – 3 1/2 tbsp (50 g) butter.

Dice the bread and soak it in the room temperature milk. Remove it when it's softened, letting any excess liquid drip off.

Boil the beet greens in salted water. Strain them, squeeze them dry, and chop them. Mix the bread with the greens, the eggs, and the flour (enough to create a smooth but firm dough).

Bring a large pot of water to a boil and season it with salt. Drop spoonfuls of dough into the water.

When the gnocchi float to the surface, strain them and combine them with foaming melted butter and lots of grated Parmigiano.

Strangolapreti di Bergamo
Strangolapreti di Bergamo

Servings 4
Difficulty *Low*
Prep Time *1h*
Cook Time *10'*

For the pasta: 1.43 lbs (650 g) stale bread (about 32 slices or 10 1/2 cups cubed) – 1/3 cup (45 g) flour – 2 egg yolks – 2 1/2 cups (600 ml) whole milk – 0.77 lbs (350 g) chard (about 10 cups raw) – breadcrumbs to taste – nutmeg to taste – salt and pepper to taste.
For the topping: 5 1/2 tbsp (80 g) butter – 1/3 cup + 1 tbsp (40 g) Parmigiano Reggiano cheese, grated – 3 sage leaves.

Soak the bread in the milk for at least 1 hour. In the meantime, blanch the chard in lightly salted water, squeeze it dry, and chop it up. Melt the butter with the sage leaves in a small pan, making sure they don't burn.

When enough time has passed, remove the bread from the milk. Let any excess liquid drip off and squeeze it lightly. Combine it with the chard and egg yolks in a food processor and blend well.

Transfer the blended mixture to a flat surface and knead in the flour. Add a pinch of nutmeg, salt, and freshly ground pepper. If the dough becomes too soft, add a few tablespoons of breadcrumbs. Form long ropes as thick as your finger. Cut them crosswise into small gnocchi, about 3/4 inch (2 cm) long. Boil them in salted water and remove them with a perforated spoon as soon as they float to the surface. Arrange them in a baking dish and cover them with a layer of grated Parmigiano and melted butter.

Turtunett
Turtunett

Servings 4
Difficulty *Low*
Prep Time *1h*
Cook Time *3-4'*

0.88 lbs (400 g) potatoes (about 2 small) – 2.8 oz (80 g) Fontina cheese, diced – 2/3 cup (80 g) flour – 1 tsp minced parsley.
For the sauce: 2/3 cup (150 ml) heavy cream – 8 sage leaves – 7 tbsp (100 g) butter – 1/3 cup + 1 tbsp (40 g) Parmigiano Reggiano cheese, grated – salt to taste.

Boil, peel, and mash the potatoes, then let them cool. Add the flour, parsley and Fontina, and mix well to form a dough. Roll out long cylinders as thick as your finger and cut them crosswise into pieces about 3/4 inch (2 cm) long. Place each one on a fork and press down gently in the center, so the tines leave an imprint on the bottom and the ends curl slightly.
To make the sauce, combine the butter and cream in a pan over medium heat. Add the sage leaves for flavor and let it simmer until the sauce has thickened. Season with salt to taste.
Boil the gnocchi (*turtunett*) in salted water. As soon as they float to the surface, remove them with a perforated spoon and add them to the sauce. Mix well, letting everything cook together for 1 minute. Top the *turtunett* with grated Parmigiano and serve them hot.

Chef's tips
Use "old" potatoes for this recipe.

STUFFED PASTA

THE TRADITION OF PREPARING FISH DISHES WITH A FLOUR AND EGG DOUGH IS AN ANCIENT ONE. TOOLS FOR MIXING AND ROLLING DOUGH ARE DEPICTED IN RELIEF ON AN ETRUSCAN TOMB AT THE CERVETERI NECROPOLIS. AND IT SEEMS THAT THE GREEK PLAYWRIGHT ARISTOPHANES DESCRIBED AN "ANCESTOR" OF THE *TORTELLO* IN THE 5TH CENTURY BC. LIKE MANY OF THEIR COOKING AND EATING CUSTOMS, THE ROMANS INHERITED THE TRADITION OF USING DOUGH FROM THE GREEKS, WITH THE CITIES OF MAGNA GRAECIA ACTING AS INTERMEDIARIES. AS CATO THE ELDER TEACHES IN HIS TREATISE *DE AGRICOLTURA*, DATING TO THE 2ND CENTURY BC, "...KNEAD THOROUGHLY WITH YOUR HANDS, ROLL OUT, AND SPREAD OUT IN A BASKET TO DRY..."

DURING THE MIDDLE AGES, SALIMBENE DA PARMA MENTIONED LASAGNA AND RAVIOLI IN HIS *CHRONICLE*. BUT STUFFED PASTA REALLY BEGAN TO FLOURISH WITH THE SPECTACULAR CREATIONS OF COURT CHEFS DURING THE RENAISSANCE. AND FROM THERE, THE TASTE FOR THIS CULINARY ART FINALLY MADE ITS WAY TO US.

LIKE ALL FRESH PASTAS, STUFFED PASTAS ARE THE OFFSPRING OF TRADITION AND

REGIONAL CONVENTION. THE DOUGH IS ARTFULLY ROLLED OUT, AND FILLINGS MADE FROM ALL SORTS OF INGREDIENTS ARE ADDED. CHEESES, MEATS, VEGETABLES, AND FRAGRANT HERBS FUSE TOGETHER IN A DELICIOUS BLEND THAT IS DESTINED TO FILL THE VARIOUS SHAPES OF *RAVIOLI, TORTELLI, TORTELLINI*, AND *AGNOLOTTI*, WHETHER THEY'RE CUT INTO SQUARES WITH A PASTRY WHEEL OR STAMPED OUT IN CIRCLES WITH A PASTRY CUTTER.

THERE'S NO REGION OF ITALY THAT ISN'T REPRESENTED BY A STUFFED PASTA RECIPE: ROBUST *AGNOLOTTI* FROM PIEDMONT, DELICATE *ANOLINI* FROM PARMA WITH A RICH PARMESAN CHEESE FILLING, THE MORE SERIOUS *CAPPELLETTI* FROM EMILIA, THE MATERNAL *TORTELLINI* FROM MODENA AND BOLOGNA, *CAPPELLACCI* FROM FERRARA, *OFELLE* FROM FRIULI AND VENETO, *PANSOTTI* FROM GENOA, *TORDELLI* FROM TUSCANY, AND THE LIST GOES ON.

ALL THESE DELICACIES ARE SUCH A SUBLIME EXPERIENCE FOR THE PALATE THAT TASSONI ATTRIBUTED THE SHAPE OF TORTELLINI TO ONE VERY LUCKY CHEF'S GLIMPSE OF VENUS'S NAVEL, AS IF TO SAY THAT STUFFED PASTAS WERE BORN OF DIVINE INSPIRATION.

Agnolotti
Agnolotti

Servings 4
Difficulty **High**
Prep Time
2h and 30'
Cook Time 5'

For the pasta: 2 1/3 cups (300 g) Italian "00" flour – 3 eggs.
For the filling: 0.77 lbs (350 g) lean beef, chopped into medium-sized pieces – 5.3 oz (150 g) spinach, cooked (about 3/4 cup + 1 tbsp) – 3.5 oz (100 g) onion (about 1 medium onion) – 2 tbsp (30 g) butter – 1 egg yolk – 2 1/2 tbsp (20 g) flour – 3.5 oz (100 g) fresh tomato purée (about 1/3 cup + 1 tbsp) – 1/3 cup + 1 tbsp (40 g) Parmigiano Reggiano cheese, grated – beef broth as needed – 1 sprig of rosemary – 1 garlic clove – nutmeg to taste – salt and pepper to taste.
For the topping: 1/3 cup + 1 tbsp (40 g) Parmigiano Reggiano cheese, grated – 2 tbsp (30 g) butter.

Heat the butter in a saucepan on medium heat. As soon as it's melted, sauté the whole peeled garlic clove and sliced onion. When they start to turn golden brown, add the meat. Cook it on low heat. Sprinkle a tablespoon of flour over the meat and season with salt and pepper to taste. Add the tomato sauce and enough broth to completely cover the meat. Cook it all on low heat for about 1 1/2 hours, until the meat is tender but not falling apart, then remove the pan from the heat.

Meanwhile, pour the flour onto a work surface and create a well in the center. Drop the eggs into the well and mix them into the flour until a smooth and homogenous dough forms. Cover it with a cloth or wrap it in plastic and let it sit for 20 minutes.

When the meat is done, remove it from the sauce so you can use it for the agnolotti filling. Put the meat in a food processor with the spinach (boiled for a few minutes and thoroughly strained), an egg yolk, a good amount of grated Parmigiano, and a pinch of nutmeg. Blend well and season with salt and pepper. With a rolling pin or pasta machine, flatten the dough into 2 sheets, each 1/32 inch (1 mm) thick. Drop teaspoonfuls of dough onto one of the sheets, about 1 1/2-2 inches (4-5 cm) apart. Lay the second sheet on top and press down around the filling to seal the agnolotti. Then use a pastry wheel or a very sharp knife to cut between them. Strain the sauce that the meat cooked in earlier and let it cool (dilute it with a few tablespoons of broth if necessary). Boil the agnolotti in salted water for 5 minutes and remove them with a perforated spoon. First coat them in melted butter, then combine them with the sauce. Finish with a generous sprinkling of Parmigiano and serve them hot.

Filling Directions

Pasta Directions

Agnolotti "del plin"
al burro e salvia
Agnolotti "del Plin" with Butter and Sage

Servings 4
Difficulty Medium
Prep Time 1h
Cook Time 2'

For the pasta: 2 1/3 cups (300 g) Italian "00" flour – 3 eggs.
For the filling: 2 tbsp (30 ml) extra-virgin olive oil – 7 oz (200 g) leg of pork – 7 oz (200 g) veal shoulder – 7 oz (200 g) spinach (about 6 2/3 cups raw) – 1/2 cup (50 g) Parmigiano Reggiano cheese, grated – 1 egg – 5.3 oz (150 g) onion (about 1 large onion) – 1 sprig of rosemary – 1 garlic clove – 1 bay leaf – nutmeg to taste – salt and pepper to taste
For the vegetable broth: 1.4 oz (40 g) carrots (about 1 small carrot) – 1.4 oz (40 g) celery, including a few leaves (about 1 medium stalk) – 2.6 oz (75 g) onion (about 1 small onion) – 4 1/4 cups (1 L) water – salt to taste
For the topping: 3 1/2 tbsp (50 g) butter – 2 sprigs of sage – Parmigiano Reggiano cheese, grated (optional).

Clean the carrot, onion, and celery (leave a few leaves on the stalk) for the vegetable broth. Boil them in 4 1/4 cups of water for at least 30 minutes, seasoning with salt. When the broth is done, strain it and use it as a base for this recipe.

Pour the flour onto a work surface or into a bowl and create a well in the center. Break the eggs and pour them into the well. Start incorporating them into the flour with a fork, then use your hands to continue mixing until the dough is consistent in density and color. Wrap it in plastic and refrigerate it for 30 minutes.

Sauté the sliced onion, whole garlic clove, bay leaf, sprig of rosemary, and diced meats (pieces about 1/3-1/2 inch or 1 cm) in the oil.

When the meats are thoroughly browned, add the cleaned and rinsed spinach with a pinch of salt and pepper and a ladleful of broth. Make sure all the liquid has been absorbed, then remove the pan from the heat.

When the meat has cooled, blend it with the egg and the grated Parmigiano in a food processor. Add a pinch of nutmeg and salt to taste.

Take the dough out of the refrigerator and cut it into 3/4-1 inch (2-3 cm) slices. Use a rolling pin or pasta machine to make thin sheets about 4 inches (10 cm) wide. Place teaspoonfuls of filling in a line down the center of each sheet, a little more than 2 inches (6 cm) apart. Fold the dough over to cover the filling. To make the "plin" (which means "pinch" in the Piedmontese dialect) use two fingers to pinch around the spoonfuls of filling and seal the agnolotti. Remove any excess dough and use a fluted pastry wheel to cut them into rectangles.

Melt the butter in a wide, shallow pan with the sprigs of sage, being careful not to let it burn. Meanwhile boil the "plin" in salted water for 1-2 minutes and remove them with a perforated spoon. Sauté them briefly in the butter and sage, then transfer them to serving plates and sprinkle with Parmigiano to taste.

Agnolotti "del plin" Directions

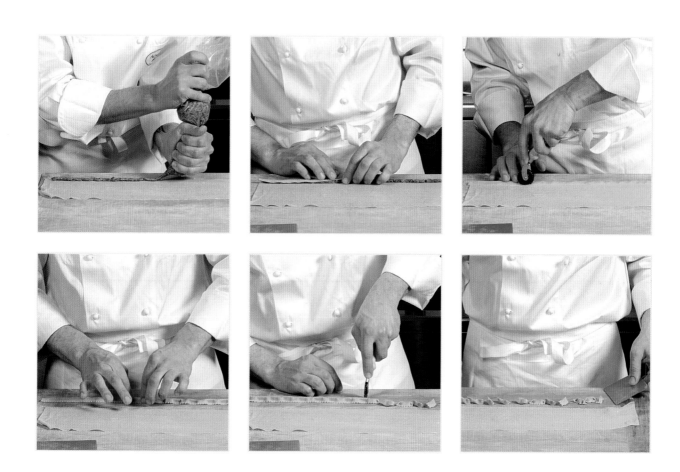

Balanzoni
Balanzoni

Servings 4
Difficulty *Medium*
Prep Time
1h and 20'
Cook Time 3-4'

For the pasta: 2 1/3 cups (300 g) Italian "00" flour – 2.6 oz (75 g) spinach, cooked and thoroughly drained (about 1/3 cup + 1 1/2 tbsp cooked) – 2 eggs.
For the filling: 10.5 oz (300 g) ricotta – 1.8 oz (50 g) spinach (about 1 2/3 cups raw) – 1 1/2 tbsp (20 g) butter – 2.8 oz (80 g) mortadella – 1 egg – 1/2 cup (50 g) Parmigiano Reggiano cheese, grated – 2-3 basil leaves – nutmeg to taste – salt and pepper to taste.
For the topping: 1/3 cup (70 g) butter – 1 sprig of sage – 1 (1 oz/30 g) slice of mortadella – Parmigiano Reggiano cheese, grated.

Combine the flour with the chopped spinach and the eggs. Mix until a consistent dough forms. Wrap it in plastic and refrigerate the dough for 30 minutes before using it.

Blanch the spinach for the filling in lightly salted water. Strain it and squeeze out any excess water, then sauté it briefly in the butter. Chop it up and mix it with the ricotta, egg, chopped basil, Parmigiano, and chopped mortadella. Season with a pinch of salt, pepper, and nutmeg.

Flatten a sheet of dough to 1/32 inch (1 mm) thick. Use a pastry bag to distribute equidistant portions (about 1 teaspoon each) of filling. Use a round pastry cutter to cut out 2 1/2-2 3/4 inch (6-7 cm) circles, making sure the filling is in the center. Fold them over into half-moon shapes and seal the edges well with a fork.

Boil the balanzoni in salted water and remove them after about 4 minutes. Transfer them directly to a pan with the butter, sage, and mortadella (cut into strips). Let it all cook together briefly, sprinkle with Parmigiano, and serve.

Caramelle ripiene di taleggio
Caramelle Stuffed with Taleggio in Creamy Cabbage Sauce

Servings 4
*Difficulty **High***
Prep Time
1h and 30'
Cook Time 5'

For the yellow pasta: 3/4 cup + 1 tbsp (100 g) Italian "00" flour – 1 egg.
For the green pasta: 3/4 cup + 1 tbsp (100 g) Italian "00" flour – 1 oz (25 g) spinach-cooked, strained, and chopped (about 2 tbsp) – half an egg.
For the red pasta: 3/4 cup + 1 tbsp (100 g) Italian "00" flour – 1.6 oz (45 g) beets, cooked and puréed (about 3 tbsp) – half an egg.
For the black pasta: 3/4 cup + 1 tbsp (100 g) Italian "00" flour – 0.18 oz (5 g) cuttlefish ink – half an egg.
For the topping: 1.1 lbs (500 g) Taleggio cheese – 0.66 lbs (300 g) cabbage – 5.3 oz (150 g) onion (about 2 small onions) – 3 tbsp (50 ml) red wine – 1 1/2 tbsp (20 g) butter – 1 1/4 cups (300 ml) water – 1 garlic clove – 1 sprig of rosemary – salt to taste.

To make the yellow pasta, pour the flour onto a marble or wooden work surface and create a well in the center. Drop the eggs into the well and work them into the flour until the dough is smooth and homogenous. Wrap it in plastic and let it rest for at least 30 minutes before working with it further. For each of the other colors, break the egg into a bowl first. Beat it with a fork and pour half of it into the flour. Add the "colorant" indicated above and mix it all together, then do the same as you did with the yellow dough.

Roll each dough color out to a thickness of 1/32 inch (1 mm) and cut it into 2 x 3 inch (8 x 5 cm) rectangles.

Remove the Taleggio rind and cut the cheese into 1/2 x 1 inch (1.5 x 3 cm) strips. Wrap each strip of cheese in a rectangle of dough and twist the ends closed like a candy wrapper.

Clean the cabbage and cut it into strips, and slice the onion. Melt the butter in a pan and sauté the onion for about 2 minutes. Add the cabbage and the wine. When all the wine has evaporated, add the water. Cook for 15 minutes, then purée the mixture until it's creamy and somewhat dense. Season with salt to taste.

Boil the caramelle in salted water for 4-5 minutes. Strain them and combine them with the cabbage sauce and rosemary (stripped from the stem).

Casonsei di Brescia
Brescian "Casonsei"

Servings 4
Difficulty **Medium**
Prep Time *1h*
Cook Time 5'

For the pasta: 2 1/3 cups (300 g) Italian "00" flour – 3 eggs.
For the filling: 0.44 lbs (200 g) ground beef – 1 cup + 2 1/2 tbsp (125 g) bread-crumbs – 1 1/4 cups (125 g) Grana Padano cheese, grated – 3 1/2 tbsp (50 g) but-ter – 1 egg – 1 tbsp minced parsley – 1 garlic clove – 3-4 tbsp water – salt to taste.
For the topping: 3 1/2 tbsp (50 g) butter – 1/2 cup (50 g) Grana Padano cheese, grated – 8 sage leaves.

To make the pasta, pour the flour onto a work surface and create a well in the center. Drop the eggs into the well and work them into the flour until a smooth and consistent dough forms. Cover it with a cloth or wrap it in plastic and let it rest for 20 minutes.

In the meantime, brown the butter in a pan. Add the ground beef and stir well with a wooden spoon. Add a few tablespoons of water, followed by the grated cheese and breadcrumbs. Season with salt to taste, mix it all together, and cook it on low heat for about 15 minutes. Remove the pan from the heat and let the contents cool. Stir in the egg, then add the garlic (minced) and parsley.

Use a pasta machine to flatten the dough to a thickness of 1/32 inch (1 mm). Cut out 1 1/2 x 3 inch (4 x 8 cm) rectangles and drop a spoonful of filling in the middle of each one. Roll them up diagonally and fold the ends in toward the center to seal in the filling and create the traditional "casonsei" shape.

Boil them in salted water and strain them well. Toss them with lots of browned butter, sage leaves (cut into thin strips), and grated Grana Padano. Serve them very hot on preheated plates.

Casunziei di erbetta rossa all'ampezzana
Ampezzo-Style Red "Casunziei"

Servings 4
Difficulty *Medium*
Prep Time *1h*
Cook Time *5'*

For the pasta: 2 1/3 cups (300 g) all-purpose flour – 3 eggs.
For the filling: 0.88 lbs (400 g) beets (about 5 beets) – 0.33 lbs (150 g) rutabaga (about 1 small rutabaga) – 1 clove, ground – 1 garlic clove – 3 tbsp (40 ml) extra-virgin olive oil – warm water as needed – nutmeg to taste – salt and pepper to taste.
For the topping: 1/2 cup (50 g) Grana Padano cheese, grated – 3 1/2 tbsp (50 g) butter – poppy seed to taste.

Pour the flour onto a work surface and create a well in the center. Break the eggs and pour them into the well. Carefully work them into the flour until the dough is firm and consistent. Wrap it in plastic and let it rest for 20 minutes before working with it further.

Boil the beets and rutabaga separately in lightly salted water. When they're cooked, peel them and pass them through a fine mesh strainer. Season the purée with a handful of salt, a pinch of nutmeg and ground pepper, and the ground clove. Mix it all together thoroughly, then drizzle some olive oil in a pan and lightly sauté the filling with the 2 whole garlic cloves (to be removed later).

To make the "casunziei" roll the pasta out into sheets, 1/32 inch (1 mm) thick. Use a round pastry cutter to stamp out 2 3/4-3 inch (7-8 cm) circles.

Drop a teaspoonful of filling in the center of each one and fold them over into half-moons. Press down lightly with your fingers to make sure all the air gets out and the edges are well sealed.

Carefully drop the "casunziei" into boiling salted water and let them cook. Remove them with a perforated spoon and transfer them serving plates. Coat the "casunziei" with a generous amount of grated cheese and brown butter, and top it off with poppy seed.

Fagottini di melanzane al timo e Pecorino toscano
Eggplant Fagottini with Thyme and Tuscan Pecorino

Servings 4
Difficulty Medium
Prep Time
1h and 20'
Cook Time 4-5'

For the pasta: 2 1/3 cups (300 g) Italian "00" flour – 3 eggs.
For the filling: 0.88 lbs (400 g) eggplant (just under 5 cups cubed) – 3.5 oz (100 g) fresh ricotta – 1/2 cup (50 g) Parmigiano Reggiano cheese, grated – 1 egg – salt and pepper – 3 1/2 tbsp (50 ml) extra-virgin olive oil – 2 sprigs of thyme.
For the topping: 2.5 oz (70 g) Tuscan Pecorino cheese – 2 sprigs of thyme – 3 1/2 tbsp (50 ml) extra-virgin olive oil.

Mix the flour and eggs until a smooth and consistent dough forms. Wrap it in plastic and refrigerate it for 30 minutes before working with it further.

Peel and cube the eggplant. Preheat the oven to 350° F (180° C). Put the eggplant in a pan with a drizzle of olive oil, a pinch of salt and pepper, and half the thyme (stripped from the stem). Cover the pan with aluminum foil and bake the eggplant for about 25 minutes, until it's very tender. Chop the eggplant very finely with a knife and mix it with the ricotta, egg, and Parmigiano.

Roll the pasta dough out to a thickness of about 1/32 inch (1 mm) and cut it into 2 x 2 inch (5 x 5 cm) squares. Use a pastry bag to place about 1 teaspoon of filling in the center of each square. Fold the corners toward the center and pinch them together to seal the fagottini.

Boil them in salted water and remove them with a perforated spoon. Toss them with the olive oil and remaining thyme (stripped from the stem). Transfer the fagottini to serving plates and top them with flakes of Pecorino.

Filling Directions

Fagottini Directions

Pansotti di patate alle olive taggiasche
Potato Pansotti with Taggiasca Olives

Servings 4
Difficulty **Medium**
Prep Time *1h*
Cook Time *3-4'*

For the pasta: 2 1/3 cups (300 g) all-purpose flour – 2 whole eggs – 3 egg yolks – 1 egg white – 2 tsp (10 ml) extra-virgin olive oil – salt to taste.
For the filling: 0.88 lbs (400 g) potatoes (about 2 medium) – 1 cup (100 g) Parmigiano Reggiano cheese, grated – 2.1 oz (60 g) black taggiasca olives, pitted (about 13 large) – grated nutmeg to taste – salt to taste.
For the topping: 1 1/4 cups (300 ml) heavy cream – 2/3 cup (60 g) Parmigiano Reggiano cheese, grated – 3.5 oz (100 g) shelled walnuts (about 3/4 cup + 1 1/2 tbsp chopped) – 1/2 garlic clove.

Mix the flour with the 2 whole eggs, 2 yolks, oil, and a pinch of salt on a flat work surface. Wrap the dough in plastic and refrigerate it for 30 minutes.

Boil the unpeeled potatoes in salted water. Peel them and mash them well. Mix the mashed potatoes with the roughly chopped olives, grated Parmigiano, and a pinch of salt and nutmeg.

Take the dough out of the refrigerator and use a rolling pin or pasta machine to roll it out to a thickness of 1/32-1/16 inch (1.5 mm). Lightly beat the egg white and brush it over the dough. Cut it into 2 1/3 inch (6 cm) squares and use a pastry bag to place about 1 teaspoon of filling in the center of each one. Fold them over on the diagonal and press down around the edges to form triangular tortelli, or pansotti.

Thicken the heavy cream in a pot with the garlic clove, then add the crushed walnuts. Remove the garlic before adding the sauce to the pasta.

Bring a pot of water to a boil and add a handful of coarse salt. Add the pansotti and let them boil for 3-4 minutes. Then remove them with a perforated spoon and transfer them directly to the pot of heavy cream and walnuts. Let them cook with the sauce for a minute, sprinkle them with Parmigiano, and serve.

Ravioli di crostacei
Shrimp and Lobster Ravioli in Creamy Artichoke Sauce with Prosciutto and Pecorino

Servings 4
Difficulty High
Prep Time
1h and 30'
Cook Time 4-5'

For the pasta: 2 1/3 cups (300 g) Italian "00" flour – 3 eggs.
For the filling: 0.55 lbs (250 g) shrimp – 0.33 lbs (150 g) locust lobster – 1 tbsp minced parsley – 1 garlic clove.
For the topping: 3 artichokes, about 0.33–0.44 lbs (150-200 g) each – 0.44 lbs (200 g) potatoes (about 1 medium) – 2.5 oz (70 g) carrots (about 1 1/2 small) – 2.5 oz (70 g) celery (about 2 medium stalks) – 2.5 oz (70 g) yellow onion (about 1 small) – 2.8 oz (80 g) prosciutto (dry-cured), thickly sliced – 2.8 oz (80 g) Pecorino cheese – 2 basil leaves – 3 1/2 tbsp (50 ml) extra-virgin olive oil (preferably Ligurian) – salt and pepper to taste.

Pour the flour onto a work surface and create a well in the center. Add the eggs and mix until a smooth and consistent dough forms. Wrap it in plastic and refrigerate for 30 minutes.

Clean and shell the shrimp and lobster. Sauté them over medium heat with the garlic, minced parsley, and a bit of oil. Once they're cooked, chop them up.

Use a rolling pin or pasta machine to roll the dough out to 1/32 inch (1 mm) thick. Cut it into 2 3/4-3 inch (7-8 cm) squares and place a bit of filling in the center of each one. Fold them over to shape the classic rectangular ravioli. Press down gently with your fingertips to remove any air bubbles and seal the edges well.

Clean the artichokes, removing the stems, tips, tough outer leaves, and fuzzy center. Clean, peel, and dice the other vegetables. Drizzle some olive oil into a pan over medium heat and let the vegetables cook until they start to soften. Add the artichokes, basil, a pinch of salt and pepper, and enough water to cover everything. Let it stew for about 15 minutes (the vegetables should become very soft). When the vegetables are done, purée them. Strain the purée and transfer it to a large bowl.

Julienne the prosciutto and sauté it in a bit of oil.

Boil the ravioli in salted water for 4-5 minutes. Strain them and add them to the bowl of purée. Sprinkle them with Pecorino flakes and crispy prosciutto, and drizzle cold-pressed olive oil on top.

Ravioli alla genovese
Genoese Ravioli

Servings 4
Difficulty High
Prep Time
1h and 35'
Cook Time 4-5'

For the pasta: 2 1/3 cups (300 g) Italian "00" flour – 3 eggs.
For the filling: 3.5 oz (100 g) chicken – 1.76 oz (50 g) pork sausage – 0.88 oz (25 g) lard – 4 tbsp (25 g) fresh breadcrumbs – 3.9 oz (110 g) borage – 3.9 oz (110 g) chard (about 3 cups) – 1 oz (30 g) spinach (about 1/4 cup) – 1/3 cup + 1 1/2 tbsp (100 ml) milk – 3 tbsp (20 g) Parmigiano Reggiano cheese, grated – 2 eggs – nutmeg to taste – salt and pepper to taste.
For the topping: 3/4 cup + 1 1/2 tbsp (200 ml) drippings from a roast – 1 1/2 tbsp (20 g) butter – 1/3 cup + 1 tbsp (40 g) Parmigiano Reggiano cheese, grated – 2 sprigs of fresh thyme.

Pour the flour onto a work surface and create a well in the center. Add the eggs and mix until the dough is smooth and consistent. Cover it with a cloth or wrap it in plastic and let it sit for 20 minutes.

In the meantime pass the chicken, sausage, lard, breadcrumbs (soaked in milk and squeezed to remove excess liquid), and herbs (washed, blanched, and cooled) through a food mill. Transfer the mixture to a bowl and incorporate the grated Parmigiano. Season with salt, pepper, and a pinch of nutmeg. Add the eggs and mix well.

Use a rolling pin or pasta machine to roll the dough out into 2 sheets, each 1/32 inch (1 mm) thick. Drop teaspoonfuls onto the first sheet, about 1 1/2-2 inches (4-5 cm) apart. Lay the second sheet on top and press down gently with your fingers to eliminate air bubbles and seal the dough around the filling. Use a pastry wheel or very shape knife to cut out square ravioli, about 2 1/3 x 2 1/3 inches (6 x 6 cm).

Boil them in lightly salted water for about 4-5 minutes. Strain them and combine them with the melted butter, thyme (stripped from the stem), and roast drippings (very hot). Top them with grated Parmigiano.

Ravioli con Pecorino
Ravioli with Pecorino in Veal Reduction Sauce

Servings 4
Difficulty **High**
Prep Time **2h**
Cook Time **10'**

For the pasta: 2 1/3 cups (300 g) Italian "00" flour – 3 eggs.
For the filling: 14 oz (400 g) ricotta – 1/2 cup (50 g) Parmigiano Reggiano cheese, grated – 1 tbsp minced parsley – salt and pepper to taste.
For the veal reduction: 2.2 lbs (1 kg) veal bones – 7 oz (200 g) celery (about 3 large stalks) – 2.8 oz (80 g) carrots (about 1 1/2 small) – 5.3 oz (150 g) onion (about 2 small) – 1/3 cup + 1 1/2 tbsp (100 ml) white wine – 1 tsp cornstarch – 1 cup (250 ml) water.
For the garnish: 2.1 oz (60 g) Pecorino cheese, in flakes.

To make the veal reduction, roast the veal bones and roughly chopped vegetables in a preheated oven at 450° F (230° C). When they're well roasted, transfer them to a large pot along with any drippings. Deglaze the pan with the wine and add it to the pot, letting it reduce by half. Then add 1 cup (250 ml) of water and let it cook until it reaches the desired consistency (it should take about 1 hour and 45 minutes total). Filter the reduction with a fine mesh strainer and add a teaspoon of cornstarch (diluted in 1-2 tablespoons of water) to thicken it further.

In the meantime, make the pasta. Pour the flour onto a work surface and create a well in the center. Drop the eggs into the well and mix until a consistent dough forms. Cover it with a cloth or wrap it in plastic and let it sit for 20 minutes.

Combine the ricotta, Parmigiano, and parsley to make the filling. Mix well and season with salt and pepper to taste.

Use a rolling pin or pasta machine to roll the dough out into 2 sheets, each 1/32 inch (1 mm) thick. Drop teaspoonfuls of filling onto the first sheet, about 1 1/2-2 inches (4-5 cm) apart. Lay the second sheet on top and press down gently with your fingertips to remove any air bubbles and seal the dough around the filling. Use a pastry wheel or very shape knife to cut out square ravioli, about 2 1/3 x 2 1/3 inches (6 x 6 cm).

Boil the ravioli in salted water for about 4-5 minutes. Strain them and combine them with the hot veal reduction sauce. Top them with Pecorino flakes.

Ravioli di Parmigiano
Parmesan Ravioli in Fresh Tomato Sauce

Servings 4
Difficulty **Medium**
Prep Time **1h**
Cook Time **4-5'**

For the pasta: 2 1/3 cups (300 g) Italian "00" flour – 3.2 oz (90 g) spinach, cooked and squeezed dry (about 1/2 cup) – 2 eggs.
For the filling: 2 cups (200 g) Parmigiano Reggiano cheese, grated – 7 oz (200 g) cow's milk ricotta – 1 egg – 1 tbsp minced parsley – salt to taste.
For the topping: 0.55 lbs (250 g) cherry tomatoes on the vine – 0.35 oz (10 g) thyme, fresh or dry (about 4 tbsp) – 1.4 oz (40 g) carrots (about 3/4 small) – 1.4 oz (40 g) celery (about 1 medium stalk) – 1.4 oz (40 g) yellow onion (about 1/2 small) – 3.5 oz (100 g) prosciutto (dry-cured) – 8 basil leaves – 1/3 cup + 1 1/2 tbsp (100 ml) extra-virgin olive oil – salt and pepper to taste.

Pour the flour onto a work surface and create a well in the center. Break the eggs and drop them into the well along with the spinach (thoroughly squeezed dry and chopped up). Mix them together until the dough is smooth and consistent in density and color. Cover it with a cloth or wrap it in plastic and let it sit for 30 minutes.

Chop the carrots, celery, and onion. Peel the tomatoes, remove the seeds, and cut them into quarters.

Sauté the vegetables and thyme in half the oil for a few minutes. Season with salt and pepper to taste and let them cook for another 15-20 minutes. Then purée the sauce and filter it with a fine mesh strainer. Cut the prosciutto into small strips and fry it with enough oil to coat the bottom of the pan. Julienne the basil. In a large bowl mix the Parmigiano, ricotta, egg, and parsley. Add salt to taste.

Use a rolling pin or pasta machine to roll the dough out to 1/32 inch (1 mm) thick. Cut it into 6 x 16 inch (15 x 40 cm) pieces. Drop teaspoonfuls of filling onto the dough, about 1 1/2 inches (4 cm) apart. Lay another sheet of dough on top and press down gently with your fingertips to eliminate air bubbles and seal the dough around the filling. Use a round pastry cutter to stamp out the ravioli.

Boil them in salted water for 4-5 minutes. Remove them with a perforated spoon and toss them in the pan with the remaining oil.

Spread a layer of tomato sauce on a preheated plate and arrange the ravioli on top. Sprinkle it with parsley and crispy prosciutto.

Ravioli di patate con noci e pinoli
Potato Ravioli with Walnuts and Pine Nuts

Servings 4
Difficulty **Low**
Prep Time *1h*
Cook Time *3-4'*

For the pasta: 2 1/3 cups (300 g) Italian "00" flour – 3 eggs.
For the filling: 0.88 lbs (400 g) potatoes (about 2 medium) – 1 cup (100 g) Parmigiano Reggiano cheese, grated – 1 egg – grated nutmeg to taste – salt to taste.
For the sauce: 8 walnuts, shelled – 1.4 oz (40 g) toasted pine nuts (about 5 tbsp) – 3/4 cup + 1 tbsp (80 g) Parmigiano Reggiano cheese, grated – fresh marjoram to taste – 7 tbsp (100 g) butter.

Pour the flour onto a work surface and create a well in the center. Break the eggs and drop them into the well. Mix them together until the dough is smooth and dense. Wrap it in plastic and refrigerate it for 30 minutes.

Boil the unpeeled potatoes in salted water. As soon as they're cooked, strain them and peel them. Mash them thoroughly with a potato masher. Mix them with the egg, Parmigiano, a handful of salt, and a pinch of nutmeg.

Use a rolling pin or pasta machine to roll the dough out into sheets, 1/32 inch (1 mm) thick. Use a pastry bag to pipe teaspoonfuls of filling onto a sheet of dough at regular intervals. Lay another sheet of dough on top and press down gently with your fingertips to eliminate air bubbles and seal the dough around the filling. Use a fluted pastry wheel to cut out square ravioli, about 1 1/2-2 inches (4-5 cm) each.

Boil the ravioli in salted water and combine them with the butter (melted in a small nonstick pot), Parmigiano, stripped marjoram leaves, roughly chopped walnuts, and toasted pine nuts. To toast the pine nuts, just toss them in a very hot nonstick pan for 1-2 minutes.

Ravioli di pollo
Chicken Ravioli

Servings 4
Difficulty Medium
Prep Time 1h
Cook Time 4-5'

For the pasta: 2 1/3 cups (300 g) Italian "00" flour – 3 eggs.
For the filling: 1/2 cup (50 g) Parmigiano Reggiano cheese, grated – 0.55 lbs (250 g) chicken breast – 0.22 lbs (100 g) fresh porcini mushrooms – 3.5 oz (100 g) fresh ricotta – 3.5 oz (100 g) spinach (about 3 1/3 cups raw) – 3 eggs – 3 1/2 tbsp (50 g) butter – 3 1/2 tbsp (50 ml) extra-virgin olive oil – 1/3 cup + 1 1/2 tbsp (100 ml) fortified wine, such as Marsala – 1 bay leaf – nutmeg to taste – salt and pepper to taste
For the sauce: 1/3 cup + 1 1/2 tbsp (100 ml) heavy cream – 0.66 lbs (300 g) fresh porcini mushrooms – 1 oz (30 g) toasted pine nuts (3 1/2 tbsp) – 1 spring onion – 2 tbsp (30 ml) extra-virgin olive oil – 1 tbsp minced parsley – salt and pepper to taste.

Mix the flour and eggs until a smooth dough forms. Wrap it in plastic and let it sit for 30 minutes.

In the meantime, dice the chicken breast. Carefully clean the mushrooms with a damp cloth and dice them. Then clean the spinach.

Melt the butter with the oil in a small rondeau (a low terracotta casserole) over medium heat. After a few seconds, add the chicken. When it's uniformly browned, add the mushrooms and let them sauté for a few minutes. Then add the spinach and season with salt and pepper. Let it cook for 5 minutes, add the Marsala, and let all the liquid evaporate over high heat.

Blend it all with a meat grinder or food processor. Then mix in the ricotta, Parmigiano, eggs, and a pinch of nutmeg.

Roll the dough out to a thickness of 1 /32 inch (1 mm). Cut it into 2 1/3 inch (6 cm) squares and drop a teaspoon of filling in the center of each one. Fold them over and seal around the edges, pressing gently with your fingertips to remove any air bubbles.

Start the sauce by mincing the spring onion and sautéing it in the oil. When it softens, add the diced mushrooms and let them cook for 2 minutes. Then add the cream and let it thicken, seasoning with salt and pepper to taste.

Boil the tortelli in salted water and remove them with a perforated spoon. Combine them with the mushroom sauce, parsley, and toasted pine nuts (toss them in a very hot nonstick pan for 1-2 minutes to toast them).

Raviolone di ricotta al timo e burro
Ricotta Ravioli with Butter and Thyme

Servings 4
*Difficulty **Low***
Prep Time 45'
Cook Time 5'

For the pasta: 1 2/3 cups (200 g) Italian "00" flour – 2 eggs.
For the filling: 7 oz (200 g) ricotta – 1/3 cup (30 g) Parmigiano Reggiano cheese, grated – 5 eggs – 1 egg white – nutmeg to taste – salt and pepper to taste.
For the topping: 4 tbsp (60 g) butter – 1/3 cup + 1 tbsp (40 g) Parmigiano Reggiano cheese, grated – fresh thyme to taste.

On a work surface or in a bowl, mix the flour and eggs until the dough is smooth and consistent. Wrap it in plastic and refrigerate it for about 30 minutes.

Sift the ricotta and mix it with the grated Parmigiano, 1 whole egg, a handful of salt, and a pinch of pepper and nutmeg.

Roll the dough out into 1/32 inch (1 mm) discs and brush them with the beaten egg white.

Use a pastry bag to distribute the filling over the dough, creating 4 rings, each with a 4-inch (10 cm) diameter. Drop an egg yolk in the center of each ring.

Cover each disc with another sheet of pasta and seal around the filling, pressing down gently with your fingers. Stamp out the ravioloni with a round pastry cutter that's big enough to fit around the edges.

Melt the butter in a nonstick pan, flavoring it with the stripped thyme leaves.

Boil the stuffed pasta in salted water for 4-5 minutes. Remove it with a perforated spoon and coat it with Parmigiano and thyme-flavored butter.

Ravioli di ricotta, asparagi e zafferano
Asparagus and Ricotta Ravioli with Saffron

Servings 4
Difficulty Medium
Prep Time 1h
Cook Time 4-5'

For the pasta: 2 1/3 cups (300 g) Italian "00" flour – 3 eggs.
For the filling: 1.1 lbs (500 g) green asparagus – 10.5 oz (300 g) ricotta – 1 cup (100 g) Parmigiano Reggiano cheese, grated – 1 shallot – 2 tbsp (30 ml) extra-virgin olive oil – nutmeg to taste – salt and pepper to taste – water as needed.
For the vegetable broth: 1.4 oz (40 g) carrots (about 3/4 small) – 1.4 oz (40 g) celery, including a few leaves (about 1 medium stalk) – 2.6 oz (75 g) onion (about 1 small) – 4 1/4 cup (1 L) water – salt to taste.
For the topping: 3 1/2 tbsp (50 ml) vegetable broth – 1/3 tsp (0.25 g) powdered saffron (or 1 pistil tip).

Start by making the vegetable broth. Wash and peel half a carrot, half an onion, and half a celery stalk with a few leaves still attached. Boil them for at least 30 minutes in 4 1/4 cups (1 L) of water, seasoning with salt to taste. When the broth is done, strain it and use it for the pasta sauce.

Pour the flour and create a well in the center. Break the eggs and drop them into the well. Mix them together until the dough is smooth and dense. Wrap it in plastic and refrigerate it for 30 minutes.

Clean the asparagus and eliminate the tougher parts from the stems, setting aside 4 of them to use as a garnish later. Slice the rest of them into rounds. Heat some oil in a pan and sauté the minced shallot with the asparagus. Add 2 tablespoons of water and let it cook on low heat for 10 minutes. Mix the ricotta with a handful of salt and a pinch of pepper and nutmeg. Then add the cooked asparagus and Parmigiano. Blend it all in a food processor and add more salt and pepper if necessary.

Roll the dough out to 1/32 inch (1 mm) thick, then stamp out 3-3 1/2 inch (8-9 cm) discs. Use a pastry bag to place some filling in the center of each one. Lightly brush the edges with water and fold the ravioli over into a half-moon shape. Bring 3 1/2 tablespoons (50 ml) of broth to a boil and let it cook for 5 minutes. Add the saffron and remove the pot from the heat, setting it aside. Take the asparagus you set aside earlier and use a potato peeler to peel off thin strips for garnishing. Blanch them and immediately run very cold water over them. Season the strips with a drizzle of olive oil and a pinch of salt. Boil the ravioli in salted water for 4-5 minutes. Remove them with a perforated spoon and distribute them among individual serving plates. Drizzle them with the saffron broth and garnish with blanched asparagus strips.

Ravioli di ricotta e spinaci
Spinach and Ricotta Ravioli

Servings 4
Difficulty Medium
Prep Time 1h
Cook Time 4-5'

For the pasta: 2 1/3 cups (300 g) Italian "00" flour – 3 eggs.
For the filling: 10.5 oz (300 g) sifted ricotta – 10.5 oz (300 g) spinach (cooked and squeezed dry), about 1 2/3 cups – 1 1/2 cups (150 g) Parmigiano Reggiano cheese, grated – 3 egg yolks – nutmeg to taste – salt and pepper to taste.
For the topping: 3 tbsp (40 g) butter – 1/4 cup + 1 tbsp (40 g) flour – 2 1/2 cups (600 ml) heavy cream – salt and pepper to taste.
For the garnish: 1/3 cup + 1 1/2 tbsp (100 ml) unsweetened whipped cream – 2 egg yolk – 1 cup (100 g) Parmigiano Reggiano cheese, grated.

Pour the flour onto a work surface and create a well in the center. Break the eggs and drop them into the well. Mix them together until the dough is smooth and dense. Cover it with a cloth and let it sit for 30 minutes.

Start the filling by briefly sautéing the spinach (already boiled and thoroughly squeezed dry) in the butter. Season it with salt and pepper and let it cool.

Sift the ricotta into a bowl. Mix in the grated Parmigiano, a handful of salt, and a pinch of pepper and nutmeg. Finely chop the spinach and add it to the ricotta along with the three egg yolks. For a more uniform filling, you can blend the mixture in a food processor.

Use a rolling pin or pasta machine to roll the dough out to 1/32 inch (1 mm) thick. Cut it into 4 -inch (10 cm) squares and place a bit of filling in the center of each one. Fold them on the diagonal to form triangular ravioli. Gently press down with your fingertips to eliminate air bubbles and seal the edges.

Make the roux next. Melt the butter in a small pot and whisk in the flour. Add the cream and let it thicken, still whisking, until the sauce is creamy and consistent. Season it with salt and pepper to taste.

Boil the ravioli in salted water for 4-5 minutes. Remove them with a perforated spoon, combine them with the roux, and transfer them to serving plates. Gently fold the yolks and Parmigiano into the whipped cream, being careful not to let it deflate. Place a generous spoonful on each plate and caramelize it in the oven or with a kitchen blowtorch. Serve immediately.

Tortelli al radicchio con fonduta all'Asiago
Radicchio Tortelli with Asiago Fondue

Servings 4
Difficulty Medium
Prep Time
1h and 30'
Cook Time 3-4'

For the pasta: 2 1/3 cups (300 g) Italian "00" flour – 3 eggs.
For the filling: 2.2 lbs (1 kg) radicchio – 3.5 oz (100 g) onion (about 1 1/2 small) – 1/3 cup (30 g) Parmigiano Reggiano cheese, grated – 2 oz (60 g) prosciutto di Parma – 1/3 cup + 2 tbsp (50 g) breadcrumbs – 1/3 cup + 1 1/2 tbsp (100 ml) extra-virgin olive oil – 1 egg – nutmeg to taste – salt and pepper to taste.
For the fondue sauce: 2 1/2 tbsp (35 g) butter – 2 1/2 tbsp (20 g) flour – 1 1/4 cups (300 ml) milk – 0.55 lbs (250 g) fresh Asiago cheese – salt.
For the garnish: 1 tbsp minced parsley – 2 radicchio leaves.

Pour the flour onto a work surface and create a well in the center. Add the eggs and mix until a smooth and homogenous dough forms. Wrap it in plastic and refrigerate it for 30 minutes.

Clean the radicchio and cut it into thin strips. Sauté it in the oil with the sliced onion, and season with salt and pepper. When it's cooked, combine it with the diced prosciutto, the egg, and the grated Parmigiano. If the dough is too wet, add some breadcrumbs. Season it with a pinch of ground nutmeg.

Roll the dough out to a thickness of about 1/32 inch (1 mm). Stamp out 3-inch (8 cm) circles and use a pastry bag to place some filling in the center of each one. Fold them over into half-moons and seal the edges of the tortelli.

Start the fondue by preparing a roux with the butter and flour, then add the hot milk and let it thicken. Add the diced Asiago, let it melt, and season with salt to taste.

Boil the tortelli in salted water for about 4-5 minutes. Spread some fondue on each plate and serve the tortelli on top.

Garnish with julienned radicchio and minced parsley to taste.

Tortelli alle erbette
Chard Ravioli

Servings 4
Difficulty *Low*
Prep Time 50'
Cook Time 3-4'

For the pasta: 2 1/3 cups (300 g) Italian "00" flour – 3 eggs.
For the filling: 10.5 oz (300 g) ricotta – 1.5 lbs (700 g) chard – 1 2/3 cups + 2 tbsp (180 g) Parmigiano Reggiano cheese, grated – 1 whole egg – nutmeg to taste – salt and pepper to taste.
For the topping: 5 tbsp (70 g) butter – 2/3 cup (60 g) Parmigiano Reggiano cheese, grated.

Wash the chard, remove the stems, and boil the green part of the leaves in lightly salted water Strain them and thoroughly squeeze them dry. Chop them up and mix them with the ricotta, whole egg, grated Parmigiano, a pinch of salt, and a generous pinch of nutmeg. Stir it all together until the mixture is thick and homogenous.
Work the eggs into the flour on a flat surface until the dough is firm and dense. Roll it out into sheets about 1/16 inch (1.5 mm) thick. Cut them into 2 3/4 inch (7 cm) squares and place about 1 teaspoon of filling in the center of each one. Fold them over to form rectangular tortelli. Gently press down with your fingertips to eliminate air bubbles and seal the edges well.
Boil the tortelli in salted water and remove them with a perforated spoon. Coat them with melted butter and grated Parmigiano, and serve them nice and hot.

Tortelli alle pere
Pear Tortelli with Prosciutto, Balsamic Vinegar, and Almonds

Servings 4
Difficulty Medium
Prep Time 1h
Cook Time 3-4'

For the pasta: 2 1/3 cups (300 g) Italian "00" flour – 2 eggs – 2.8 oz (80 g) beets, cooked and puréed (about 1 medium).

For the filling: 10.5 oz (300 g) pears, diced (about 2 cups) – 10.5 oz (300 g) ricotta – 1/3 cup + 1 tbsp (40 g) Parmigiano Reggiano cheese, grated – salt and pepper to taste.

For the topping: 4.2 oz (120 g) sliced prosciutto (dry-cured) – 4 sprigs of thyme – 0.7 oz (20 g) slivered almonds (about 3 tbsp) – 1.4 oz (40 g) Parmigiano Reggiano cheese, in flakes – 3 1/2 tbsp (50 g) butter – 3 tbsp (40 ml) Modena balsamic vinegar.

Mix the flour with the eggs and beet purée until a smooth and consistent dough forms. Wrap it in plastic and refrigerate it for 30 minutes.

Mix the diced pears with the ricotta and the Parmigiano, and season with salt and pepper to taste. Roll the pasta dough out to 1/32 inch (1 mm) thick. Cut it into 2-2 1/3 inch (5-6 cm) squares and drop a teaspoonful of dough in the center of each one. Fold them over into triangles and seal the edges well. Then wrap them around your index finger and bring the ends together.

Melt the butter in a nonstick pan and add the prosciutto, cut into strips about 1/3-1/2 inch (1 cm) wide. Sauté it for a few minutes, then add the balsamic vinegar. Let it cook for another 3-4 minutes, until it reaches a syrupy consistency.

Meanwhile boil the tortelli in salted water and strain them when they're *al dente*. Combine them with the sauce and add the thyme (stripped from the stem). Distribute the pasta among serving plates and top it with almonds and flakes of Parmigiano.

Tortello cremasco
Crema-Style Tortelli

Servings 4
Difficulty Low
Prep Time 50'
Cook Time 5'
one day for filling to sit

For the pasta: 2 1/3 cups (300 g) Italian "00" flour – 2/3 cup (150 ml) warm water.

For the filling: 0.55 lbs (250 g) dark amaretti cookies – 1.76 oz (50 g) raisins (about 1/3 cup packed) – 1.76 oz (50 g) candied citron – 1 egg – 1 hard tack biscuit – salt to taste.

For the topping: 5 1/2 tbsp (80 g) butter – 1 cup (100 g) Grana Padano cheese, grated.

Make the filling first. Crush the amaretti and chop the other ingredients. Mix them all together thoroughly and let the mixture sit for at least one day.

Mix the flour with the warm water until a consistent dough forms. Wrap it in plastic and refrigerate it for at least 20 minutes. Then roll the dough out to about 1/32 inch (1 mm) thick. Stamp out circles 4 inches (10 cm) in diameter, and use a pastry bag to place some filling in the center of each one. Fold them over into half-moons and seal the edges well, using your thumb and forefinger (or pressing down with the back of a knife) to pinch it like a pie crust.

Boil the tortelli in a large amount of salted water for about 5 minutes. Strain them and coat them with lots of melted butter (browned in a nonstick pan) and grated Grana Padano.

Tradition calls for adding a crushed mint to the ingredients. The original recipe for this traditional dish from Crema is still a subject of debate among the locals.

Tortelli d'anatra
Duck Tortelli

Servings 4
Difficulty **High**
Prep Time **1h**
Cook Time 5'

For the pasta: 2 1/3 cups (300 g) Italian "00" flour – 3 eggs.
For the filling: 2 duck thighs (deboned) – 2.8 oz (80 g) carrots (about 1 1/2 small) – 2.5 oz (70 g) celery (about 2 medium stalks) – 4.2 oz (120 g) yellow onion (about 1 medium) – 3/4 cup + 1 1/2 tbsp (200 ml) red wine – 1 egg – 3 tsp (5 g) unsweetened cocoa powder – 1 tbsp Italian "00" flour – 1 tsp cornstarch – 1/2 cup (50 g) Parmigiano Reggiano cheese, grated – 2 tbsp (30 ml) extra-virgin olive oil – 2 sprigs of thyme – 1 bay leaf – water as needed – salt and pepper to taste.

Mix the flour and eggs until a consistent dough forms. Wrap it in plastic and refrigerate it for 30 minutes.

Peel and julienne the onions. Wash and chop the celery and carrots.

Pour the oil into a saucepan and set it on medium heat. Add the onion, carrots, celery, bay leaf, and thyme. Sauté them until they're golden brown, then add the chopped duck. When the duck is well browned, add the flour and cocoa. Season with salt and pepper, then add the red wine and let it reduce. Keep adding water, one ladleful at a time, until the meat starts to fall apart. Then use a fine strainer to remove the duck from the sauce.

Let the sauce come to a boil. Thicken it with the cornstarch, dissolved in 1-2 tablespoons of cold water.

When the duck has cooled, pass it through a meat grinder and mix it with the eggs and Parmigiano. Roll the pasta out to a thickness of 1/32 inch (1 mm). Cut it into 3-inch (8 cm) squares and use a pastry bag to place some duck filling in the center of each one. Fold them over into triangles and seal the edges well. Fold down the top corner and curve the triangle around your index finger, bringing the 2 bottom corners together.

Boil the tortelli in salted water for about 5 minutes, then strain them and combine them with the sauce. Top them with grated Parmigiano and ground pepper.

Tortelli di branzino
Sea Bass Tortelli with Carpet Shell Clams and Broccoli

Servings 4
Difficulty **Medium**
Prep Time
1h and 20'
Cook Time 4-5'

For the pasta: 2 1/3 cups (300 g) Italian "00" flour – 2.6 oz (75 g) spinach (boiled, squeezed dry, and chopped), about 1/3–1/2 cup – 2 eggs.
For the filling: 1 (2.2 lbs/1 kg) sea bass – 1.76 oz (50 g) sliced white bread (about 2–3 slices) – 3 1/2 tbsp (50 ml) heavy cream – 1 egg – 2 sprigs of marjoram – 1/2 tbsp minced parsley – salt and pepper to taste.
For the topping: 0.44 lbs (200 g) broccoli – 1.1 lbs (500 g) carpet shell clams – 1 garlic clove – 1/2 tbsp minced parsley – salt to taste.

Mix the flour with the chopped spinach and the egg until a consistent dough forms. Wrap it in plastic and refrigerate it for 30 minutes.

Skin and fillet the fish, removing all the bones, and chop the marjoram. Remove the crust from the bread and soak it in the cream.

Pour the oil into a pan and cook the sea bass on low heat with a pinch of salt and pepper. When it's done (it should take about 10 minutes to cook), let it cool. Then chop it up and mix it with the soaked bread (lightly squeezed to remove excess liquid), marjoram, half the parsley, and the egg.

Use a pasta machine or rolling pin to roll the pasta out to a thickness of 1/32 inch (1 mm). Cut out squares, about 2 1/3 inches (6 cm), and place a bit of fish filling in the center of each one. Fold them over to make rectangular tortelli and seal them well.

Wash the broccoli and divide it into florets, removing the stems. Boil it in salted water, strain it, and quickly run cold water over it to cool it off.

Thoroughly flush out the clams, then cook them in a covered saucepan with a drizzle of olive oil until they open. Remove the shells, filter the remaining liquid from the saucepan, and set it aside.

Drizzle some oil in a skillet on medium heat. Add the halved garlic clove, the broccoli, and the clams. Sauté them together, adding the liquid from the clams toward the end.

Boil the tortelli for 4-5 minutes in salted water. Strain them and transfer them to the pan with the clam sauce. Let everything cook together for a minute and top it off with the remaining minced parsley.

Tortelli di cavolfiore
Cauliflower Tortelli with Shrimp and Toasted Pine Nuts

Servings 4
Difficulty **Medium**
Prep Time
1h and 30'
Cook Time 4-5'

For the pasta: 2 1/3 cups (300 g) Italian "00" flour – 3 eggs.
For the filling: 0.88 lb (400 g) cauliflower – 3.5 oz (100 g) fresh Caprino cheese – 1/2 cup (50 g) Parmigiano Reggiano cheese, grated – salt and pepper to taste.
For the topping: 2 tbsp (30 ml) extra-virgin olive oil – 16 shrimp – 1.4 oz (40 g) toasted pine nuts (about 5 tbsp) – 1 garlic clove – 1 tbsp minced parsley – salt to taste.

Mix the flour and eggs until a smooth and consistent dough forms. Wrap it in plastic and refrigerate it for 30 minutes.

Wash the cauliflower and divide it into florets, removing the stems. Boil it in salted water, strain it, and let it cool. Mix it with the Caprino and the Parmigiano, breaking the cauliflower into small pieces. Season with salt and pepper to taste.

Roll the pasta out to 1/32 inch (1 mm) thick. Stamp out circles, about 3 inches (8 cm) in diameter and use a pastry bag to place some filling in the center of each one. Fold them over into half-moons and seal the edges. Fold down the top part of the rounded side and curve the half-moon around your index finger, bringing the 2 corners together.

Remove the shells and devein the shrimp, then dice them. Peel the garlic and slice it very thinly.

Heat the oil in a pan and add the garlic (careful not to let it brown) and shrimp. Let them cook for 2-3 minutes and season with salt to taste.

Boil the tortellini in salted water for 4-5 minutes. Strain them and transfer them to the pan with the shrimp. Add the parsley and pine nuts and let it all cook together for a minute. To toast the pine nuts, just toss them in a very hot nonstick pan for 30 seconds.

Tortelli di patate con prosciutto di Parma
Potato Tortelli with Prosciutto di Parma

Servings 4
Difficulty Low
Prep Time 1h
Cook Time 4-5'

For the pasta: 2 1/3 cups (300 g) Italian "00" flour – 3 eggs.
For the filling: 5.3 oz (150 g) prosciutto di Parma – 0.66 lbs (300 g) potatoes (about 1 1/2 medium) – chives to taste – 1/2 cup (50 g) Parmigiano Reggiano cheese, grated – 1 egg – nutmeg to taste – salt to taste.
For the topping: 1/4 cup (60 ml) extra-virgin olive oil – 2.1 oz (60 g) basil (about 2 1/2 cups whole leaves) – 1 tsp cornstarch.

Wash, boil, and peel the potatoes. Mash them with a potato masher and let them cool. Mix them with the egg, nutmeg, finely chopped prosciutto, about 1 tablespoon of chives, and the grated Parmigiano. Season with salt to taste.

Carefully mix the eggs and flour until a consistent dough forms. Use a pasta machine or rolling pin to flatten it to 1/32 inch (1 mm) thick. Distribute small spoonfuls of filling over half the dough, about 1-1 1/2 inches (3-4 cm) apart. Fold the empty half over the half with the filling. Press lightly with your fingers to get all the air out and make sure the dough is well sealed around the filling. Use a very sharp knife or a fluted pastry wheel to cut out the individual tortelli.

Boil the basil in salted water for 30 seconds, then strain it and blend it with the oil in a food processor. Heat the basil oil in a pan and let it thicken. Dissolve the cornstarch in 1-2 tablespoons of water and add it to the oil. Be careful not to let it boil.

Boil the tortelli in a large amount of salted water for 4-5 minutes and coat them with the fragrant basil oil.

Chef's tips
To perfectly seal the tortelli, you can use a small brush to moisten the edges with a bit of water or lightly beaten egg white before you fold them closed.

Tortelli di zucca al burro
Pumpkin Tortelli with Butter

Servings 4
Difficulty Low
Prep Time 45'
Cook Time 3-4'

For the dough: 2 1/3 cups (300 g) all-purpose flour – 3 eggs.
For the filling: 2.2 lbs (1 kg) pumpkin – 5.3 oz (150 g) Parmigiano Reggiano cheese, grated (about 1 1/2 cups) – 1 egg – 1/2 cup (50 g) crushed *amaretti* cookies, about 8 cookies – 2 tbsp (40 g) Mostarda di Cremona – 2 tbsp breadcrumbs – nutmeg to taste – salt to taste.
For the topping: 5 1/2 tbsp (80 g) butter – 2.1 oz (60 g) Parmigiano Reggiano cheese, grated (about 2/3 cup).

Pour the flour onto a work surface and create a well in the center. Break the eggs into the well and carefully mix them into the flour until a smooth and consistent dough forms. Cover it in plastic wrap and let the dough sit for about 20 minutes before working with it.

Cut the pumpkin into large chunks, remove the seeds, and bake it at 350°F (180°C) for about 25 minutes. Once the pumpkin is tender, remove the skin and pass it through a food mill to create a purée.

Combine the pumpkin purée with the egg, Parmigiano Reggiano, a pinch of grated nutmeg, and a handful of salt. Mix it all together, adding 1-2 tablespoons of breadcrumbs to thicken the mixture if it isn't dense enough.

Using a pasta machine or rolling pin, flatten the dough into sheets just under 1/16 of an inch (1 mm). Drop small spoonfuls (about 1 teaspoon) of the pumpkin filling onto a sheet of pasta, about 3 inches (8 cm) apart. Lay another sheet of pasta on top and use a fluted pastry wheel to cut 2 1/2 inch (6 cm) squares around the filling. Use a fork to seal the tortelli edges well, so that no filling escapes while the pasta cooks.

Boil the tortelli in salted water and remove them with a perforated spoon. Transfer them to a heated pan and toss them with the melted butter and Parmigiano Reggiano.

Tortellini con besciamella
Tortellini in Béchamel Sauce

Servings 4
Difficulty High
Prep Time 2h
Cook Time 10-15'

For the pasta: 2 1/3 cups (300 g) Italian "00" flour – 3 eggs.

For the filling: 3.5 oz (100 g) mortadella – 3.5 oz (100 g) Parma prosciutto – 3.5 oz (100 g) pork loin – 4.2 oz (120 g) Parmigiano Reggiano cheese, very aged – 1 1/2 tbsp (20 g) butter (or ox marrow) – 1 egg – nutmeg – salt to taste.

For the béchamel sauce: 3/4 cup + 1 1/2 tbsp (200 ml) milk – 1 1/2 tbsp (20 g) butter – 2 tbsp (15 g) flour – nutmeg to taste – salt to taste.

For the ragù: 2 tbsp (30 ml) extra-virgin olive oil – 1 oz (30 g) celery (about 1 medium stalk) – 1.76 oz (50 g) carrots (about 1 small) – 2.1 oz (60 g) onion (about 1 small) – 0.7 oz (20 g) pancetta – 3.5 oz (100 g) ground pork – 4.2 oz (120 g) ground beef – 1.76 oz (50 g) chicken livers – 1/3 cup (80 ml) red wine – 3 1/2 tbsp (60 g) tomato paste – 2 cups (0.5 L) water – 1 bay leaf – salt and pepper to taste.

For the topping: 2/3 cup (60 g) Parmigiano Reggiano cheese, grated – black truffles to taste.

Mix the flour and egg until a smooth and consistent dough forms. Wrap it in plastic and refrigerate it for 30 minutes.

In the meantime, make the filling. Finely chop the meat and cold cuts, and combine them with the Parmigiano, egg, and softened butter. Season with salt to taste and a bit of grated nutmeg.

Roll the pasta into sheets, about 1/32 inch (1 mm) thick. Cut them into 1-inch (3 cm) squares and place about 1/2 teaspoon of filling in the center of each one. To shape the tortellini, fold each square over into a triangle and seal the edges. Fold the top corner down and curve the triangle around your little finger, bringing the other two corners together in the middle.

Clean and chop the onion, carrot, and celery. Drizzle some oil in a saucepan and sauté the vegetables with the bay leaf on medium heat. Then add the meat, chopped cold cuts, and livers (cleaned and diced). Turn up the heat so everything cooks thoroughly. Once the meat is browned, season with salt and pepper and add the red wine. Let it evaporate completely, then turn down the heat

and add the tomato paste. Add enough water to completely cover the contents of the pan and let it simmer for at least 30 minutes.

Preheat oven to 350° F (180° C).

Meanwhile make the béchamel. Melt the butter in a pot and add the flour, whisking continuously. Let it cook on low heat for 3-4 minutes. Slowly pour in the heated milk, and season with salt and grated nutmeg. Let the sauce cook until it's dense and creamy.

Boil the tortellini in salted water for 4-5 minutes. Strain them and transfer them to a buttered baking dish. Cover them with the ragù and béchamel sauces. Sprinkle grated Parmigiano on top.

Bake them for 10-15 minutes. When the surface is golden and bubbling, remove the tortellini from the oven and serve them with shaved truffles.

Filling Directions

Tortellini in brodo di cappone
Tortellini in Chicken Broth

Servings 4
Difficulty Medium
Prep Time
3h and 30'
Cook Time 5'

For the pasta: 2 1/3 cups (300 g) Italian "00" flour – 3 eggs.
For the filling: 0.22 lbs (100 g) mortadella – 0.22 lbs (100 g) prosciutto di Parma – 0.22 lbs (100 g) pork loin – 1 cup + 3 tbsp (120 g) Parmigiano Reggiano cheese, very aged – 1 1/2 tbsp (20 g) butter (or ox marrow) – 1 egg – nutmeg to taste – salt to taste.
For the broth: Half a chicken, about 3.3 lbs (1.5 kg) – 0.66 lbs (300 g) beef flank steak – 1.1 lbs (500 g) beef bones – 5.3 oz (150 g) onion (about 2 small) – 2.5 oz (70 g) celery (about 2 medium stalks) – 2.8 oz (80 g) carrots (about 1 1/2 small) – 1 bunch of parsley – 1 gallon + 5 cups (5 L) water – coarse salt to taste.

Mix the flour and eggs until a smooth and consistent dough forms. Wrap it in plastic and refrigerate it for 30 minutes.

Pour the water in to a large pot and add the whole vegetables, peeled and cleaned, with the parsley. Add the meat and bones (well rinsed). Remove any remaining feathers from the chicken, rinse it well, and add it to the pot.

Bring it to a boil and let it simmer, covered, for about 3 hours on low heat. Skim any foam that rises to the surface. Add a small handful of coarse salt about halfway through. When it's done, strain the broth with a fine mesh strainer and add more salt if necessary.

Then make the filling. Finely chop the cold cuts and mix them with the Parmigiano, egg, softened butter, and a pinch of salt and nutmeg.

Roll the pasta out into sheets about 1/32 inch (1 mm) thick and cut them into 1-inch (3 cm) squares. Place half a teaspoon of filling in the center of each square and fold them on the diagonal. Bring the corners together to shape the tortellini.

Boil the tortellini in the filtered broth and serve them hot.

FRESH PASTA

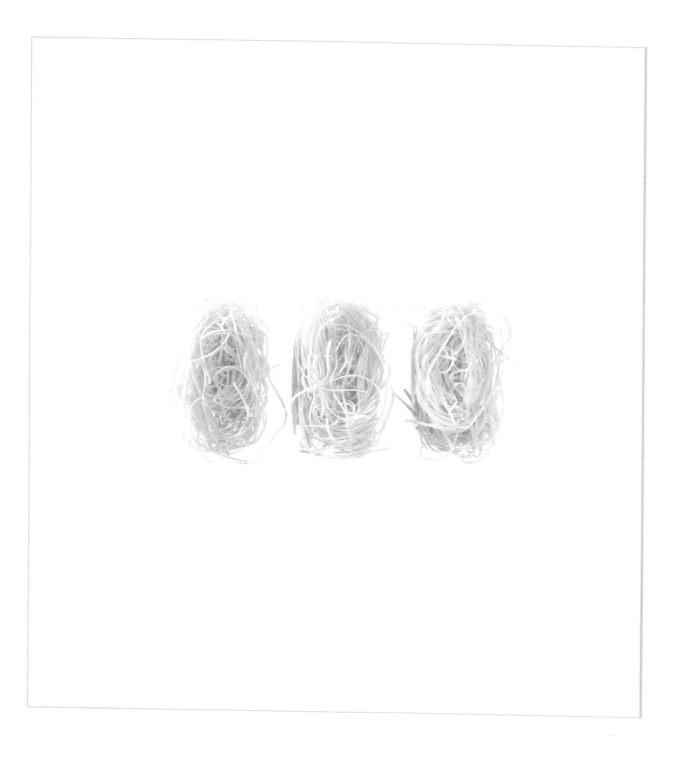

SINCE ANCIENT TIMES, DIFFERING CLIMACTIC CONDITIONS THROUGHOUT THE ITALIAN PENINSULA HAVE FAVORED THE CULTIVATION OF VARIOUS TYPES OF GRAINS. THESE DIFFERENCES HAVE HAD NOTABLE REPERCUSSIONS ON REGIONAL CULINARY TRADITIONS. SINCE DURUM WHEAT WAS MORE COMMON IN SOUTHERN ITALY, DRIED SEMOLINA PASTAS PREVAILED. COMMON WHEAT WAS MORE PREVALENT IN THE PO VALLEY AND NORTHERN ITALY, SO FRESH PASTA MADE FROM WHITE FLOUR AND EGGS BECAME THE NORM.

EGGS ARE ESSENTIAL BECAUSE THEY PROVIDE THE PROTEINS NECESSARY TO CONTAIN THE HIGH LEVELS OF STARCH IN THIS TYPE OF FLOUR. WITHOUT THEM, IT WOULD DISPERSE INTO THE WATER AND MAKE THE PASTA VERY STICKY. THE EGGS ALSO ARE ALSO RESPONSIBLE FOR A NOTICEABLE DIFFERENCE IN FLAVOR. THIS IS THEN PERFECTLY BALANCED, ON A PURELY GASTRONOMIC LEVEL, BY THE SAUCES.

THE FINE SKILL OF ROLLING OUT PASTA DOUGH WITH A ROLLING PIN, OR *CANNELLA*, WAS ONCE THE RESULT OF A LONG APPRENTICESHIP THAT BEGAN IN CHILDHOOD. BECAUSE OF THE IMPORTANCE ATTRIBUTED TO THIS ART, EGG-BASED PASTA DOUGH IS A SOURCE OF PRIDE IN REGIONAL ITALIAN TRADITIONS.

THIS DOUGH PRODUCES *TAGLIATELLE, FETTUCCINE, TAGLIOLINI,* AND *MAL-TAGLIATI,* ALL OF WHICH HAVE NAMES THAT INDICATE THE MODE OF PRODUCTION – CUTTING OR SLICING. THERE ARE ALSO *REGINETTE, PAPPARDELLE* AND *LASAGNETTE* – "FESTOONED" PASTAS CREATED WITH A *SPERONELLA,* OR PASTRY CUTTER. THEN THERE ARE THE SHAPES MADE FROM SMALL RECTANGLES, LIKE *FARFALLE,* WHICH ARE HAND-PINCHED IN THE CENTER AND THEREFORE ALSO KNOWN AS *STRICCHETTI* (FROM *STRINGERE,* "TO TIGHTEN").

EATEN ON SPECIAL OCCASIONS, FRESH PASTA IS A RICH FOOD THAT CALLS FOR A RICH SAUCE. AND THE RECIPES ARE INFINITE BECAUSE IT'S GOOD WITH MEATS, MUSHROOMS, VEGETABLES, CREAM OR TRUFFLES, WILD GAME, AND EVEN PAIRS WELL WITH MORE HUMBLE LEGUMES.

FINALLY, EGG AND FLOUR DOUGH IS ALSO USED FOR "GRATED" PASTAS. SIMPLE YET FULL OF TASTE, THEY'RE STILL FREQUENTLY SERVED IN BEEF BROTH THROUGHOUT ITALY.

Bigoli ai porcini
Bigoli with Goose Breast and Porcini Mushrooms

Servings 4
Difficulty *Medium*
Prep Time 40'
Cook Time 15'

For the pasta: 2 1/3 cups (300 g) all-purpose flour – 3 eggs.
For the topping: 0.55 lbs (250 g) goose breast, deboned – 3 tbsp (40 g) butter – 1 lb (450 g) fresh porcini mushrooms – 1 onion – 1 tbsp minced parsley – 2 tbsp (30 ml) extra-virgin olive oil – 1 garlic clove – grated zest of 1 orange – salt – pepper – 1/3 cup + 1 tbsp (40 g) Parmigiano Reggiano cheese, grated.

Pour the flour onto a work surface and create a well in the center. Break the eggs and drop them into the well. Start working them into the flour with a fork, then use your fingers and palms to continue working the dough until it's smooth and consistent. Wrap it in plastic and let it sit for about 20 minutes.

To make the bigoli, pass the dough through a pasta machine on the appropriate setting or through a meat grinder with 1/8-inch (3-4 mm) holes.

Clean and rinse the mushrooms, then cut them into thick slices. Separately mince the garlic and onion and sauté them in a bit of oil. Add the mushrooms and let them cook over medium heat, adding a bit of water if they get too dry. Season with salt and pepper to taste.

Remove all the skin from the goose breast. Use a very sharp knife to cut it lengthwise into strips, then crosswise into cubes. Heat the butter in a deep pot. When it starts to foam, add the diced goose. Let it cook until all the liquid has evaporated and the meat is golden brown. Season generously with salt and pepper.

Meanwhile heat a large amount of water in a pot. When it reaches a boil, add a handful of coarse salt along with the pasta. When the pasta is done, strain it and combine it with the goose and mushrooms. Let everything cook together for a few seconds, mixing well. Add the Parmigiano, parsley, and grated orange zest. Serve the bigoli very hot.

Bigoli in salsa
Bigoli with Anchovy Sauce

Servings 4
Difficulty *Low*
Prep Time 35'
Cook Time 10'

For the pasta: 2 1/3 cups (300 g) all-purpose flour – 3 eggs.
For the topping: 1 medium onion (or 2-3 garlic cloves) – 3.5 oz (100 g) anchovies, packed in salt – 1/4 cup + 2 tsp (70 ml) extra-virgin olive oil – salt and pepper to taste.

Pour the flour onto a work surface and create a well in the center. Break the eggs into the well and start to incorporate them into the flour with a fork. Then use your fingers and palms to continue mixing until a smooth, consistent dough forms. Wrap it in plastic and let it rest for about 20 minutes.

To make the bigoli, pass the dough through a pasta machine on the appropriate setting or through a meat grinder with 1/8 inch (3-4 mm) holes.

Rinse the salt-packed anchovies well and remove the innards and bones. Peel and *julienne* the onion. Pour half the oil into a large pan on low heat and sauté the onion. When it starts to turn golden brown, add the anchovies. Half a minute later add 3-4 tablespoons of water and let it simmer until the fish dissolves.

Boil the bigoli in a large pot of salted water. When they're *al dente*, strain them and toss them in the pan with the sauce, letting everything cook together for another 1-2 minutes (this type of pasta maintains its consistency well). Add a few tablespoons of water if it gets too dry.

For a stronger, more intense flavor, replace the onion with 2-3 well-crushed garlic cloves.

Cavatielli con cozze e patate
Cavatielli with Mussels and Potatoes

Servings 4
Difficulty Low
Prep Time 1h
Cook Time 3-4'

For the pasta: 1 3/4 cups (300 g) re-milled durum wheat semolina – 2/3 cup (150 ml) water.
For the sauce: 1.1 lbs (500 g) mussels – 0.8 lbs (360 g) tomatoes, very ripe (about 3 medium tomatoes) – 0.44 lbs (200 g) potatoes (about 1 medium potato) – 3 1/2 tbsp (50 ml) extra-virgin olive oil – 1 tbsp minced parsley – hot red pepper (fresh or dried) to taste – 1 garlic clove – salt to taste.

Mix the semolina and warm water until the dough is smooth and elastic. Wrap it in plastic and refrigerate it for 15 minutes.

Form long cylinders as thick as your finger and cut them into 1/3-1/2 inch (1 cm) pieces. Use a knife with a rounded tip to roll the pieces back and forth on the work surface, pressing down gently in the middle so the edges curl up.

Scrape the mussels clean and rinse them thoroughly. Peel the tomatoes, remove the seeds, and dice them.

Heat 2/3 of the oil in a pan with the whole garlic clove and hot red pepper (dry or fresh) to taste, being careful not to toast them. Add the mussels and let them cook. When they open, add the tomatoes and half the parsley. Season with salt and let it all cook for 5 more minutes. Remove the garlic clove and some of the shells.

Dice the potato and boil it in salted water with the cavatelli. Strain them both when the pasta is *al dente* and combine them with the mussel sauce. Mix some cold-pressed olive oil with minced parsley and drizzle it on top.

Cavatielli con ricotta dura
Cavatielli with Tomatoes and Hard Ricotta

Servings 4
Difficulty *Low*
Prep Time *1h*
Cook Time *5-6'*

For the pasta: 1 3/4 cups (300 g) re-milled durum wheat semolina – 2/3 cup (150 ml) water.
For the sauce: 2.2 lbs (1 kg) tomatoes (about 5-6 large) – 5.3 oz (150 g) aged ricotta – 3 1/2 tbsp (50 ml) extra-virgin olive oil – 1 garlic clove – 1 bunch of basil – salt – pepper.

Let the water warm up to room temperature and mix it with the flour in a large bowl. When the dough is smooth and elastic, wrap it in plastic and refrigerate it for 15 minutes.
Shape the dough into long cylinders as thick as your finger and cut them into 1/3-1/2 inch (1 cm) pieces. Use a knife with a rounded tip to roll the pieces back and forth on the work surface, pressing down gently in the middle so the edges curl up.
Wash the tomatoes, remove the seeds, and dice them.
Heat the oil in a pan over medium heat. Add the whole garlic clove and be careful not to let it overcook. Add the tomatoes, season with a pinch of salt and pepper, and let it cook for 15 minutes. Then add the basil leaves (hand-torn) and let it cook for a few more minutes. Remember to remove the garlic clove at the end.
Meanwhile heat a large amount of water in a pot. When it reaches a boil, add a handful of coarse salt along with the cavatielli. Strain the pasta after 5-6 minutes and combine it with the tomato sauce. Sprinkle it with grated ricotta and drizzle cold-pressed olive oil on top.

Chef's tips
A traditional wooden cutting board is the ideal surface for making this kind of pasta. The dough won't slide around, making it easier to give the cavatielli their characteristic shape.

Crema di piselli con tagliolini
Black Tagliolini with Creamy Pea Sauce

Servings 4
*Difficulty **Medium***
Prep Time
1h and 30'
Cook Time 4'

For the pasta dough: 2 2/3 cups (330 g) Italian "00" flour – 0.5 oz (15 g) cuttlefish ink – 3 eggs.

For the sauce: 4 1/4 cups (1 L) vegetable broth – 14 oz (400 g) peas, fresh or frozen – 1 1/2 tbsp (20 ml) extra-virgin olive oil – 2 oz (60 g) onion (about half a medium onion) – 1.4 oz (40 g) celery (about 1 medium stalk) – 3 cups + 3 tbsp (750 ml) water – salt and pepper to taste

For the topping: 10.5 oz (300 g) cherry tomatoes (about 18) – 8.8 oz (250 g) cuttlefish – 3.2 oz (90 g) onion (about 1 medium onion) – 8 basil leaves – 1 tbsp minced parsley – 1 garlic clove – dry white wine to taste – salt to taste – pepper to taste.

Pour the flour onto a work surface and create a well in the center. Break the eggs and pour them into the well, then add the cuttlefish ink. Mix it all into the flour, working the dough until it's smooth and consistent. Wrap it in plastic and let it sit for 30 minutes.

Meanwhile clean and rinse the cuttlefish, then clean the onion and celery. Julienne the cuttlefish along with the vegetables.

Quarter the tomatoes and cut the basil into strips. Mince the garlic and parsley separately.

Place a small *rondeau* (a low terracotta casserole) over low heat and add 1 1/2 tablespoons (20 ml) of olive oil, half the onion, the basil, and the garlic. Let everything cook together and soften, then add the cuttlefish. After three minutes add 1/4 cup + 2 teaspoons (70 ml) of wine. When the liquid has been completely absorbed, add the tomatoes and season with salt and pepper. Cook for another 10 minutes on low heat.

Drizzle some oil in a separate pan and briefly sauté the celery with the rest of the onion on medium heat. Add enough water to cover everything (about 3 cups/750 ml) and let it come to a boil, then add the peas. When the peas are tender, pureé the contents of the pan and season with salt to taste.

For the tagliolini, use a pasta machine or rolling pin to roll the dough out to a thickness of just under 1/16 inch (1.5 mm). Cut the sheets of pasta into strips 1/16-inch (2 mm) wide.

Boil the pasta in salted water. Strain it when it's *al dente* and toss it with the cuttlefish sauce and minced parsley. For serving, place a ladleful of creamy pea sauce in each bowl and arrange the tagliolini in the middle, forming a small "nest".

Fettuccine al mascarpone
Fettuccine with Mascarpone

Servings 4
Difficulty *Low*
Prep Time 35'
Cook Time 3-4'

For the pasta: 2 1/3 cups (300 g) Italian "00" flour – 3 eggs.
For the topping: 7 oz (200 g) mascarpone – 2.8 oz (80 g) ham – 1 egg yolk – 1/2 cup (50 g) Parmigiano Reggiano cheese, grated.

Mix the flour and eggs until a smooth, consistent dough forms. Wrap it in plastic and refrigerate it for 30 minutes.

Put the mascarpone in a large bowl and add a few spoonfuls of hot water to soften it. Then use a wooden spoon to stir in the egg yolk until it's smooth and creamy. Cut the ham into short, thin strips and add it to the mascarpone along with half the grated Parmigiano.

Remove the dough from the refrigerator and use a rolling pin or pasta machine to flatten the dough into sheets about 1/32 inch (1 mm) thick. Cut the sheets into strips about 1/4 inch (6 mm) wide, laying out the finished fettuccine on a lightly floured surface.

Boil the pasta in a large pot of lightly salted water. When it's *al dente*, strain it and transfer it to the bowl with the mascarpone. Mix well to thoroughly combine the pasta and sauce. Serve it immediately in heated plates and top it with the remaining Parmigiano.

Fettuccine al ragù d'anatra
Fettuccine with Duck Ragù

Servings 4
*Difficulty **Medium***
Prep Time
1h and 10'
Cook Time 3-4'

For the pasta: 2 1/3 cups (300 g) Italian "00" flour – 3 eggs.
For the topping: 10.5 oz (300 g) crushed tomatoes – 1 (1.76 oz/50 g) slice of prosciutto di Parma – 0.55 lbs (250 g) duck breast – 2.8 oz (80 g) onion (about 1 small onion) – 1.76 oz (50 g) carrots (about 1 small carrot) – 1 oz (30 g) celery (about 2 medium stalks) – 1/3 cup + 1 1/2 tbsp (100 ml) extra-virgin olive oil – 2/3 cup (150 ml) red wine – 1 garlic clove – a few sage leaves – 1 sprig of rosemary – salt and pepper to taste – beef broth as needed.

Mix the flour and eggs until a smooth, consistent dough forms. Wrap it in plastic and refrigerate it for 30 minutes.

In the meantime, pour half the oil into a saucepan and sauté the whole garlic clove with the chopped onion, carrot, and celery. Add the ham (cut into strips), sage, and rosemary. Use a separate pan to brown the finely chopped duck breast in the rest of the oil, then add it to the vegetables. Pour in the red wine and cook everything together on high heat until all the liquid is absorbed. Add the tomatoes and season with salt and pepper to taste. Cook the sauce for about another 30 minutes, adding a bit of broth if it gets too dry.

Take the dough out and use a pasta machine or rolling pin to flatten it into 1/32-inch (1 mm) sheets. Then cut them into 1/4-inch (6 mm) strips. Lay the fettuccine out on a lightly floured surface.

Boil the pasta in salted water. Strain it and mix it with the duck ragù.

Fettuccine alla boscaiola
Fettuccine alla Boscaiola

Servings 4
Difficulty Low
Prep Time 1h
Cook Time 3-4'

For the pasta: 2 1/3 cups (300 g) Italian "00" flour – 3 eggs.
For the topping: 14 oz (400 g) fresh porcini mushrooms – 3 1/2 tbsp (50 ml) extra-virgin olive oil – 1 garlic clove – 1 tbsp minced parsley – salt and pepper to taste – 1/3 cup + 1 tbsp (40 g) Parmigiano Reggiano cheese, grated (optional).

Mix the flour and eggs until a smooth and consistent dough forms. Wrap it in plastic and refrigerate it for 30 minutes.

Carefully clean the mushrooms with a damp cloth, removing any dirt. Cut them into 1/32-1/16 inch (1-2 mm) slices. Mince the garlic and sauté it in the oil, then add the mushrooms and cook them on high heat. Add the minced parsley and season with salt and pepper. Continue to cook for another few minutes, but don't let the mushrooms get too soft.

Take the dough out of the refrigerator and use a pasta machine or rolling pin to roll out 1/32-inch (1 mm) sheets. Cut them into 1/4-inch (6 mm) strips and lay the fettuccine out on a lightly floured surface.

Boil the pasta in salted water and strain it when it's *al dente*. Mix it with the mushroom sauce and top it with Parmigiano to taste.

Fettuccine con la ricotta
Fettuccine with Ricotta

Servings 4
Difficulty Low
Prep Time 50'
Cook Time 5'

For the pasta: 2 1/3 cups (300 g) all-purpose flour – 3 eggs.
For the topping: 14 oz (400 g) fresh ricotta – 1 1/2 tbsp (20 ml) extra-virgin olive oil – salt and pepper (freshly ground) to taste.

Mix the eggs and flour until a smooth and consistent dough forms. Cover it with a cloth and let it sit for 30 minutes. Use a rolling pin or pasta machine to roll the dough out to a thickness of 1/16 inch (1.5 mm). Fold it over on itself several times and cut it into 1/4 inch (6 mm) wide strips. Lay the fettuccine out on a lightly floured surface (don't let them overlap too much) and let them dry. Boil the fettuccine in lightly salted water. While the pasta cooks, sift the ricotta into a large bowl. Mix it with the olive oil and 1/4 cup + 1 tablespoon (70 ml) of pasta water, and season with ground pepper to taste. Strain the pasta when it's *al dente* and combine it with the ricotta. Mix well and serve immediately.

Chef's tips
You can enhance the ricotta sauce with a handful of grated Pecorino or Parmigiano and replace the black pepper with hot red pepper.

Fettuccine con panna, rafano e limone
Fettuccine with Lemon, Cream and Horseradish

Servings 4
Difficulty Low
Prep Time 50'
Cook Time 5'

For the pasta: 2 1/3 cups (300 g) all-purpose flour – 3 eggs.
For the topping: 3/4 cup + 1 1/2 tbsp (200 ml) heavy cream – 1 tsp grated horse-radish – zest of half a lemon – 1 ladleful of beef broth – 0.009 oz (0.25 g) saffron (about 1/3 tsp) – salt and pepper to taste.

Mix the flour and eggs until a smooth and consistent dough forms. Cover it with a cloth and let it sit for 30 minutes. Use a rolling pin or pasta machine to roll out sheets of dough just under 1/16 inch (1.5 mm) thick. Fold each sheet over onto itself several times and cut it into 1/4 inch (6 mm) wide strips. Lay the fettuccine out on a floured surface to dry, being careful not to let them overlap too much. Peel and finely grate the horseradish. Combine 2/3 of the lemon zest with the broth and heavy cream in a large pot. Bring the mixture to a boil, stirring continuously. Turn down the heat and let the sauce thicken, then season with salt and pepper.
Boil the fettuccine and strain them when they're still *al dente*. Transfer them to the pot with the cream sauce. Dissolve the saffron in 2 tablespoons of pasta water, then add it to the pot.
Cook everything together on high heat, mixing well. Add the horseradish and remaining lemon zest at the very end.

Fettuccine con salsa al Grana Padano
Fettuccine with Grana Padano Sauce

Servings 4
Difficulty Low
Prep Time 50'
Cook Time 5'

For the pasta: 2 1/3 cups (300 g) all-purpose flour – 3 eggs.
For the topping: 1 1/2 cups (150 g) Grana Padano cheese, grated – 4 tsp (10 g) flour – 1 2/3 cups (400 ml) milk – 8 sage leaves – 2/3 tbsp (10 g) butter – nutmeg to taste – salt to taste.

Mix the eggs and flour until a smooth and consistent dough forms. Cover it with a cloth and let it sit for 30 minutes. Use a rolling pin or pasta machine to roll the dough out to about 1/32-1/16 inch (1.5 mm) thick. Fold it over several times and slice it into strips about 1/4 inch (6 mm) wide. Lay the fettuccine on a lightly floured surface to dry, being careful not to let them overlap too much.

Toast the flour in a saucepan for a few seconds. Then slowly add half the milk, whisking continuously to avoid lumps. Let the sauce thicken over low heat, stirring continuously and slowly adding the rest of the milk. As soon as it reaches the consistency of heavy cream, add a pinch of salt and nutmeg. Then stir in the grated cheese.

Mix well and let it cook for another few minutes before turning off the heat. The sauce should be relatively thin.

Boil the fettuccine in salted water. Strain them when they're *al dente* and add them to the pan of sauce. Add 1/4 cup + 1 tablespoon (70 ml) of pasta water, a few flakes of softened butter, and the sage leaves. Mix well, letting everything cook together for 1-2 minutes, and serve.

Garganelli "al nero" alla cervese
Black Garganelli alla Cervese

Servings 4
Difficulty *Medium*
Prep Time *1h*
Cook Time 5'

For the pasta: 2 2/3 cups (330 g) Italian "00" flour – 0.5 oz (15 g) cuttlefish ink – 3 eggs.
For the topping: 1.1 lbs (500 g) cuttlefish – tbsp tomato paste – 1/3 cup + 1 1/2 tbsp (100 ml) extra-virgin olive oil – 1/3 cup + 1 1/2 tbsp (100 ml) dry white wine – 2 tbsp (30 ml) wine vinegar – 1 garlic clove – 1 onion – 1 tbsp minced parsley – 2 basil leaves – salt and pepper to taste – water as needed.

Pour the flour onto a work surface and create a well in the center. Break the eggs and drop them into the well, add the cuttlefish ink, and mix until the dough is smooth and consistent in color and consistency. Wrap it in plastic and let it sit for 30 minutes.

Clean and rinse the cuttlefish, and chop it very finely with a knife (or put it through a meat grinder). Mince the garlic and onion separately. Heat 2/3 of the oil in a saucepan on medium heat. When the oil is hot, add the onion, garlic, and basil (torn up by hand). As soon as the onion begins to soften, add the cuttlefish and let it brown. Then add the tomato paste and season with salt and pepper to taste. Pour in the white wine and wait for all the liquid evaporate, then add 1/2 cup + 1 1/2 tablespoons (140 ml) of water and let it cook for another 10-15 minutes.

Take the dough out of the refrigerator and use a rolling pin or pasta machine to roll out very thin sheets. Cut the sheets into 1-inch (2.5 cm) squares. Starting from one corner, roll each square around a cylindrical stick (no wider than a pencil) and then over a weaving comb. Arrange the finished garganelli on a lightly floured cardboard tray.

Boil the pasta in salted water and strain it when it's *al dente*. Combine it with the sauce and top it with minced parsley and a drizzle of cold-pressed olive oil.

Garganelli al prezzemolo con ragù di branzino
Parsley Garganelli with Sea Bass Ragù

Servings 4
Difficulty Medium
Prep Time 1h
Cook Time 12'

For the pasta: 2 1/3 cups (300 g) Italian "00" flour – 3 eggs – 1 tbsp minced parsley.
For the ragù: 1 sea bass (about 2.2 lbs/1 kg) – 8.8 oz (250 g) red bell pepper (about 2 medium) – 7 oz (200 g) spring onions (about 13 medium) – 1 garlic clove – 1/3 cup + 1 1/2 tbsp (100 ml) white wine – 3 1/2 tbsp (50 ml) extra-virgin olive oil – salt and pepper to taste.

Pour the flour onto a work surface and create a well in the center. Break the eggs and pour them into the well. Add the parsley and mix it all together until a smooth and consistent dough forms. Wrap it in plastic and refrigerate it for 30 minutes.

Clean, skin, fillet, rinse, and dice the sea bass.

Clean the bell peppers and dice them. Clean the spring onions and slice them very thinly.

Heat the oil in a pan. Add the spring onions and whole garlic clove, letting them cook for 2-3 minutes. Then add the sea bass and peppers. Let everything brown together for another couple of minutes. Season with salt and pepper and add the white wine. Let it evaporate, remove the garlic, and keep the sauce warm.

Take the dough from the refrigerator and use a rolling pin or pasta machine to flatten it into sheets, each 1/32 inch (1 mm) thick. Cut the sheets into 1-inch (2.5 cm) squares. Starting from one corner, roll each square around a thin stick (no larger than a pencil) and then over a weaving comb. Arrange the resulting garganelli on a lightly floured paper or cardboard surface.

Boil the pasta in salted water. Strain it when it's *al dente* and combine it with the sea bass and pepper ragù.

Garganelli con salsiccia, piselli e peperoni
Garganelli with Sausage, Peas, and Peppers

Servings 4
Difficulty *Low*
Prep Time *40'*
Cook Time *5'*

For the pasta: 2 1/3 cups (300 g) all-purpose flour – 3 eggs – Alternatively: 12.3 oz (350 g) egg garganelli, already made.
For the topping: 0.44 lbs (200 g) fresh sausage – 3.5 oz (100 g) peas, fresh or frozen (about 2/3 cup) – 10.5 oz (300 g) crushed tomatoes – 1 bell pepper, diced – 2 tbsp (30 g) butter – 1/2 cup (50 g) Parmigiano Reggiano cheese, grated – salt – pepper.

Pour the flour into a bowl or onto a work surface and create a well in the center. Break the eggs and pour them into the well. Mix until the dough is smooth and consistent. Wrap it in plastic and refrigerate it for 30 minutes.

Heat the butter in a pan over low heat. Once it's melted, add the sausage (removed from the casing and broken up) and let it brown. Add the diced pepper, followed by the crushed tomatoes. Season with salt and pepper and let the sauce cook on low heat for 20 minutes. Then take it off the stove, but keep it warm.

Take the dough out of the refrigerator and use a rolling pin or pasta machine to roll it out into very thin sheets. Cut the sheets into 1-inch (2.5 cm) squares. Starting from one corner, roll each square around a thin stick (no larger than a pencil) and then over a weaving comb. Arrange the resulting garganelli on a lightly floured paper or cardboard surface.

Boil the peas and pasta together in salted water. When the pasta is *al dente*, strain them both thoroughly and combine them with the sauce in a large serving bowl. Stir in the grated Parmigiano and serve immediately.

Lasagne al papavero
Poppy Seed Lasagna

Servings 4
Difficulty Low
Prep Time 40'
Cook Time 2-3'

For the pasta: 2 1/3 cups (300 g) Italian "00" flour – 3 eggs.
For the topping: 5 1/2 tbsp (80 g) butter – 2 1/2 tbsp (30 g) sugar – 3 1/2 tbsp (30 g) poppy seed.

Pour the flour onto a work surface and create a well in the center. Work in the eggs until a smooth and consistent dough forms. Wrap it in plastic and let it rest for 20 minutes. Use a pasta machine to flatten it to a thickness of about 1/32 inch (1 mm) and cut it into 1-1 1/2 inch (3-4 cm) wide strips.
Grind the poppy seed and sugar together. Melt the butter in a small nonstick pot, add the ground sugar and poppy seed, and let it all brown.
Boil the pasta in salted water, strain it when it's *al dente*, and combine it with the seasoned butter.

Interesting fact
This recipe for lasagna with poppy seed, sugar, and butter reflects the influence of Austrian, Hungarian, Jewish, Slavic, and East Asian cuisine on that of Trieste.

Maccheroni "al pettine"
"Comb" Macaroni with Culatello, Gorgonzola, and Arugula

Servings 4
Difficulty Medium
Prep Time 45'
Cook Time 5'

For the pasta: 2 1/3 cups (300 g) Italian "00" flour – 3 eggs.
For the topping: 5.3 oz (150 g) sliced Culatello (a variety of prosciutto) – 2.8 oz (80 g) arugula (4 cups) – 3.5 oz (100 g) Gorgonzola cheese – 1/3 cup + 1 tbsp (40 g) Parmigiano Reggiano cheese, grated – salt and pepper to taste.

Pour the flour onto a work surface and create a well in the center. Break the eggs and drop them into the well. Mix them together until the dough is smooth and consistent. Wrap it in plastic and let it sit for 30 minutes.

Cut the Culatello into strips, 3/4-1 inch (2-3 cm) wide. Dry sauté it in a nonstick pan until it's crispy.

Dice the Gorgonzola and melt it in a pot over low heat. Add a bit of water, Parmigiano, and roughly chopped arugula. Season with salt and pepper to taste.

Take the dough out of the refrigerator and use a rolling pin or pasta machine to roll it out to a thickness of 1/32 inch (1 mm). Cut it into 1-inch (2.5 cm) squares. Starting from one corner, wrap each square around a thin cylinder, no bigger than a pencil, and roll it over a weaving comb.

Arrange the "comb" macaroni on a lightly floured cardboard tray.

Boil the macaroni in salted water. Strain it when it's *al dente* and combine it with the Gorgonzola sauce. Top each serving with crispy Culatello.

Maltagliati "al nero"
Black Maltagliati with Seafood, Turnip Greens, and Cured Fish Roe

Servings 4
Difficulty Medium
Prep Time 40'
Cook Time 4-5'

For the pasta: 2 2/3 cups (330 g) Italian "00" flour – 0.5 oz (15 g) cutttlefish ink – 3 eggs.
For the topping: 1.4 oz (40 g) mullet roe – 0.66 lbs (300 g) mussels – 0.66 lbs (300 g) carpet shell clams – 0.66 lbs (300 g) turnip greens (about 5 cups) – 1 "cluster" tomato – 3 tbsp (40 ml) extra-virgin olive oil – salt and pepper to taste.

Pour the flour onto a work surface and create a well in the center. Break the eggs and pour them into the center. Add the cuttlefish ink and mix it all together until the dough is smooth and consistent in color and consistency. Wrap it in plastic and refrigerate it for 30 minutes.

Scrape the mussels well and rinse them several times along with the clams to remove any impurities. Cook them both in a saucepan over high heat until they open. Remove the shells and filter the liquid from the pan. Blanch the tomatoes, remove the skin and seeds, and dice them. Clean the turnip greens and roughly chop them.

Drizzle some extra-virgin olive oil in a pan and place it over medium heat. Add the tomatoes, clams, and mussels. Let them cook together for 4-5 minutes.

Take the dough out of the refrigerator. Use a rolling pin or pasta machine to roll it out into sheets about 1/32 inch (1 mm) thick. Let it dry for a few minutes, then cut it into diamonds. Lay the maltagliati out on a lightly floured tray or work surface.

Heat a large pot of water. When it reaches a boil, add a handful of coarse salt and immerse the turnip greens. As soon as the water returns to a boil, add the pasta. Strain them both when the pasta is *al dente*. Add them to the pan of seafood sauce and let everything cook together for a minute.

Top each serving with mullet roe, very thinly sliced. Drizzle with cold-pressed olive oil to taste.

Maltagliati al sugo di carciofi
Maltagliati in Artichoke Sauce

Servings 4
Difficulty Low
Prep Time 45'
Cook Time 4-5'

For the pasta: 2 1/3 cups (300 g) all-purpose flour – 2/3 cup (150 ml) water.
For the topping: 4 artichokes, about 0.33–0.44 lbs (150-200 g) each – 1 tbsp minced parsley – 3 1/2 tbsp (50 ml) dry white wine – 3 1/2 tbsp (50 ml) vegetable broth – 2/3 cup (60 g) Parmigiano Reggiano cheese, grated – 3 tbsp (40 ml) extra-virgin olive oil – 1 garlic clove – salt and pepper to taste.

Mix the flour and eggs until the dough is smooth and consistent. Cover it with a cloth and let it sit for 30 minutes. Roll it out until it's very thin and fold it over on itself several times. Cut it into irregular diamonds. Lay the maltagliati out on a lightly floured surface, being careful not to let them overlap too much.

Clean the artichokes and slice them, not too thinly. Cook them in a skillet with the oil, garlic, minced parsley, and salt and pepper to taste. Add the white wine and let it evaporate completely. Then add a bit of broth and let the artichokes finish cooking (it should take about 10 minutes).

Boil the pasta in salted water and strain it when it's *al dente*. Combine it with the artichokes and grated Parmigiano, and serve it hot.

Maltagliati alle erbe
Herbed Maltagliati with Green Tomato, Robiola, and Hazelnut Pesto

Servings 4
Difficulty Medium
Prep Time 50'
Cook Time 5'

For the pasta: 2 1/3 cups (300 g) Italian "00" flour – 3 eggs – 1.76 oz (50 g) fresh mixed herbs, minced (marjoram, thyme, rosemary, chives), about 1 cup.
For the pesto: 0.8 lbs (360 g) green tomatoes (about 3 medium) – 1.76 oz (50 g) hazelnuts, toasted and crushed (about 1/2 cup) – 1/2 cup (50 g) Pecorino cheese, grated – 1 garlic clove – 3 1/2 tbsp (50 ml) extra-virgin olive oil – salt and pepper to taste.
For the Cream Sauce: 3.5 oz (100 g) fresh Robiola cheese – 1/3 cup + 1 1/2 tbsp (100 ml) milk.

Wash the herbs, carefully dry them with paper towels, and mince them.

Mix the flour, eggs, and herbs until a smooth and consistent dough forms. Cover it with a cloth and let it sit for 30 minutes. Roll it out to 1/32 inch (1 mm) thick and fold it over on itself several times. Cut it into irregular diamonds. Lay the maltagliati out to dry on a lightly floured surface, being careful not to let them overlap too much.

Combine the Robiola and milk in a food processor and blend until the mixture is soft and creamy. Wash the tomatoes, cut them into quarters, and remove the seeds. Combine all the pesto ingredients in a deep container and roughly blend them with an immersion blender.

Boil the pasta in salted water and strain it when it's *al dente*. Mix it with the pesto and serve it with the Robiola sauce.

Chef's tips
While making the pesto, use the pulse setting so that the sauce doesn't overheat. This will result in a nicer color and a better flavor. It's also a good idea to freeze the container for 10 minutes before using it with immersion blender.

Pasta Directions

Cream and Pesto Directions

Maltagliati romagnoli
Maltagliati Romagnoli

Servings 4
Difficulty Low
Prep Time 40'
Cook Time 4-5'

For the pasta: 1 2/3 cups (200 g) Italian "00" flour – 2 eggs – 1/3 cup + 1 tbsp (40 g) Parmigiano Reggiano cheese, grated – zest of 1 lemon – nutmeg to taste.
For the topping: 1.1 lbs (500 g) spinach – 21 oz (600 g) tomato purée – 5.3 oz (150 g) onion (about 1 cup chopped) – 2.8 oz (80 g) carrots (about 2/3 cup chopped) – 2.5 oz (70 g) celery (about 2/3 cup chopped) – 4 1/4 cups (1 L) beef broth – 1/2 tbsp (50 ml) extra-virgin olive oil – salt to taste.

To make this pasta combine the flour, eggs, cheese, lemon zest, and a pinch of salt and nutmeg. Mix them together until a dense and consistent dough forms. If it's too dry, add a few drops of water. Cover the dough with a cloth and let it sit for about 30 minutes. Roll it out to a thickness of 1/32 inch (1 mm) and cut it into diamonds, which will become the *maltagliati*.

Chop up the onion, celery, and carrot. Sauté them in the olive oil, then add the tomato purée and let it cook for 15-20 minutes. Add the raw spinach (washed and finely chopped) and let it cook for another 15 minutes.

Boil the *maltagliati* in the broth. As soon as they float to the surface, add the spinach sauce to the pot. Season with salt to taste and serve immediately.

Chef's tips
Grate the lemon zest, rich in essential oil (contained in the oleiferous glands), but be careful not to grate the pith (the white part, which is bitter and inedible). Use only untreated lemons and wash them well before grating.

Orecchiette con cavolfiore
Orecchiette with Cauliflower

Servings 4
Difficulty *Low*
Prep Time 10'
Cook Time 3-4'

For the pasta: 1 3/4 cups (300 g) re-milled durum wheat semolina – 2/3 cup (150 ml) hot water.
For the sauce: 0.88 lbs (400 g) tomatoes (about 3 medium tomatoes) – 1.3 lbs (600 g) cauliflower – 3.5 oz (100 g) cacioricotta cheese – 3 1/2 tbsp (50 ml) extra-virgin olive oil – 1 garlic clove – salt and pepper to taste.

Mix the flour with enough hot water to form a smooth and elastic dough. Wrap the dough in plastic and refrigerate it for at least 15 minutes.

Shape the dough into long ropes as thick as your finger and cut them crosswise into pieces about 3/4 inch (2 cm) long. Use the rounded tip of a butter knife to slide them over the work surface. Then use your thumb to create a depression in the center of each one, creating the typical concave orecchiette shape.

Clean the cauliflower and divide it into florets. Wash them and boil them in lightly salted water. Peel the tomatoes, remove the seeds, and finely chop them. Meanwhile sauté the whole garlic clove in the oil. When it's a nice golden brown, add the tomatoes. Season generously with salt and pepper and let it cook for 10 minutes on high heat. If necessary, add some of the water from the cauliflower.

When the cauliflower is almost cooked, add the orecchiette and let them boil together for about 3-4 minutes. Then strain them and combine them both with the tomato sauce. Serve with lots of grated cacioricotta.

Orecchiette con cavolo romano
Orecchiette with Romanesco Cabbage and Scampi Tails

Servings 4
Difficulty Low
Prep Time 25'
Cook Time 12'

For the pasta: 1 1/2 cups (250 g) re-milled durum wheat semolina – 1/2 cup (125 ml) warm water.

For the topping: 12 scampi tails – 0.66 lbs (300 g) Romanesco cabbage – 2 oil-packed anchovy fillets – 1 hot red pepper – 1 garlic clove – 3 tbsp (40 ml) extra-virgin olive oil – salt to taste – ground pepper to taste.

Mix the semolina and water until a smooth, consistent dough forms. Cover it with plastic wrap and let it sit for at least 15 minutes. Form long cylindrical strips about as thick as your finger, and slice them crosswise into 1/3-1/2 inch (1 cm) pieces. Use the rounded tip of a butter knife to drag them over the work surface. Then use your thumb to create a depression in the center of each one.

Clean the cabbage and cut it into florets. Remove the scampi heads and peel off the shells, leaving only the very tip attached.

Sauté the garlic (unpeeled), whole hot pepper, and anchovy fillets in a wide, shallow pan with 3 tablespoons of olive oil. Add 3-4 tablespoons of water, and when the anchovies have dissolved, turn off the heat.

Meanwhile, heat the water for the orecchiette. When it reaches a boil, add the pasta with a handful of coarse salt. When the pasta is about halfway done, add the Romanesco cabbage florets.

A couple of minutes before the orecchiette are ready, brown the scampi tails in 1 tablespoon of olive oil on high heat. Once they're cooked, add salt to taste and turn off the heat.

Strain the pasta and florets (preferably with a very fine strainer that will catch all the cabbage remnants), and toss them with the anchovy mixture. Season with freshly ground pepper and garnish with scampi tails.

Orecchiette con cime di rapa
Orecchiette with Turnip Greens

Servings 4
Difficulty Low
Prep Time 45'
Cook Time 5-6'

For the pasta: 1 1/2 cups (250 g) re-milled durum wheat semolina – 1/2 cup (125 ml) warm water.
For the topping: 0.66 lbs (300 g) turnip greens, cleaned – 2 oil-packed anchovies – 1 hot red pepper – 1 garlic clove, thinly sliced – 4 tbsp (60 ml) extra-virgin olive oil – salt to taste – ground pepper to taste.

Mix the semolina and water until a smooth, consistent dough forms. Cover it with plastic wrap and let it sit for at least 15 minutes. Form long cylindrical strips about as thick as your finger, and slice them crosswise into 1/3-1/2 inch (1 cm) pieces. Use the rounded tip of a butter knife to drag them over the work surface. Then use your thumb to create a depression in the center of each one. Clean the turnip greens, removing any of the tougher stems.

In a wide, shallow pan, sauté the sliced garlic, the whole hot pepper, and anchovies with 3 tablespoons of olive oil. Then add 3-4 tablespoons of water. When the anchovies have dissolved, turn off the heat.

Meanwhile heat a large pot of water for the orecchiette. When it reaches a boil add the pasta, greens, and a handful of coarse salt.

A few minutes before straining the orecchiette, warm up the anchovy sauce.

Strain the pasta (preferably with a very fine strainer to catch all turnip green remnants) and add it to the anchovies. Carefully mix everything together, season with freshly ground pepper, and serve immediately.

Orecchiette con pomodoro
Orecchiette with Fresh Tomatoes, Taggiasca Olives and Eggplant Purée

Servings 4
*Difficulty **Low***
Prep Time 50'
Cook Time 12'

For the pasta: 1 1/2 cups (250 g) re-milled durum wheat semolina – 1/2 cup (125 ml) warm water.

For the topping: 1 eggplant – 2 ripe tomatoes – 3.5 oz (100 g) taggiasca olives (about 23 large olives) – 1 garlic clove – black pepper to taste – 1/3 cup (80 ml) extra-virgin olive oil – basil to taste – vegetable broth as needed.

Mix the semolina and water until a smooth, consistent dough forms. Cover it with plastic wrap and let it sit for at least 15 minutes. Form long cylindrical strips about as thick as your finger, and slice them crosswise into 1/3-1/2 inch (1 cm) discs. Use the rounded tip of a butter knife to drag them over the work surface. Then use your thumb to create a depression in the center of each one.

Wrap the entire eggplant, skin and all, in aluminum foil. Bake it in a convection oven at 350° F (180° C) for at least 30 minutes, until it's very tender.

Blanch the tomatoes, peel them, remove the seeds, and dice them.

Sauté the diced tomatoes and the whole garlic clove with some olive oil and a pinch of pepper in a wide, shallow pan. Pit the olives and slice them in half. After the other ingredients have cooked together for 5 minutes, add the olives to the sauce. Then tear up some basil leaves and add those as well.

Boil the orecchiette in salted water. In the meantime, peel the eggplant and purée the pulp with a dash of olive oil (preferably fruity) and enough broth to create a smooth, creamy texture. Mix the orecchiette with the tomato and olive sauce. Spread some eggplant purée on each plate, top it with a portion of pasta, and serve.

Paglia e fieno con piselli
"Straw and Hay" with Peas

Servings 4/6
Difficulty Low
Prep Time 40'
Cook Time 4-5'

For the pasta
Green Pasta: 1 cup + 3 tbsp (150 g) Italian "00" flour – 1.2 oz (35 g) spinach (cooked, squeezed dry, and chopped), about 3 tbsp – 1 egg.
Yellow Pasta: 1 2/3 cups (200 g) Italian "00" flour – 2 eggs.
For the topping: 5.6 oz (160 g) peas (about 1 cup) – 5 oz (140 g) prosciutto (dry-cured) in one piece – 0.88 oz (25 g) onion, minced (about 2 1/2 tbsp) – 2 tbsp (30 g) butter – 1/3 cup + 1 tbsp (40 g) Parmigiano Reggiano cheese, grated – 3 1/2 tbsp (50 ml) beef broth – salt and pepper to taste.

Pour the flour onto a cutting board or marble counter and create a well in the center. Break the eggs and pour them into the well. Work them into the flour one at a time and mix until the dough is soft and consistent. Wrap it in plastic and let it sit for 30 minutes before using it. Do the same for the green pasta, adding the spinach together with the eggs.

Roll the dough out to a thickness of 1/32 inch (1 mm) and cut it into 1/4 inch (5-7 mm) strips.

Sauté 1 tablespoon of minced onion with a pat of butter on low heat. When it's softened, add the prosciutto (cut into thin strips) and season with salt and pepper. Add a few tablespoons of broth and let it cook on high heat for 5 minutes, stirring occasionally. Blanch the peas and add them at the end.

Boil the pasta in salted water and strain it when it's *al dente*. Combine it with the sauce and a bit of pasta water. Sprinkle it with grated Parmigiano and serve it immediately.

Paparele e bisi
Paparele e Bisi

Servings 4
Difficulty Low
Prep Time 30'
Cook Time 3-4'

For the pasta: 2 1/3 cups (300 g) Italian "00" flour – 3 eggs.
For the topping: 1.76 lbs (800 g) fresh peas (about 5 1/2 cups) – 1.76 oz (50 g) pancetta – 2.8 oz (80 g) onion (about 1 small onion) – 2 tbsp (30 g) butter – 1/3 cup + 1 tbsp (40 g) Parmigiano Reggiano cheese, grated – 1 1/2 tbsp (20 ml) extra-virgin olive oil – 1 tsp minced parsley – salt to taste.

Mix the eggs and flour until a smooth and consistent dough forms. Wrap it in plastic and refrigerate it for at least 30 minutes.
Use a pasta machine to roll the dough out to a thickness of 1/32 inch (1 mm). To make the *paparele* (fettuccine), cut it into long strips 1/8-1/4 inch (0.5 cm) wide.
Shell the peas, mince half the onion, and dice the pancetta. Sauté the onion and pancetta in the olive oil, then add the peas and pour in enough water to cover everything. Sprinkle the parsley on top and let it all cook on medium heat until the peas are tender and the liquid has sufficiently thickened. Boil the pasta in salted water and strain it when it's *al dente*. Combine it with the peas and butter (cut into small pieces). Add the grated Parmigiano to bring it all together and mix well to coat the pasta.

Chef's tips
If the pea sauce is too thin, you can temper a teaspoon of cornstarch with about 3 tablespoons of cold water, then add it to the peas and let it all boil together for a few minutes.

Pappardelle
al ragù di cinghiale
Pappardelle with Wild Boar Ragù

Servings 4
Difficulty *Low*
Prep Time *3h*
Cook Time *4-5'*

For the pasta: 2 1/3 cups (300 g) Italian "00" flour – 3 eggs.
For the wild boar ragù: 0.66 lbs (300 g) wild boar – 1.76 oz (50 g) whole peeled tomatoes – 1.4 oz (40 g) carrot (about 1/3 cup chopped) – 2.6 oz (75 g) onion (about 1/2 cup chopped) – 2.5 oz (70 g) celery (about 2/3 cup chopped) – 3 tsp (5 g) unsweetened cocoa powder – 1 bay leaf – 2 juniper berries – 3 sprigs of thyme – 1 sprig of marjoram – 1 cup (250 ml) red wine – 1/3 cup (80 ml) extra-virgin olive oil – salt to taste – white pepper to taste.

Mix together the flour and eggs until a smooth and consistent dough forms. Wrap it in plastic and refrigerate it for 30 minutes. Roll it out to a thickness of 1/32 inch (1 mm) and cut it into 1/3-inch (8 mm) wide pappardelle.
Cut the boar into 3/4-inch (2 cm) cubes and marinate it in the wine for 2 hours.
Mince all the vegetables and herbs. Chop up the whole peeled tomatoes and strain the marinated boar. Pour the oil into a pot on medium heat and add the vegetables, boar, cocoa powder, and tomatoes. Season with salt and pepper and cover the pot. Let it cook for about 45 minutes, adding a bit of water if needed.
Boil the pappardelle in salted water and strain them when they're *al dente*. Combine them with the ragù and mix well.

Chef's tips
Wild boar ragù is very good, perhaps best, when reheated, so make it a day early if you can.

Pappardelle al ragù di salsiccia e peperoni
Pappardelle with Sausage and Pepper Ragù

Servings 4
Difficulty Low
Prep Time 1h
Cook Time 10'

For the pasta: 2 1/3 cups (300 g) all-purpose flour – 3 eggs.
For the sauce: 1/4 cup (60 ml) extra-virgin olive oil – 2 shallots – 0.44 lbs (200 g) sausage – 3.5 oz (100 g) red bell pepper (about 1 medium pepper) – 3.5 oz (100 g) yellow bell pepper (about 1 medium pepper) – 10.5 oz (300 g) crushed tomatoes – 3.5 oz (100 g) black olives (about 23 large olives) – salt and pepper to taste.

Mix the flour and eggs until a smooth and homogenous dough forms. Wrap it in plastic and refrigerate it for 30 minutes.

Roll the dough out to a thickness of 1/16 inch (1.5 mm). Cut it into 1/3-inch (8 mm) strips and lay out the pappardelle on a lightly floured surface.

Thinly slice the shallots and cut the peppers into diamonds (removing the seeds and inner membrane). Sauté the shallots in half the oil, and when they're well browned add the peppers.

Use your hands to remove the sausage from the casing, then cook it in the remaining oil. When it's thoroughly browned, drain the fat and add the sausage to the peppers.

Add the crushed tomatoes to the sauce, season with salt to taste, and cook for another 15 minutes. Add the black olives at the end.

Meanwhile boil the pappardelle in salted water and strain them when they are *al dente*. Combine them with the sausage and pepper ragù, and serve immediately.

Pasta e fagioli
Pasta e Fagioli

Servings 4
Difficulty Low
Prep Time 50'
Cook Time
1h and 10'

For the pasta: 2 1/3 cups (300 g) Italian "00" flour – 3 eggs.
For the beans: 2.2 lbs (1 kg) fresh borlotti beans – 1.1 lbs (500 g) red potatoes (about 2 1/2 medium potatoes) – 0.33 lbs (150 g) "lardo" (cured pork fat) – 3.5 oz (100 g) onion (about 1 1/2 small onions) – 1 sprig of rosemary – 1 tsp minced parsley – 1 garlic clove – 1/3 cup + 1 1/2 tbsp (100 ml) white wine – 6 1/3 cups (1.5 L) beef broth – 1 1/2 tbsp (20 ml) extra-virgin olive oil – salt and pepper to taste – Parmigiano Reggiano cheese, grated (to taste).

Mix the eggs and flour until a smooth and consistent dough forms. Cover it with a cloth and let it sit for 30 minutes. Use a rolling pin or pasta machine to roll the dough out into a 1/16 inch (1.5 mm) sheet. Fold it over on itself several times and cut it into tagliolini about 3/4 inch (2 cm) wide. Lay them out to dry on a well-floured cloth, making sure not to let them overlap too much.

Sauté the pounded "lardo" with the garlic clove, minced onion, and beans in a saucepan. Add the white wine and let it evaporate. Add the beef broth and season with salt to taste. Peel and dice the potatoes and add them to the pan. Let it cook for 1 hour on medium heat, then pass about 1/3 of the beans and all the potatoes through a sieve. Season with salt to taste and add the pasta to the soup.

About 4-5 minutes before the soup is done, add the chopped rosemary and parsley and drizzle with cold-pressed olive oil. Sprinkle with freshly ground pepper and grated Parmigiano to taste. Serve the pasta and bean soup in individual bowls.

Pici con ragù toscano
"Pici" with Tuscan Ragù

Servings 4
Difficulty Low
Prep Time 50'
Cook Time 10'

For the pasta: 2 1/3 cups (300 g) all-purpose flour – 2/3 cup (150 ml) warm water.
For the ragù: 0.88 lbs (400 g) beef – 2.8 oz (80 g) tomato paste (about 5 tbsp) –
3.5 oz (100 g) onions (about 2/3 cup chopped) – 2.8 oz (80 g) carrots (about 2/3
cup chopped) – 2.5 oz (70 g) celery (about 2/3 cup chopped) – 1/3 cup + 1 tbsp
(40 g) Pecorino cheese, grated – 2 sprigs of rosemary – 3 1/2 tbsp (50 ml) red wine
– 3 1/2 tbsp (50 ml) extra-virgin olive oil – salt and pepper to taste.

Combine the flour and water, mixing until a smooth, dense dough forms. Cover it with a cloth and let it rest for about 20 minutes. Roll it out to a thickness of 1/8-1/4 inch (5 mm) and cut it into thin ribbons, about 12 inches (30 cm) long and 1/4-1/3 inch (1 cm) wide. Then roll each ribbon, keeping the ends between your fingers and pulling outward very slightly. "Pici" is long, thick, hand-rolled, cylindrical pasta. Keep it covered with a cloth as you roll out each ribbon, and make sure the strands are completely separated.

Chop the carrots, celery, and onion. Heat the oil in a pan and sauté the vegetables. Dice the meat and add it to the pan when they start to turn golden brown. Let the meat brown for a few minutes and season with salt and pepper. Add the wine and a sprig of rosemary. When all the liquid has evaporated, add the tomato paste. Cover the ragù and cook it on low heat for 30 minutes. If it gets too dry, add a few tablespoons of hot water.

Boil the "pici" in salted water and strain them. Combine them with the ragù, the remaining rosemary (stripped from the stem), and the Pecorino.

Pizzoccheri valtellinesi
Pizzoccheri Valtellinesi

Servings 4
Difficulty **Medium**
Prep Time 40'
Cook Time 7-10'

For the pasta: 1 2/3 cups (200 g) buckwheat flour (black) – 1/3 cup + 1 1/2 tbsp (60 g) Italian "00" flour – 1/2 cup + 1 tbsp (135 ml) water, room temperature.
For the topping: 0.77 lbs (350 g) white cabbage – 0.55 lbs (250 g) potatoes (about 1 medium) – 8.8 oz (250 g) Valtellina Casera cheese (not too aged) – 2 garlic cloves – 1 sprig of sage – 7 tbsp (100 g) butter – salt to taste.

Mix the black and white flours together on a flat surface. Add the room temperature water and knead the dough for at least 15 minutes, until it's soft to the touch. Roll it out to a thickness of about 1/16 inch (2 mm) and cut it into strips 2 3/4 inches (7 cm) long. Lay the strips on top of each other and cut them crosswise into tagliatelle about 1/4 inch (6-7 mm) wide.

Thinly slice the Casera cheese and place it back in the refrigerator. Set a large pot of water to boil over high heat. Clean the cabbage and roughly chop the leaves, or slice them into 2-inch (5 cm) strips. Wash, peel, and dice the potatoes. When the water reaches a boil, add salt to taste and toss in the cabbage, making sure it's fully submerged. After 5 minutes, add the potatoes and the "pizzoccheri" (tagliatelle) at the same time. Let them cook for 7-10 minutes.

While they cook, melt the butter in a small pan with the whole garlic cloves and roughly chopped sage. When the butter is completely melted, remove the garlic.

Before straining them, taste the "pizzoccheri" to make sure they're soft but not overcooked. Then use a perforated spoon to remove a portion of pasta and vegetables from the pot and spread it in the bottom of a casserole dish. Layer some Casera cheese on top, then add another layer of pasta and vegetables, followed by more cheese. Continue until all the ingredients are finished. Drizzle the melted butter on top and serve.

It may seem like too much, but in the traditional Teglio recipe for "pizzoccheri" each serving is literally drowning in melted butter.

Quadrucci con le vongole
Quadrucci with Clams

Servings 4
Difficulty **Medium**
Prep Time 50'
Cook Time 4-5'

For the pasta: 2 2/3 cups (330 g) Italian "00" flour – 0.5 oz (15 g) cuttlefish ink – 3 eggs.
For the topping: 1.1 lbs (500 g) clams – ripe tomatoes – 1 tbsp minced parsley – 1/3 cup + 1 1/2 tbsp (100 ml) dry white wine – hot red pepper to taste – 1 garlic clove – 3 1/2 tbsp (50 ml) extra-virgin olive oil – salt to taste.

Pour the flour onto a work surface and create a well in the center. Break the eggs and drop them into the well. Add the cuttlefish ink and mix everything together until the dough is smooth and consistent in color and texture. Wrap it in plastic and let it sit for 30 minutes.

Place the clams in a pot with half the oil, the whole garlic clove, minced parsley, white wine, and a piece of hot pepper (amount at your discretion). Let them cook over high heat until they open. Remove some of the shells and filter the remaining liquid from the pot.

Peel the tomatoes, remove the seeds, and dice them. Heat the remaining oil in another pan and add the tomatoes. Season with salt to taste and let them cook for 2-3 minutes. Add the clams along with their liquid.

Take the dough out of the refrigerator and use a rolling pin or pasta machine to roll out thin sheets. Cut the sheets into 3/4 inch (2 cm) squares.

Boil the pasta in salted water and add it to the pan of clam sauce. Let everything cook together for a minute, mixing well.

Spaghetti alla chitarra con ragù d'agnello
Chitarra Spaghetti with Lamb Ragù

Servings 4
Difficulty **Medium**
Prep Time *1h*
Cook Time 6-7'

For the pasta: 1 cup (200 g) durum wheat flour – 1/3 cup + 2 1/2 tsp (100 g) Italian "00" flour – 3 eggs.
For the topping: 0.66 lbs (300 g) lamb – 3 tbsp (40 ml) extra-virgin olive oil – 0.7 oz (20 g) onion (about 1/3 small) – 7 oz (200 g) crushed tomatoes – 1.1 lbs (500 g) bell peppers (about 4 medium) – 1.4 oz (40 g) Pecorino cheese – salt and pepper to taste – 1 bay leaf – fresh thyme.

Combine the two flours with the eggs on a flat surface or in a bowl. Mix until a smooth and consistent dough forms. Wrap it in plastic and let it sit for at least 30 minutes.

With a rolling pin or pasta machine, roll the dough out to about 1/8 inch (3 mm) thick. To make this traditional square spaghetti you will need a chitarra (guitar), a pasta-making tool that's named for the instrument it so closely resembles.

Mince the onion. Clean the peppers dice them (pieces should be about 1/3-1/2 inch or 1 cm). Dice the lamb as well.

Brown the lamb on medium heat with half the extra-virgin olive oil and the bay leaf.

When it's uniformly browned, add the onion and peppers and let it all stew together for 5 minutes. Then add the tomatoes and let it cook for another 15 minutes. Season with salt and pepper to taste.

Boil the pasta in salted water and strain it when it's al dente. Add it to the lamb ragù along with the Pecorino, the remaining oil, and the thyme (stripped from the stem). Let everything cook together for a minute and serve it very hot.

Strascinati con la menta
Strascinati with Mint

Servings 4
Difficulty Low
Prep Time 45'
Cook Time 5-6'

For the pasta: 1 1/3 cup (250 g) durum wheat flour – 1/2 cup (125 ml) warm water.
For the topping: 2.8 oz (80 g) pounded lard – 4-5 fresh mint leaves – hot pepper to taste – 2 tbsp (30 ml) extra-virgin olive oil – 1 garlic clove – 2-3 sweet peppers, dried (optional).

Make the dough by mixing the flour and warm water. Cut the dough into pieces and roll them into small cylinders. Then dice the cylinders. Stretch out each piece little bit and flatten it on a grooved cutting board (called a *cavarola*) by pressing down gently with three fingers.

Let the strascinati dry on a lightly floured surface for a few minutes. Then boil the pasta in salted water and strain it when it floats to the surface.

While the pasta cooks, sauté the garlic in the lard and oil until it's well browned. Then add hot pepper to taste. If you prefer a red sauce, you can also add 2-3 dried sweet peppers, crumbled up or ground in a food processor. Just before adding the sauce to the pasta, add a few mint leaves for extra flavor.

Strozzapreti con cavoletti di Bruxelles
Strozzapreti with Brussels Sprouts

Servings 4
Difficulty Low
Prep Time 45'
Cook Time 5-6'

For the strozzapreti: 2 1/3 (300 g) Italian "00" flour – 1 egg white – 1/2 cup (120 ml) milk.

For the topping: 10 Brussels sprouts – 3.2 oz (90 g) shallots (about 1/2 cup + 1 tbsp diced) – 3 tbsp (40 ml) extra-virgin olive oil – 1 sprig of chives – 1/3 cup + 1 tbsp (40 g) Parmigiano Reggiano cheese, grated – salt and pepper to taste.

Mix the flour with the egg white and milk until the dough is smooth and consistent. Wrap it in plastic and let it sit for 20 minutes.

Roll the dough out to 1/16 inch (2 mm) thick and cut it into strips about 1/3-1/2 x 2 inches (1 x 5 cm). Roll each strip between your palms to shape the strozzapreti.

Clean and rinse the Brussels sprouts and boil them in salted water for about 10 minutes. Strain them, let them cool, and cut them into quarters.

Dice the shallots and sauté them in a bit of oil over low heat. Add the Brussels sprouts and season with salt and pepper to taste.

Boil the pasta in salted water for about 5-6 minutes and strain it when it is al dente. Add it to the Brussels sprouts along with the Parmigiano and a pinch of minced chives. Let it all cook together for a minute and serve.

Chef's tips
When buying the Brussels sprouts, make sure they're firm and solid with a delicate aroma and vivid color. Always boil them in salted water for 5 minutes before using them in any dish, which will make them more easily digestible.

Tagliatelle al ragù alla bolognese
Tagliatelle in Bolognese Sauce

Servings 4
Difficulty *Low*
Prep Time
1h and 30'
Cook Time 3-4'

For the tagliatelle: 2 1/3 cups (300 g) Italian "00" flour – 3 eggs.
For the topping: 2/3 cup (160 ml) water – 5.3 oz (150 g) pork shoulder – 5.3 oz (150 g) beef – 5.3 oz (150 g) pounded lard – 1.4 oz (40 g) carrots (about 1/2-1 small) – 1.4 oz (40 g) celery (about 1 medium stalk) – 1.4 oz (40 g) yellow onion (about 1/2 small) – 3.2 oz (90 g) tomato paste (5 1/2 tbsp) – 1/3 cup + 1 tbsp (40 g) Parmigiano Reggiano cheese, grated – 1/3 cup + 1 1/2 tbsp (100 ml) red wine – 1/3 cup + 1 1/2 tbsp (100 ml) extra-virgin olive oil – 2 bay leaves – black pepper to taste – salt to taste.

Mix the flour and eggs until a smooth and consistent dough forms. Wrap it in plastic and refrigerate it 30 minutes.

Take the dough out of the refrigerator and use a rolling pin or pasta machine to roll it out to a thickness of 1/32 (1 mm). Cut it into strips about 1/8-1/4 inch (5 mm) wide and lay the tagliatelle out on a lightly floured surface.

Chop up the meat and vegetables. Combine the oil, pounded lard, chopped vegetables, and hand-torn bay leaf in a saucepan over medium heat.

When they've started to turn golden brown, add the ground meat and let it brown over high heat. Then add the red wine and let all the liquid evaporate completely. Turn down the heat, add the tomato paste, and season with a handful of salt and a pinch of ground pepper. Add the water and let it cook on low heat for about 1 hour.

Boil the pasta in salted water and strain it when it's *al dente*. Combine it with the ragù and grated Parmigiano. Mix well and serve.

Tagliatelle al ragù di salsiccia
Tagliatelle with Sausage Ragù

Servings 4
Difficulty Low
Prep Time 1h
Cook Time 3-4'

For the tagliatelle: 2 1/3 cups (300 g) Italian "00" flour – 3 eggs.
For the topping: 0.66 lbs (300 g) sausage – 7 oz (200 g) leeks (about 2–2 1/2) – 14 oz (400 g) crushed tomatoes – 1 1/2 tbsp (20 g) butter – 2 tsp (10 ml) extra-virgin olive oil – fennel seeds to taste – fresh dill to taste – salt to taste – Parmigiano Reggiano cheese, grated, to taste (optional).

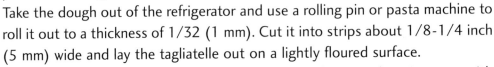

Mix the flour and eggs until a smooth and consistent dough forms. Wrap it in plastic and refrigerate it 30 minutes.

Take the dough out of the refrigerator and use a rolling pin or pasta machine to roll it out to a thickness of 1/32 (1 mm). Cut it into strips about 1/8-1/4 inch (5 mm) wide and lay the tagliatelle out on a lightly floured surface.

Slice the white, tender part of the leeks into rounds. Stew them in a pan with the butter, seasoning lightly with salt. Brown the sausage in a separate pan with the fennel seeds and oil. Once the fat has melted, add the sausage to the leeks. Then add the crushed tomatoes, season with salt to taste, and let it cook for 15 minutes.

Boil the pasta in salted water and strain it when it's *al dente*. Combine it with the sausage ragù and fresh dill. Sprinkle it with grated Parmigiano to taste.

Tagliatelle con funghi, bresaola e rucola
Tagliatelle with Mushrooms, Bresaola, and Arugula

Servings 4
Difficulty Low
Prep Time 50'
Cook Time 3-4'

Per le tagliatelle: 2 1/3 cups (300 g) Italian "00" flour – 3 eggs.
For the topping: 0.66 lbs (300 g) white button mushrooms – 3.5 oz (100 g) sliced bresaola – 2/3 cup (150 ml) heavy cream – 1.76 oz (50 g) arugula (about 2 1/2 cups) – 1/3 cup + 1 tbsp (40 g) Parmigiano Reggiano cheese, grated – 3 1/2 tbsp (50 ml) white wine – 2 tbsp (30 ml) extra-virgin olive oil – salt and pepper to taste.

Mix the flour and eggs until a smooth and consistent dough forms. Wrap it in plastic and refrigerate it 30 minutes.

Take the dough out of the refrigerator and use a rolling pin or pasta machine to roll it out to a thickness of 1/32 (1 mm). Cut it into strips about 1/8-1/4 inch (5 mm) wide and lay the tagliatelle out on a lightly floured surface.

Clean and slice the mushrooms and cut the bresaola into strips. Wash the arugula and roughly chop it.

Sauté the bresaola in the oil over medium heat. As soon as it starts to turn golden brown, add the white wine and let it evaporate. Then add the mushrooms and let them cook with the bresaola. Season with salt and pepper to taste, add the cream, and let the sauce thicken.

Meanwhile boil the pasta in salted water. Strain it when it's *al dente* and transfer it directly to the pan with the sauce. Let everything cook together for a minute and top it off with the grated Parmigiano and chopped arugula.

Tagliatelle con zucca
Tagliatelle with Pumpkin, Honey Mushrooms, Rabbit, and Fennel Seed

Servings 4
Difficulty Low
Prep Time 1h
Cook Time 3-4'

For the tagliatelle: 2 1/3 cups (300 g) Italian "00" flour – 3 eggs.
For the topping: 5.3 oz (150 g) pumpkin (about 1 1/3 cups cubed) – 0.44 lbs (200 g) rabbit – 0.55 lbs (250 g) honey mushrooms – 1 tsp fennel seeds – 3 1/2 tbsp (50 ml) extra-virgin olive oil – 1 garlic clove – 3 1/2 tbsp (50 ml) white wine – salt and pepper to taste – 1 bunch of fresh dill or 1 tsp minced parsley (optional).

Mix the flour and eggs until a smooth and consistent dough forms. Wrap it in plastic and refrigerate it 30 minutes.

Take the dough out of the refrigerator and use a rolling pin or pasta machine to roll it out to a thickness of 1/32-1/16 inch (1.5 mm). Cut it into strips about 1/8-1/4 inch (5 mm) wide and lay the tagliatelle out on a lightly floured surface.

Clean the mushrooms and sauté them in a bit of oil with the whole garlic clove (which will be removed before adding the pasta). Season with a pinch of salt and pepper.

Clean the pumpkin, remove the seeds, and cube it. Sauté it in a bit of oil and season it with salt and pepper to taste.

Cube the rabbit meat and sear it in a skillet with the fennel seeds. When it's well browned, season with salt and pepper to taste and add the white wine. When the wine has completely evaporated, add the mushrooms and pumpkin. Add more salt and pepper if necessary and let it cook for another 5 minutes.

Boil the tagliatelle in salted water. Strain them when they're *al dente* and combine them with the sauce. Garnish with a bunch of fresh dill or minced parsley at your discretion.

Tagliatelle di polenta
Polenta Tagliatelle with Deer Ragù, Porcini Mushrooms, and Berries

Servings 4
Difficulty Medium
Prep Time 1h and 30'
Cook Time 4-5'
Marinating 5-6h

For the pasta: 1 1/3 cups (180 g) superfine polenta – 1/3 cup (60 g) re-milled durum wheat semolina – 1/3 cup + 2 tbsp (60 g) Italian "00" flour – 3 eggs.
For the topping: 0.66 lbs (300 g) porcini mushrooms – 1.1 lbs (500 g) deer meat, diced – 5.3 oz (150 g) onion (about 2 small onions) – 2 cups + 1 1/2 tbsp (500 ml) red wine – 1 oz (30 g) fresh blueberries (about 1/4 cup) – 5 juniper berries – sprigs of thyme – 1 sprig of rosemary – 1 tsp minced parsley – 1 clove – 1 garlic clove – 1/2 tbsp (50 ml) extra-virgin olive oil – salt and pepper to taste.

Slice half the onion and combine it with the wine and the spices. Marinate the deer meat in this mixture for 5-6 hours.

Combine the flours and mix them with the egg until a consistent dough forms. Wrap it in plastic and refrigerate it for 30 minutes.

Roll the dough out to a thickness of 1/16 inch (1.5 mm) and cut it into strips 1/8 inch (4 mm) wide.

Mince the remaining onion and sauté it in 2/3 of the oil with 1 thyme sprig, 1 rosemary sprig, and the whole garlic clove (to be removed when the sauce is done). Strain the deer meat well and add it to the pan. Brown everything together for 4-5 minutes. Filter the marinade with a mesh strainer and add it to the pan. Season with salt and pepper and cook the sauce on low heat for 40 minutes.

Use a knife to remove any clumps of dirt from the mushrooms, then clean them with a damp cloth. Cut them into thick slices and sauté them in the remaining oil with a thyme sprig and half the parsley. Season with salt and pepper and let them cook for 5 minutes.

Boil the pasta in salted water and strain it when it's *al dente*. Combine it with the deer ragù, the remaining parsley, and the mushrooms. Add the blueberries at the very end.

Tagliatelle in crema di fagioli
Tagliatelle with Bean Purée in Mullet and Thyme Sauce

Servings 4
Difficulty *Medium*
Prep Time
1h and 30'
Cook Time 3-4'

For the tagliatelle: 2 1/3 cups (300 g) Italian "00" flour – 3 eggs.
For the topping: 0.44 lbs (200 g) Lamon beans (a variety of Borlotti beans) – 2.8 oz (80 g) carrots (about 1 1/2 small) – 2.5 oz (70 g) celery (about 2 medium stalks) – 5.3 oz (150 g) onion (about 2 small) – 4 medium-sized mullet – 0.25 lbs (120 g) cherry tomatoes (about 7) – 2 tbsp (30 ml) white wine – 3/4 cup + 1 1/2 tbsp (200 ml) extra-virgin olive oil – 4 1/4 cups (1 L) water – 2 sprigs of thyme – 1 garlic clove – salt and pepper to taste.

Mix the flour and eggs until a smooth and consistent dough forms. Wrap it in plastic and refrigerate it for 30 minutes.

Take the dough out of the refrigerator and use a pasta machine or rolling pin to roll it out to 1/32-1/16 inch (1.5 mm) thick. Cut it into strips about 1/8-1/4 inch (5 mm) wide and lay the tagliatelle out on a lightly floured surface.

Clean and dice the vegetables. Strip the thyme from one of the stems and mince it together with the garlic. Drizzle some olive oil in a saucepan sauté the vegetables and thyme. When they start to turn golden brown, add the beans (if you're using dried, soak them overnight before using them). Add the water and let it simmer until the beans have softened to mush. Season with salt to taste, pass it all through a vegetable mill, and keep it warm.

Clean, fillet, and chop the mullet. Drizzle some olive oil in a pan and sauté the mullet with the other sprig of thyme (stripped from the stem). Add the tomatoes, season with salt and pepper, and let it cook for a few minutes. Add the white wine and let it evaporate completely on high heat.

Boil the tagliatelle in salted water and strain them when they're *al dente*. Transfer them directly to the pan with the fish, letting everything cook together for a minute.

Spread some of the bean purée on each plate and arrange the tagliatelle on top. Drizzle with extra-virgin olive oil, sprinkle with ground pepper, and serve.

Tagliatelle verdi al pomodoro fresco
Green Tagliatelle with Fresh Tomato Sauce

Servings 4
Difficulty **Low**
Prep Time 50'
Cook Time 10'

For the pasta: 2 1/3 cups (300 g) all-purpose flour – 3 oz (90 g) spinach, boiled and strained (about 1/2 cup cooked) – 2 eggs.
For the sauce: 2 tbsp (30 ml) extra-virgin olive oil – 2.2 lbs (1 kg) ripe tomatoes – 3.5 oz (100 g) onion (about 2/3 cup chopped) – 1 garlic clove – 1 bunch of basil – 1/3 cup + 1 tbsp (40 g) Parmigiano Reggiano cheese – salt to taste.

Mix together the flour, eggs, and spinach (boiled, strained, and chopped up) until a consistent dough forms. Cover it in plastic wrap and refrigerate it for 30 minutes.

Use a pasta machine or rolling pin to flatten the dough to just under 1/16 of an inch (1.5 mm) thick. Cut it into 1/8-inch (4 mm) strips, then lay the tagliatelle out on a lightly floured surface. Peel the tomatoes, remove the seeds, and dice them. Mince the onion and sauté it in the oil with the whole garlic clove. When the onion turns golden brown, add the diced tomato and season with salt to taste. After 10 minutes, remove the garlic clove from the sauce and add the basil (roughly chopped).

Boil the tagliatelle in salted water. When they're *al dente*, strain them and mix them with the tomato sauce. Sprinkle grated Parmigiano on top.

Tagliatelle verdi con prosciutto e limone
Green Tagliatelle with Prosciutto and Lemon

Servings 4
Difficulty *Low*
Prep Time 50'
Cook Time 4-5'

For the pasta: 2 1/3 cups (300 g) Italian "00" flour – 2.6 oz (75 g) spinach, cooked and squeezed dry (just under 1/2 cup) – 2 eggs.
For the topping: 5.3 oz (150 g) prosciutto (dry-cured), in thick slices – 3 1/2 tbsp (50 g) butter – 2 lemons – salt and pepper to taste.

Mix the flour with the eggs and chopped spinach until a consistent dough forms. Wrap it in plastic and refrigerate it for 30 minutes.

Flatten the dough into sheets 1/16 inch (1.5 mm) thick. Cut the sheets into 1/8 inch (4 mm) strips. Cut the prosciutto into strips the same width as the tagliatelle. Remove the rind of one lemon (being very careful to take only the yellow part) and cut it into matchstick slices. Grate the other lemon peel.

Boil the tagliatelle in salted water. In the meantime sauté the prosciutto in the butter, but don't let it dry out. Add a ladleful of pasta water and the grated lemon zest. Season with salt and pepper to taste.

Strain the pasta and add it to the sauce, stirring well to combine. Top it with some sliced lemon peel and a pinch of ground pepper.

Chef's tips
You can boil the sliced lemon rind in unsalted water for 1 minute to soften it.

Tagliolini agli scampi
Tagliolini with Scampi in Rosemary-Chickpea Sauce

Servings 4
Difficulty Medium
Prep Time 1h
Cook Time 2-3'

For the pasta: 2 1/3 cups (300 g) Italian "00" flour – 3 eggs.
For the topping: 12 scampi – 4 sun-dried tomatoes – 14 oz (400 g) chickpeas, cooked – 1/3 cup + 1/3 cup + 1 1/2 tbsp (100 ml) white wine – 1/4 cup (60 ml) extra-virgin olive oil – 2 sprigs of rosemary – 1 garlic clove – salt and pepper to taste.

Mix the eggs and flour until a smooth and consistent dough forms. Wrap it in plastic and refrigerate it for 30 minutes.

Roll the dough out to a thickness of 1/32 inch (1 mm) and cut it into strips 1/16-1/8 inch (2-3 mm) wide.

Purée the chickpeas with some of the water they were packed (or cooked) in, until they're somewhat dense with a smooth and creamy texture. Season them with salt and pepper.

Clean and devein the scampi, removing all the heads. Remove the tails from 8 of the scampi and dice them. Leave the other 4 whole, with tails.

Heat half the oil in a pan with the whole garlic clove. Crush the scampi heads with a meat tenderizer and add them to the pan. When they're well browned, add the white wine. Let all the liquid evaporate, then add a ladleful of water. Let it cook for another ten minutes, then pour it all through a fine mesh strainer and add the filtered liquid back to the pan. Add the diced scampi, season with salt and pepper, and cook for another 2 minutes.

Drizzle some olive oil in another pan and sear the whole scampi tails for 1 full minute on each side, seasoning them with salt and pepper.

Boil the tagliolini in salted water and strain them when they're *al dente*. Transfer them to the pan of scampi sauce and cook them together for a minute, mixing so the pasta is well coated.

Spread a layer of chickpea purée on each plate and arrange the tagliolini in the center. Garnish with whole scampi tails and a few sun-dried tomato slices.

Drizzle a bit of cold-pressed olive oil over each portion, topping it with a pinch of chopped rosemary and ground pepper.

Tagliolini al nero con broccoli e vongole veraci
Black Tagliolini with Broccoli and Carpet Shell Clams

Servings 4
Difficulty *Low*
Prep Time 50'
Cook Time 2-3'

For the pasta dough: 2 2/3 cups (330 g) Italian "00" flour – 0.5 oz (15 g) cuttlefish ink – 3 eggs.
For the topping: 0.55 lbs (250 g) broccoli – 1.1 lbs (500 g) carpet shell clams – 3 1/2 tbsp (50 ml) extra-virgin olive oil – 1 garlic clove – 1 tbsp minced parsley – salt and pepper to taste.

Pour the flour onto a work surface and create a well in the center. Break the eggs and pour them into the well. Add the cuttlefish ink and mix it all together until the dough is smooth and consistent in color. Wrap it in plastic and let it sit for 30 minutes.

Meanwhile clean the broccoli, cutting off the tops and peeling and dicing the stems. Boil it in lightly salted water for about 2 minutes.

Clean and rinse the clams thoroughly. Put them in a pan with half the oil, the whole garlic clove, and the parsley. Let them cook on high heat until they open. Filter the liquid from the pot with a fine mesh strainer. Add the remaining oil to the pot with the clams and sauté the broccoli. Season with salt and pepper to taste, and after a few minutes add the filtered liquid from the clams.

Roll the dough out to about 1/16-1/32 inch (1.5 mm) thick with a rolling pin or pasta machine. Cut the sheets of dough into strips about 1/8 inch (2 mm) thick wide.

Boil the pasta in salted water and add it to the sauce, mixing thoroughly.

Tagliolini al profumo di arancia
Orange Tagliolini with Fennel Cream and Salmon Carpaccio

Servings 4
Difficulty Medium
Prep Time 1h
Cook Time 3-4'

For the pasta: 2 1/3 cups (300 g) Italian "00" flour – 3 eggs – zest of 1 orange.
For the topping: 5.3 oz (150 g) onion (about 2 small onions) – 3.5 oz (100 g) smoked salmon, thinly sliced – 1.76 oz (50 g) salmon roe – 12.3 oz (350 g) fennel – a few bunches of wild fennel – 1 whole peeled orange, segments separated and diced – 2 cups (500 ml) water – 0.02 oz (0.5 g) saffron (about 3/4 tsp) – 3 1/2 tbsp (50 ml) extra-virgin olive oil – salt and pepper to taste.

Mix the flour with the eggs and orange zest until the dough is smooth and consistent. Wrap it in plastic and refrigerate it for 30 minutes.
Roll the dough out to 1/32 inch (1 mm) thick and cut it into 1/8 inch (3-4mm) strips.
Clean and dice the fennel and slice the onion. Heat the oil in a pan and sauté the vegetables for 2-3 minutes, then add just enough water to cover them. Let them stew for about 20 minutes and season with salt and pepper. Add the saffron and purée the mixture until it's dense and creamy.
Boil the tagliolini in salted water and strain them when they're *al dente*. Combine them with the fennel cream, a bit of pasta water, and the diced orange, letting it all cook together for a minute.
Serve the tagliolini over the salmon slices. Garnish with salmon roe and wild fennel, and top with ground pepper.

Tagliolini alla monferrina
Tagliolini alla Monferrina

Servings 4
Difficulty Low
Prep Time 1h
Cook Time 2'

For the pasta: 2 1/3 cups (300 g) Italian "00" flour – 8-10 egg yolks.
For the topping: 7 tbsp (100 g) butter – 1 sprig of rosemary – 1 sprig of sage – 1 sprig of thyme – half a garlic clove – 1 bay leaf – Parmigiano Reggiano cheese, grated (to taste).

Combine the flour and egg yolks (8-10 depending on the size of the eggs) until a smooth and consistent dough forms. Wrap it in plastic and refrigerate it for at least 30 minutes.

With a rolling pin or pasta machine, roll the dough out to 1/32 inch (1 mm) thick. Fold it over on itself several times and cut it into thin strips, 1/32 inch (1 mm) wide.

Melt the butter in a pan with the herbs (stripped from the stems and minced) and whole garlic clove. Leave it on low heat for a few minutes to let the flavors blend. Pour the butter through a small strainer to filter out the herbs and garlic.

Boil the tagliolini in salted water. Strain the pasta when it's *al dente* and toss it with the flavored butter. Sprinkle with grated Parmigiano to taste.

Tagliolini alla rapa rossa
Beet Tagliolini with Salmon Trout and Sunchokes

Servings 4
Difficulty **Medium**
Prep Time 50'
Cook Time 3-4'

For the pasta: 2 1/3 cups (300 g) Italian "00" flour – 2 eggs – 2.8 oz (80 g) beets, cooked and puréed (about 1 medium).
For the topping: 2 salmon trout fillets, about 0.66 lbs (300 g) – 7 oz (200 g) sunchokes – 2.1 oz (60 g) shallots – 0.25–0.28 oz (7-8 g) fresh ginger root – a few bunches of wild fennel – 1/4 cup (60 ml) extra-virgin olive oil – oil for frying as needed – salt and pepper to taste
For the reduction sauce: 3/4 cup + 1 1/2 tbsp (200 ml) red wine – 1 tbsp (10 g) sugar.

Mix the flour with the puréed beet and eggs until a smooth and consistent dough forms. Wrap it in plastic and refrigerate it for 30 minutes.

Roll the dough out to a thickness of 1/32 inch (1 mm). Cut it into strips about 1/8 inch (3-4 mm) wide.

Reduce the wine and sugar over medium heat until it reaches a syrupy consistency.

Remove the skin from the trout fillets and dice them.

Peel the sunchokes. Slice 2 of them very thinly and fry them in a large amount of boiling oil. Remove them, letting the excess oil drip off, and set them on paper towels to dry.

Dice the remaining sunchokes and boil them in salted water for 5 minutes, then strain them and let them cool.

Slice the shallots and sauté them in 4/5 of the oil. Add the trout and grated ginger to taste. Season with salt and pepper and let it cook for 5 minutes. Add the diced and boiled sunchokes at the end.

Boil the pasta in salted water and strain it when it's very *al dente*. Combine it with the sauce and serve it with the wild fennel, ground pepper, and sunchoke "chips". Garnish each plate with the wine reduction and a few drops of cold-pressed olive oil.

Tagliolini con fagiolini e cacioricotta
Tagliolini with Green Beans and Cacioricotta

Servings 4
Difficulty Low
Prep Time 40'
Cook Time 3-4'

For the pasta: 2 1/3 cups (300 g) all-purpose flour – 3 eggs.
For the topping: 0.55 lbs (250 g) green beans – 0.77 lbs (350 g) plum tomatoes (about 5 1/2) – 1 garlic clove – a few basil leaves – 1.76 oz (50 g) Cacioricotta cheese – extra-virgin olive oil to taste – salt to taste.

Pour the flour onto a marble work surface or cutting board and use your fingers to create a well in the center. Break the eggs and pour them into the well. Start working the eggs into the flour and mix until a soft and consistent dough forms. Wrap it in plastic and let it sit for 30 minutes before proceeding.

Use a rolling pin or pasta machine to roll the dough out to a thickness of 1/32 inch (1 mm). Cut it into strips about 1/8 inch (3 mm) wide.

Clean the green beans, breaking the ends off, and wash them. Cut each one into 3-4 pieces and boil them in salted water. Strain them when they're still fairly crunchy and cool them in ice water. While the beans are boiling, sauté the whole garlic clove in the olive oil. Peel the tomatoes, remove the seeds, cube them, and add them to the garlic. Then add the basil, hand-torn, followed by the beans. Season with salt and let the sauce thicken a bit.

Boil the pasta in salted water and strain it when it's *al dente*. Add it directly to the sauce, letting everything cook together for a minute. Finish by adding the aged Cacioricotta, partially grated and partially cut into thin slices.

Tagliolini con tartufi
Tagliolini with Truffles

Servings 4
Difficulty Low
Prep Time 40'
Cook Time 6'

For the pasta: 2 1/3 cups (300 g) all-purpose flour – 3 whole eggs.
For the topping: 3 1/2 tbsp (50 g) butter – 1 small truffle – 1/2 cup (50 g) Parmigiano Reggiano cheese, grated – salt to taste.

Pour the flour onto a work surface and create a well in the center. Drop the eggs in the center and work them into the flour until a smooth and consistent dough forms. Let it sit for about 30 minutes, then roll it out to about 1/32 inch (1 mm) thick and cut it into strips 1/8 inch (3 mm) wide.
Boil the tagliolini in salted water. In the meantime, melt the butter in a pot and add half the truffle, thinly sliced.
Strain the pasta when it's *al dente* and coat it with the melted butter, Parmigiano, and remaining truffle (thinly sliced). Serve it nice and hot.

Chef's tips
Wrap the truffles in a paper towel and keep them in an airtight glass container in the warmest part of the refrigerator. For best quality, eat them as soon as possible after buying them.

Tagliolini di mais ai porcini
Cornmeal Tagliolini with Porcini Mushrooms

Servings 4
Difficulty Low
Prep Time 50'
Cook Time 2'

For the pasta: 1 2/3 cups (200 g) Italian "00" flour – 2/3 cup (100 g) cornmeal – 3 eggs – 3 egg yolks.
For the topping: 3 1/2 tbsp (50 ml) extra-virgin olive oil – 1 garlic clove – 0.88 lbs (400 g) porcini mushrooms – 1 sprig of rosemary – salt to taste – 1/2 cup (50 g) Parmigiano Reggiano cheese, grated.

Combine the two flours with the eggs and egg yolks on a flat work surface or in a bowl. Mix until a smooth and consistent dough forms. If it's too dry, add a bit of water. Wrap the dough in plastic and refrigerate it for about 30 minutes.

Meanwhile clean the mushrooms with a damp cloth and dice them. Chop the rosemary and garlic separately.

Heat the oil in a pan and sauté the garlic, but don't let it brown. After a few seconds, add the mushrooms and rosemary. Season with salt and let the mushrooms cook, but don't let them get too soft.

Roll the dough out into sheets, about 1/32-1/16 inch (1.5 mm) thick. Cut them into strips about 1/16 inch (2 mm) thick.

Boil the tagliolini in salted water. Strain them when they're *al dente* and add them to the pan with the mushrooms. Let everything cook together for a minute, adding a bit of pasta water if necessary. Sprinkle with grated Parmigiano and serve.

Tonnarelli cacio e pepe
Tonnarelli Cacio e Pepe

Servings 4
Difficulty Low
Prep Time 10'
Cook Time 5'

12.3 oz (350 g) tonnarelli pasta – 1/3 cup + 1 1/2 tbsp (100 ml) extra-virgin olive oil – 7 oz (200 g) Pecorino Romano cheese, grated (about 2 cups) – coarsely ground black pepper.

Boil the tonnarelli in a large pot of salted water. When the pasta is *al dente*, strain it. Stir in the Pecorino and black pepper (use as little or as much as you want, the important thing is to make sure it's very coarsely ground). Serve immediately.

Chef's tips
Before adding it to the pasta, temper the cheese with oil and 2-3 tablespoons of pasta water. Remember to remove it from the burner before combining them. Use freshly ground black pepper for more fragrant and flavorful results.

Trofie al pesto alla genovese
Trofie with Pesto Alla Genovese

Servings 4
Difficulty Low
Prep Time 40'
Cook Time 4-5'

For the pasta: 2 cups (250 g) all-purpose flour – 1/2 cup (125 ml) warm water.
For the pesto: 1 oz (30 g) basil leaves (about 1 1/4 cups or 60 leaves) – 2/3 cup (60 g) Parmigiano Reggiano cheese, grated – 1/3 cup + 1 tbsp (40 g) aged Pecorino cheese, grated – 0.35 oz (10 g) pine nuts (about 1 tbsp) – 1 garlic clove – 3/4 cup + 1 1/2 tbsp (200 ml) Ligurian extra-virgin olive oil – salt to taste.
Additional Ingredients: 3.5 oz (100 g) green beans (about 18 beans) – 7 oz (200 g) potatoes (about 1 1/2 small potatoes).

Pour the flour onto a work surface and create a well in the center. Add the water a little at a time and mix until a smooth and elastic dough forms. Pinch off pieces the size of a chickpea and roll them into thin strips between your hands (or roll them on a work surface, exerting slight pressure with your palm). Now you have trofie pasta.

Carefully clean and rinse the basil, and set it out to dry on a towel. When it's thoroughly dried, put it in a food processor with the oil, garlic, pine nuts, and a pinch of salt. Blend well, adding the grated Parmigiano Reggiano and Pecorino toward the end. To keep the pesto fresh, transfer it to a bowl and cover it with a thin layer of olive oil.

Wash and peel the potatoes, then cut them into 1/3-1/2 inch (1 cm) cubes. Clean the green beans and cut them in half. Heat a large pot of water, and when it reaches a boil add the potatoes, green beans, and a handful of coarse salt. Let them cook for 5 minutes, then add the trofie and cook for about 5 more minutes. Remember to set aside a ladleful of pasta water and mix it into the pesto before adding it to the cooked pasta.

When the pasta is *al dente*, strain it along with the potatoes and green beans. Combine everything with the pesto and mix well.

CARLO CRACCO

CRACCO WAS BORN IN VICENZA IN 1965. HE STUDIED IN RECOARO TERME, NEAR VICENZA, AT THE I .P.C. INSTITUTE, A MEMBER OF THE EUROPEAN HOTEL AND TOURISM ASSOCIATION FOUNDED IN 1963. DURING HIS SCHOOL DAYS HE WORKED FOR THE "DA REMO" RESTAURANT (VICENZA). HIS PROFESSIONAL CAREER STARTED IN 1986 WHEN GUALTIERO MARCHESI IN MILAN EMPLOYED HIM IN THE FIRST ITALIAN RESTAURANT TO EARN THE MICHELIN THREE STARS AWARD. CRACCO LATER WORKED AT THE "MERIDIANA" IN GARLENDA (SAVONA), BELONGING TO THE RELAIS & CHÂTEAUX CHAIN. HE THEN MOVED TO FRANCE WHERE FOR THREE YEARS HE LEARNED THE ART OF FRENCH CUISINE UNDER MASTERS SUCH AS ALAIN DUCASSE (HOTEL PARIS) AND LUCAS CARTON (PARIS, SENDERENS).

ON RETURNING TO ITALY HE BECAME HEAD CHEF OF THE ENOTECA "PINCHIORRI" IN FLORENCE, WHICH EARNED THE MICHELIN THREE STARS MARK UNDER HIS LEADERSHIP. SUBSEQUENTLY, GUALTIERO MARCHESI CALLED HIM FOR THE OPENING OF HIS RESTAURANT "L'ALBERETA" IN ERBUSCO (BRESCIA), WHERE CRACCO THEN WORKED AS CHEF FOR THREE YEARS. HE SUCCEEDINGLY INAUGURATED THE "LE CLIVIE" RESTAURANT IN PIOVESI D'ALBA (CUNEO), WHICH ALSO EARNED THE MICHELIN STAR IN JUST A YEAR.

A FEW YEARS LATER, HE ACCEPTED THE INVITATION OF THE STOPPANI FAMILY, OWNER OF THE MOST RENOWNED FOOD AND WINE SHOP IN MILANO, TO OPEN THE "CRACCO PECK" RESTAURANT WHERE CRACCO TODAY WORKS AS EXECUTIVE CHEF. THE RESTAURANT HAS BEEN OPEN SINCE 2001 IN AN ELEGANT BUILDING IN THE CENTER OF MILAN. ITS CUISINE IS A CONTEMPORARY REVIVAL OF THE TRADITIONAL MILANESE SPECIALTIES, AND IT CAN PRIDE ITSELF IN ITS TWO-STAR MICHELIN, 18,5/20 ESPRESSO AND THREE FORKS GAMBERO ROSSO AWARDS. IT HAS BEEN LISTED AMONG THE TOP 50 RESTAURANTS IN THE WORLD SINCE 2007. IN JULY THAT YEAR, CRACCO BECAME THE RESTAURANT'S SOLE PROPRIETOR.

RECIPE INDEX

INGREDIENTS INDEX

All photographs are by ACADEMIA BARILLA

MY FAVORITE RECIPES

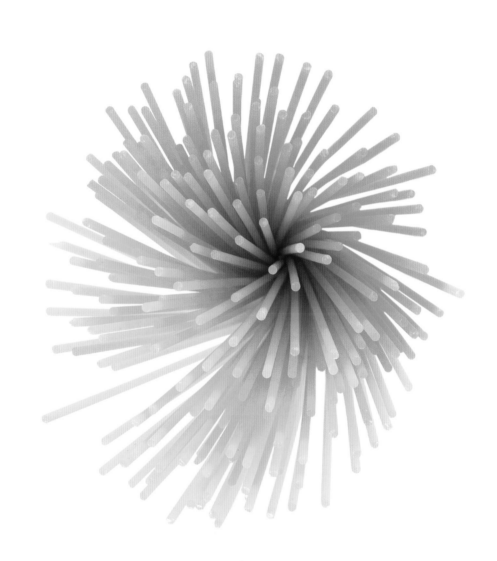